CLOCKING the GOOSE

A memoir of short stories about growing up and getting over it.

Robert Moseley

BookLocker
Trenton, Georgia

Copyright © 2025 Robert Moseley

Print ISBN: 978-1-959620-59-4
Ebook ISBN: 979-8-88531-806-8

All rights reserved. No part of this publication may be reproduced, stored in a retrieval system, or transmitted in any form or by any means, electronic, mechanical, recording or otherwise, without the prior written permission of the author.

Published by BookLocker.com, Inc., Trenton, Georgia.

BookLocker.com, Inc.
2025

First Edition

Library of Congress Cataloging in Publication Data
Moseley, Robert
CLOCKING the GOOSE: A memoir of short stories about growing up and getting over it by Robert Moseley
Library of Congress Control Number: 2024916120

For Mom, Dad, Rick, and Steve, my first teachers, and for Diane and David, whose never-ending love constantly nourishes me, and for Marion, who saw from the very first I was a writer and inspired me to tell my story with all my heart and soul.

"The first step to the knowledge of the wonder and mystery of life is the recognition of the monstrous nature of the earthly human realm as well as its glory, the realization that this is just how it is and that it cannot and will not be changed. Those who think they know how the universe could have been had they created it, without pain, without sorrow, without time, without death, are unfit for illumination."

Joseph Campbell

AUTHOR'S ACKNOWLEDGEMENTS

People rarely read this part of a book, but they should. Without the support of these folks this memoir would never have been written. First and foremost, I must thank my immediate and extended family. My brother from another mother, Joe Gibbons, partnered and inspired me in the final year of this project, gave me moral support, was an invaluable sounding board, and buffered the loneliness of writing. My buddies at TARP nudged me in the right direction and were examples of what I needed to do both positively and negatively, which were equally important. Chase Gipson played a crucial role in framing and contextualizing these stories via our many conversations about current American life. The Friends of Jung, a group I've been happily connected to in Fayetteville for the past several years, gave me a forum to share my stories and their feedback gave me the confidence to secure a publisher. Finally, my friend J. S., who prefers to remain anonymous, helped me finalize the look of the manuscript. All of you contributed to bring this project to term and every one of you has my eternal gratitude.

AUTHOR'S NOTE

Although we knew him as Dick or Dicky until he left home for college, for simplicity's sake and throughout this memoir, I refer to my oldest brother as Rick.

As to the structure of this book, there are many ways to read it.

The reader who is interested in the social context of **Clocking the Goose** had best read the Introduction, then the stories and Afterword.

If your primarily interest is my stories alone, jump right into them on page one. They stand on their own without the pre and post story elements of the book.

For readers who want more detail about my family, the Appendix provides that.

Why read THIS book?!?

As you read these accounts from my life, or more precisely as you let them intermingle with yours, we become interchangeable as the central figure in this book.

By some strange alchemy, my voice and my stories become yours.

If you're open to this viewpoint, our shared humanity makes this fusion not only possible but inevitable.

That's why the story of my life is relevant and can change yours.

We all had a childhood, good, bad or both. We all had parents, good, bad or both. Each one of us has had triumphs and tragedies. These extremes often oppress us, yet if we use them to find higher ground, they can enrich the person we become.

How we turn out in the end is rooted in our choices, especially by what we make of the challenges of our youth.

At some point in these chronicles, you will meet yourself. As you journey through this memoir, you'll discover that the struggles and the darkness of being human can provide you as much value as your positive qualities.

The physical struggle of a caterpillar to emerge from its chrysalis makes its wings strong enough to soar as a butterfly. Likewise, our emotional and spiritual difficulties are essential to our soulful growth as human beings.

For my part, I never wanted to be perfect, rich, or famous. What I needed was to become wholly human and fully alive.

Robert Moseley

If you let it, the humanity you find here can liberate you.

The goose, a symbol of divinity and goodwill, seems most awkward just before he takes wing.

We all want to fly, so in a spirit of solidarity, let's give him a nudge.

Fasten your seat belts folks, this will be a bumpy flight...

RM

CLOCKING the GOOSE
TABLE of CONTENTS

INTRODUCTION xix

PREFACE: Clocking the Goose xxvii

CHAPTER I: In My Beginning is My End 1
    Terribly Two and Tyson Park: The Battle is Joined 1
    Cowlicks and Popsicles 3
    Kindergarten and Graduation Day in a Combat Zone 5
    Life Without Training Wheels 10
    A New Model is Replacing Me and SHE'S A GIRL!?!?!? 18
    On Family Dynamics and Reversals of Fortune 20

CHAPTER II: Moving to the House on the Hill 31
    A Change of Venue: 468 North Crest Road 31
    My Father as a Son 33
    New Neighborhood, New Life, New School 36
    Starting Over with Charlotte Thurman 38
    Mrs. Johnson's Art Prize and the Ice Cream Sandwich 39
    The Sincenset 42
    A Fourth Grade Science Experiment and first time Therapy 43
    Sir George Beagle 46
    Breathing Room 48
    A Close Call 57
    I love you; I hate you-What the Hell do you do with Girls? 61
    Changing Classes 64
    Hitting My First Golf Shot 66

CHAPTER III: Broadening My Horizons 69
    My First Awakening 69

Rome	71
Cairo	74
Jerusalem	76
Tel Aviv	78
Beirut	79
Damascus	80
Athens and Santorini	81
Paris	82
You Can't Go Home Again	83
My Secret Garden	84
Warming Up with Darlene	86
Acne	88
Civil and Uncivil Protest	90
Standing up to a Bully	93
A Dead Volvo and a Violation	95
The Kimball Case	97
Captain Kirk and Being a Champion	101
Naked Bait	104
High School Daze	107
Meeting My Shadow and Discovering the Stars	107
Saved by Southern Belle	111
My First Time	115
CHAPTER IV: Fleeting First Steps On my Own	**121**
The Last Time in Your Life No One Expects Anything of You	121
The View from Rocky Top	122
Magic and Mastery at Augusta National	128
Going Door to Door	132
Comebacks, Chocolate-Chip Cookies and a Big Scare	136
My Late Drop	139
Riffraff	143

Losing Grandaddy Hawk 144
A Glimpse of the Future.. 146
Graduation to a Future Uncertain.. 148
Other Worlds, Other Possibilities: My Acting Days and the
Women in my Life 149
You Want to Be What? My Introduction to Acting..................... 150

CHAPTER V: Life and Love in The Big Apple 153
Circle in the Square... 153
Breakthrough on My Birthday 161
The Pigeon and the Nazi 164
COMING OUT OF MY BODY 165
Living the Actor's Life: Embracing Temporary Insanity........... 166
Acting with a Board Up My Ass.. 170
Potter's Field and learning to play Shakespeare 173
Marion I.. 177
Playing the Bard in the Company of Miserable Idiots............... 179
Susan Slavin's Actors and Singers Academy............................. 185
Living on the Periphery.. 195
Paula... 197
Don Quixote At the Crossroads 203
The White Crow.. 205
Marion II and MacMillan.. 208
Sherri.. 213
A New Start and The Invitation 220

CHAPTER VI: Life gets Metaphysical... 243
Loose Ends and Angelic Interventions.. 243
Gabriel.. 244
No where Man in a No Man's Land: Finding and filling
my Own Void 251
On Teaching and Being Taught... 254

Machu Picchu & an unexpected turn in a familiar direction 258
Roberto Borgatti and following my Bliss 260
Dead, Buried and Born Again; Again! 269
Becoming A Starman 274
Virginia 281
Saying Goodbye to Gabriel and Grounding His Message
in the Real World 286
MDI 287
Confessions of a Prodigal Son 292
Fayetteville I-Making a new start with Chiron 293

CHAPTER VII: Great Loss Opens Me to Deeper Ground 301
Losing Dad 301
Taking a deeper dive into WHAT'S WHAT 305
Nancy: The Feeling of Being Home, At Last 307
Losing Mom 321
Coming Home again; at least part way 326
Losing Stephen 327
The Saving Grace of a Part Time Job 332
Losing Rick 334
Covid 336
Scotland 2023 339
Marion III 346
A Forced Move becomes a Blessed New Beginning 349
Finding Diane 352
NOW 355

AFTERWORD: Getting a Good Job on Coming Full Circle 357

APPENDIX: Rounding out the picture of my immediate
family members 369
My Father-Raymond Herbert Moseley 369
My Mother-Lois Virginia Hawk Moseley 371

My Oldest Brother-Richard Paul Moseley 372
My Middle Brother-Stephen Ray Moseley 373
My Sister-Diane Louise Moseley Crabtree 375
The Corporate Cosmology of Arthur Jensen from Sidney
Lumet's film *NETWORK* 1976 376

INTRODUCTION

There's something gothic about growing up in the south. The states comprising the underbelly of the Mason-Dixon line are often celebrated for their conviviality, yet mainstream southern graciousness has a dark, inscrutable side. No less a human observer than D.H. Lawrence might have referenced this when he said; *"The essential American Soul is hard, isolate, stoic, and a killer. It has never yet melted."*

This sinister quality, like a haunted house, frames the work of southern writers from Fitzgerald, Faulkner, and Wolfe, to James Dickey, Tennessee Williams, and many, many more.

As a Tennessean raised outside the Deep South, I didn't have this understanding. But as an adult who has lived beyond the region and travelled the world, I see that many white southerners never got over losing *the war of northern aggression*, known more broadly as the American Civil War.

This loss; this gnawing resentment and shame, if now only a psychic inheritance, has passed generation to generation of mainstream southerners from Appomattox to today. It often stays with us whether we remain in our birthplace or live as far from it as possible.

There are many manifestations of this resentment; this grudge. Some good, some bad depending on how you see it and what you do with it.

At its root, many descendants of the Confederacy feel stigmatized; they feel *other* or *less than* Americans from the north, east and west. This, *otherness*, again if only psychological, has similarities to yet is vastly different from the *otherness* experienced by most Black people who have roots or grew up in Dixie.

I feel incapable of writing about the complexities of the Black experience in the region of my birth. That's a story beyond the scope of this memoir and my current understanding. But I can speak with clarity and depth about being a child in my family and that's something almost all of us can relate to.

All people who struggle with feeling *other* or *less than* share a common pain and a common need.

Unless and until they become conscious of their alienation; and then become responsible, intentional, and disciplined in addressing and integrating the emotions that go with that affliction, they never get past it.

I offer this perspective at the beginning of my memoir to show how where I came from affected the man I became and how the ghosts of my past have never completely left me.

Clocking the Goose, a collection of short stories from my life, is about how I grew up and how I'm getting over it.

At first glance, I am a person of no importance. My life has not been distinguished by great achievement of any socially significant kind, and my voice is not celebrated nor sought by anyone.

Yet amidst cultural forces that now diminish our experience of *feeling truly alive*, I cry out for a renewal of human values in an America today that prizes image over substance, political correctness over candor, corporate greed over the equitable sharing of our bounty, and never-ending commercialized excess over the preservation of healthy personal boundaries and social limits.

In this or any era, if we are to live lives of true meaning, getting past the wounds of our youth is relevant to everyone, everywhere, regardless of how or where they grew up.

We now exist in a social media culture that trivializes our hopes and dreams, as attested to by "Reality TV" shows like the Kardashian family opus, or politicizes our interactions to the point of absurdity, like all the revamped telecasts of *Bachelor, Bachelorette, and Survivor* of who gives a damn where.

We have more sophisticated means of communication than at any time in history, yet true connection and real intimacy are as rare as a moment of authentic humanity in the overhyped, repetitious, and polarizing 24-hour news cycle.

In this context, my stories call for a rebirth of integrity, humility, and common sense in our relationships and for each of us to become the authority in his or her life. Being my own authority need not be seen as insurrection and egoism run rampant. For if I decide what is best for me, I recognize and respect the same is true for you.

In this regard, I see civilization as a 24-hour agreement adults renew daily to make things work despite the never-ending challenges that mitigate against that. I strive to live in ways that makes sense to me, and I respect my fellow travelers' right and need to do the same.

Today, branding and buzz surpass substance and simple human decency. By and large, experts in contemporary America, credentialed and counterfeit, dominate our self-involved and self-indulgent culture. Yet their advice seems to produce automatons, aping woke, reactive or corporate narratives that are antithetical to healthy self-possession, self-reliance, sound judgment, and to our collective well-being.

How else can we explain the passive compliance of the critical mass of our populace who mindlessly consume pharmaceutical symptom suppressors, the taking of which are normalized by an avalanche of prime-time TV commercials, which cost hundreds or thousands of dollars per dose yet cure nothing, and produce a demon's list of toxic, sometimes terminal side effects.

There's got to be a better way.

Becoming conscious, intentional, and inner-directed people who make real contributions to their fellow humans and who enrich of our public life, is a notion hostile to the drone-like, politically correct existence our profit obsessed corporatized culture would have us adopt. Moreover, corporations use their many public service initiatives to brainwash us into believing how much they care and to *camouflage* their soul-diminishing, profit at all costs agenda.

Deep down in our hearts, we know this.

In America today, individuality is quashed in service of collective corporate standards, practices and returns. Our personal value is reduced to and determined by what we consume. We subsist under a plethora of dehumanizing "industrial complexes;" from the governmental industrial complex to the technological industrial complex, the military industrial complex, the medical industrial complex, the social media complex, and now even the entertainment industrial complex.

Sadly, most of our encounters with these multiplexes diminish our self-confidence, our enthusiasm and our humanity, no matter how faithfully we follow conventional wisdom, stay up-to-date, or how many "likes" we get.

So, my voice, undistinguished though it may be, is a solitary call for staying true to yourself; of standing in solidarity with genuine human values, whether they're popular and trending, or not.

At least, I hope it is.

At the end of the day, my voice and my experiences; my stories, are how I make myself known and my viewpoint credible. I believe the most powerful gift a person can share is his or her authentic story and that reading mine will inspire you to take account of your own.

But let me get underneath the self-liberating context I hope you bring to reading this book, get more personal than my analysis of life in America today, and focus with some precision on the feelings and facts that underpinned my upbringing.

I grew up in a haunted house; at least that's how it felt to me. A terrifying environment not troubled by the legacy of states' rights vs. federal domination, or by the curse of slavery and the ghosts of the possessed and the possessors, but by the consequences of the Great Depression and the havoc that social catastrophe twisted into my father's soul.

Raymond Herbert Moseley, the central figure in my world, was a towering figure to me. He was a warm, active, action-oriented, and accomplished man, with a deeply thoughtful, articulate, and poetic soul. Dad, in his pragmatic way, had immortal longings. He was abundantly gifted physically and intellectually; equally skilled using his hands as a craftsman, and his mind and voice as an advocate of clients who hired him for his widely acknowledged skill as an attorney.

He was also a man of compassion, common sense, and social conscience, though you only saw this if you looked at how unobtrusively he helped those in need. He never spoke of his charitable actions or donations; never blew his own horn. My father was a man of deep integrity and character, filled with flaws, contradictions, and denials, *as we all are*, but whose strength of character and desire to do good was clear to anyone with eyes to see.

And in all the most important ways he knew his quality; knew who and what he was. Dad didn't want and would disdain reviews by anyone presuming to pigeon-hole him one way or another, whether they "liked" him, or not.

Yet as gifted, humane, and self-possessed as he was, as loving and dedicated to our family as he made us feel, my father was also afflicted with a toxic rage that overwhelmed and haunted him his entire life. That rage drove him to success and renown among his peers, but it wrought chaos at home. It was like a raw, open wound that would and could not be healed, and when it erupted as it often did, everyone in our family ducked for cover however and wherever we could find it.

The reduced circumstances of his parents in the Depression era south were devastating to dad. He was traumatized even more by the shame of being perceived by some as a *ne'er do well*.

My father's dilemma, the split between his good and bad sides, gives rise to one of the most important ideas in this book; *that all of us, everywhere, are obliged to grapple with the light and darker angels of our conflicted human nature*. For if God exists deep within us, the devil lives there, too.

I believe we are meant to come to grips with this seeming impasse. That only by doing so can we become fully alive, fully human and reach the empathy, compassion, and grace essential to the preservation of a civilization worthy of the name.

Ultimately, my father's struggle with his light and darker impulses, speaks to another fundamental contention of these narratives; *that to fully realize our creed as Americans and our potential as human beings, we must develop a healthy relationship with our pain.*

Pain is meant to instruct and purify, not to be avoided at all costs. In its highest incarnation, our existential pain does not affirm humanity's original sin; it calls on us to deepen and grow.

So long as we mollycoddle ourselves in self-indulgence and entitlement, so long as we abide in trivialities like participation trophies and Reality TV, so long as we evade the elements of our personal character that keep us on the periphery of our best selves, masking our shame by how we manage our Facebook profiles, we will suffer needlessly in the shallows of what we might otherwise become.

Lastly, please know that my intention here is to heal, not to hurt; to find my way to the freedom, liberation and redemption that only come from digging deep into my soul and speaking with candor about my life. And not least, to put an end to generations of unspoken shame and pain within my family and yours by calling out what needs to be faced and transcended by people everywhere.

That said, I can only share what I experienced and perceived, and memory is a tricky biographer. Moreover, my memory is biased towards my viewpoint. This makes reality, past and present, illusive.

If, therefore, what I say here is hurtful to the survivors of those I write about or to sensibilities you hold dear, I ask for your forbearance. If I commit errors in fact, make mistakes of omission or commission, or voice things that seem cynical, wounding, or hateful, know that the tone of what I chronicle here is straight and true to my experience.

Robert Moseley

I loved my now dead family members with all my heart and soul. I believe they always knew and still know this; and that they will take this into account as I come to grips with them and myself through this memoir.

Likewise, if you disagree with my view of how we live in America today, please consider what I see and say is not tainted with malice, but imbued with hope for a happier, healthier world.

I've learned that life without love isn't worth living; that to love others I must first be true to myself, and that love is the constant act of forgiveness.

I hope my efforts here inspire you to do the same.

RM

PREFACE:
Clocking the Goose

Sometime in the early spring of 1991, my days as a professional actor, and thus my ***raison d'être*** for living and working in New York City, had come and gone. At loose ends, betwixt and between whatever new direction my life would now take, I took a break from worrying about my future to play a round of golf.

Although I never aspired to play professionally, lacking the skill and dedication to acquire it, I needed to get away from my worries by doing something I loved. Besides, you couldn't play worth a damn with your mind on anything but golf. Maybe I'd come back to my situation refreshed, with a new perspective.

Today, my first round of the season, was at Van Cortlandt Park. Vanny, as she was known by locals, was an odd golf course. The metaphor of going out, then coming in, so richly chronicled in the literature of the game, found strange expression here. At Van Cortlandt you not only went out, *but over, around, under and through* before coming back home.

Many golfers who played this eccentric relic speculated about the strangeness of the layout. Some thought the course, which opened in 1898 and so became the oldest public track in the U.S., was forced to adapt to roadways that didn't yet exist. In her earliest days, however, Vanny was surrounded by undeveloped forest and accessible only by train.

Just to get to the first tee required you to pass a lake that ran the length of an uphill par 4. Holes one and two were separated from the rolling, isolated matrix of three through seven by a tunnel routed to the north. When you finished seven, you came back through this viaduct, then walked west another hundred yards or so to play eight and nine. Upon finishing the ninth, you passed through another lengthy tree lined alleyway to ten and eleven, after which you backtracked on the route you'd taken to eight, to play the par-5 twelfth.

It makes me dizzy just recalling it.

From twelve to fourteen you headed back parallel to the first two holes, which at least made sense, but then you had to hike up the length of another long, annoying causeway to the last four holes, aptly known as the Hills.

So, if you carried your bag as I always did in those days, you were hiking the length of a 22-hole, 9,000-yard golf course that finished with some hefty slopes, after which you faced a quarter mile hike back to the clubhouse.

The byzantine routing of this labyrinth mirrored my confusion about my life. On days I played badly I felt like Sisyphus. If this golf course symbolized the current ground of my being, it would be all too easy to get lost and collapse in despair. At least Sissy knew his task, what to expect, and the ground he trod.

In my current state, I might never find my way to a new beginning.

The quirky old gal was soft today. Snow had blanketed her just three days before and the course was barely firm enough to play. I'd just come to thirteen, a hole I'd nearly aced the year before, missing the cup by half a ball's width, as evidenced by the pitch mark my ball made on the green that day. The memory of that near miss still made me wince. To this day, I've never come closer to a hole in one.

CLOCKING the GOOSE

On this new day, in a new season, of what I hoped would be a new life, a large flock of geese ambled short of the green, just beyond the far edge of a large pond fronting the tee box. From the green side of this pond the terrain covered another seventy yards up to the putting surface. Nobody liked the geese at Vanny. They got in your way, their offal was awful, fouling your shoes, cluttering the greens and on wet days like today, they made that part of the course stink.

Depending on the placement of the tee, this hole was a six, seven or eight-iron of about 160 or 175 yards to a green strongly canted from back to front. As with most old courses, the real trouble lay behind the hole. Airmail this elderly dance floor and you had no play. If, however, you kept your ball below the pin, tempering your greed to go for flags cut deep, and *IF* you could roll your rock, this could be an easy hole.

At lucky thirteen, everything depended on your tee shot.

Perhaps it was my un-tethered mood, my lusty recall of missing that ace, or a desire for payback, for now I thinned my 7-iron with a ferocious lash, sending my ball like a shin-high rocket to find neither hole nor green, but the unlucky neck of a wandering goose. I didn't like the damn things any more than I liked my life at the moment, but I didn't want to kill anyone or anything.

I was just trying to find my swing.

The poor beast was staggered. His head looped around the base of his long, whiplashed *décolletage* with a rotation so wide and wobbly I feared I'd broken the creature's neck.

So sudden and terrible was my blow, that had I been boxing, not golfing, I'd have been DQ'd for clocking my opponent with a sucker punch. Worse still, he was about to stay down for the count. For not wanting this poor goose to suffer, I pondered euthanizing him with my sand-wedge.

Sensing now that this had become much more than a salving round of golf, and debating if, when and how, to deliver the *coup de grace,* I saw the addled bird begin to right himself. The groggy loop of his head and flaccid neck gradually began to abate. Eventually, if very slowly, he recovered his composure and his stride. Then, with a shrug and a shake, he rejoined his fellows as if nothing had happened.

Relieved, I sheathed my wedge.

Down wasn't necessarily out. Perhaps I, like he, could recover from an unforeseen and staggering blow to find my way again.

THE STORIES

CHAPTER I:
In My Beginning is My End

Terribly Two and Tyson Park: The Battle is Joined

Several years ago, my dad told me a story that unlocked the beginning, if not the root, of my lifelong battle with him and with myself.

When I was two, as my father told it, we were playing together in Tyson Park. We lived in Knoxville, Tennessee, where I was born at 2:38 pm on December 12, 1952. Dad told me that I got so mad at him I held my breath till I turned blue. My rageful self-attack terrified my father. He picked me up by my feet and slapped my back with his open palm, just so I'd start breathing again.

The instant I heard his recollection it was as if I witnessed a movie of my life go black. In my mind's eye I thought, *"Aha, so this is where the battle was joined!"* It was if the tumblers inside a lock fell into place. Tracking back from this unexpected revelation, even with no specific memory of the episode myself, I began to realize why certain lines from books or films stuck with me.

For some reason I thought of Captain Ahab from Melville's <u>Moby Dick</u>,

"To the last, I will grapple with thee!"

Now, with the insight triggered by my forgotten tantrum, I knew why this sentiment resonated with me. *I had a vendetta with dad from a time before I could remember.*

My father was not an evil or abusive man, but he was very VERY controlling, and he ruled our family driven by his fear of the Great Depression that befell him as a child. Although I was too young to realize it, his mercurial nature mirrored my own. Even as a toddler, I bristled at being controlled by him or anyone

Patricide is a threatening concept, especially for a two-year old; that's probably why I couldn't remember anything before I was five. No doubt, as a toddler, I couldn't abide being manhandled, as from time to time my father was wont to do.

But why did I take my anger at dad out on myself? What was the meaning, beyond my unfettered rage, for not just this episode, but what I'm told was my infantile pattern of shutting-down and breath-holding whenever I got mad?

Answering these questions would take time.

In writing these memoirs, a start and stop process that took many years, I would come to learn that I wasn't the only one in my family with blank spots in my memory and a pattern of self-abuse.

For my father's part, he had an odd way of relating to pets, which correlated to how he interacted with me and all his sons. He would aggressively handle our family dogs or cats so severely the poor animals would try to bite or scratch him.

I saw dad behave this way with a kitten we had named Jack. My father became so enraged at being clawed, *which he damn well deserved*, that he put poor Jack in a box, drove him out to the boondocks, shook the container forcefully, dumped him out and abandoned the hapless creature to fend for himself in the wilderness.

My discovery of the Tyson Park puzzle piece now confirmed another feeling I've always had; **that a person born with a warrior spirit is imbued with that savage, unfiltered and primordial energy from birth.** I connected now in a deeper way to my unspoken, defiant, and deep-seated refusal to take action, especially when an activity was forced on me against my will.

I was just beginning to glimpse the consequences of the silent vow I made in that small and narrow little park when I was barely two.

Again, it was Melville's Ahab who prompted me to realize the vengeful oath I took that day:

"From Hell's heart, I stab at thee! For hate's sake I spit my last breath at thee!"

Now, I began to grasp the lengths to which I had gone to keep this unconscious vow.

"I will go to the end of time to beat you, you son of a bitch! I will get you if it kills me. No matter what I have to do, no matter what it costs me, you are going down!"

Such was my resolve from a time before I could remember.

Cowlicks and Popsicles

If I was a vengeful tyke, I was loving and playful, too. Like many children with an unfettered spirit, I had the ability to kill someone off, then instantly recreate them. I also had an enormous range of possibilities. Moreover, when my feelings came up, they hit me like a thunderbolt.

My mother told me I was forever getting into things and insatiably curious. Apparently, I also had a giggle/laugh that would fill a room, especially when granddaddy Hawk, mom's dad, sat me on his knee to tell me stories.

My temper was as big as my laugh and I had an appetite for danger, too. At home, for instance, I would find a way to crawl up near the stove, attracted by the redness of the eye that was cooking God knows what on any given day.

Mom told me that I definitely had to be watched.

Out in the yard, I nearly waddled onto the busy road that fronted our house, just to get one of granddaddy's cigarette wrappers that had blown into the street. The triumphal climax to my manic curiosity came when I figured out how to switch on mama's floor polisher. It bounced around like a bucking bronco, I'm sure to my utter delight, till its long power cord got tangled up in its rotating floor brushes, burning the motor out.

Then, when I was just past three, we moved from Knoxville to Chattanooga in January 1956. Looking back on this new chapter in my life, what I remember is how fully in the moment I was. My days seemed endless.

One of my fondest Chattanooga memories was when the ice cream truck came to our new neighborhood. I would hear the familiar sound of its calliope, heralding its approach to my new domain at 777 Brookfield Avenue. The appearance of the ice cream man, delightful though it was, always presented me with a challenge. I remember twisting the cowlick of my burr haircut and thinking, *"I wonder how I can get a nickel from mom today?"*

Early one Saturday, the ice cream/popsicle truck appeared anew, suddenly transformed into a flying saucer. It looked neat but caused me a BIG problem. Popsicles and Nutty Buddies were no longer a nickel:

NOW THEY COST A DIME!

As far as I was concerned this was an outrage; a grave injustice; a true national crisis.

Suddenly, *"What do I have to do to get a popsicle, today"* became *"How will I ever get a whole dime out of Mom?"* Mother was a tough nut to crack. *"What will happen to me if I'm deprived of the yummy deliciousness of my favorite banana pop? How will I go on living if I can't lick it till my gums go numb? If I can't suck on my flat popsicle stick till I get splinters in my tongue, I just can't go on!"*

Something's got to be done!

At first, mama seemed as outraged as me. I think she gave me a dime a few more times but going forward my memory of enjoying banana popsicles trailed off. I imagine I got an early lesson here in economy/scarcity.

At any rate, I learned to live without a treat I could no longer afford.

Kindergarten and Graduation Day in a Combat Zone

"Now don't forget, shake the principal's hand THEN take the diploma." These were dad's last words to me as he readied his big press camera, the one he used to take pictures of car wrecks. Why he did this I wasn't sure, but it had something to do with bankrolling Mom

to feed my popsicle habit. I knew Dad was a lawyer, but I wasn't sure what that had to do with busted cars.

Anyway, today's project was to memorialize my graduation from kindergarten, and I could feel my father's demanding presence from across the entire auditorium. There seemed to be hundreds of thousands of people attending this highly anticipated event and all us graduates were decked out in white shirts, shorts, socks, and shoes.

My appearance might have been angelic, but my thoughts were anything but. *"Stop telling me what to do! Whatever you say, I'm doin' the opposite! I'll grab my diploma from that old man and if he doesn't give it to me first, I won't shake his hand!"*

Here I was barely out of nursery school and dad was already trying to control me and everything else around me. *"Fat chance, buddy. You can't push me around. Back off!"*

Unconscious of my anger and defiance, deep down inside I felt something was wrong with me. I'd already started to second-guess myself and I wasn't even in grade school yet. Dad's concern that I get things right was such an ongoing worry for him that I began to think my first impulses must always be wrong.

I don't remember if I had directly experienced my father's ferocity yet. But I knew how demanding he could be. Dad had been an active-duty Naval aviator a few years before I was born and things were to be done in a proper way, dictated by his fighter-pilot standards. I wasn't sure what the fighter pilot thing was all about, either, but I probably saw on TV, *an instrument that fascinated me*, that flyers like dad killed their opponents in intense aerial combats.

For sure, I felt the pressure of getting things right according to his militant rules and regulations. I also recall feeling pushed by him to meet his standards quickly and efficiently. That also pissed me off.

My nature and rhythm, as opposed to my father's which seemed all fire and fury, had both quicksilver and deliberate qualities. I thought quickly and usually picked up what was happening around me fast. But I was measured and would mull over things, too. This was especially so when I wasn't sure what I was doing, or why, or when I felt pressed into service or to behave in a certain way.

Dad was always in a rush, or so it seemed to me.

The best example I can recall of our contrasting styles was manifested in my father's never-ending weekend projects. These ventures ran the gamut from getting the best photo op for my graduation today, to pouring a concrete walkway in our front yard or building a patio at the rear of our house, to extending the parking area of our driveway, to putting a full bathroom in a closet, to installing an air-conditioning system throughout our home, and on and on.

In all these projects, my older brothers, Rick, and Steve were expected to keep up with dad, who did things five-times faster than sound. So was I, and we all had to do this WITHOUT ANY INSTRUCTIONS!

I don't know how my brothers felt about this and for some reason I never asked them, but I could have used some guidance, or God forbid, a little context.

This illustrates an element of our family life that now, looking back, I find sad and still puzzles me. *None of us ever seemed to reach out to each other for help*. We all did things on our own. This might account, at least in part, for why isolation became a major theme in my life and in the lives of everyone in my entire family.

At any rate, dad never took time to clue us in. He never told us what we were working to accomplish, why, or explain how our assignments fit the overall goal. No, it was sink or swim, figure shit out for yourself, get to work, do what I tell you to do, and get it done fast and properly or there'll be hell to pay.

Not only was there a frenzied quality to the work we did but my brothers were better at adapting to pop's weekend sprints than I was. *They got with it*, one of dad's catch phrases, in ways that escaped me.

"Get with it, son. Why aren't you with me? Stop dreaming and get with me," seemed to be my father's constant complaint about me. My subconscious reply to my father's command, (that is the more reactive, R-rated version) was firmly in the realm of *"Get with you? Get with you? GO FUCK YOURSELF, YOU TYRANT!"*

In time, many years later, I came to realize what dad meant by saying *"Get with it."* He was giving me a life lesson; he was saying that, when necessary, it serves you to ignore how you feel about any particular task, *especially if you don't like doing it*, and focus all your energies on getting it done and doing it well. Don't fight the problem, align with the challenge. You might learn something that improves you. And at the very least you'll get back to doing whatever you like as quickly as possible.

This is a lesson I wish I learned much earlier than I did but it's also one he began giving me when I was four. I didn't know any four-year-old fighter pilots.

In retrospect, I think my brothers got this distinction instinctively. My fear of dad and my anger at him blinded me to this insight. Only with age and experience did I also realize that he intended his projects to make a better life for all of us and to prepare us to be successful on our own.

There is truth in this, of course, but it's also true that dad did what he wanted to do because he wanted to do it and he justified it without considering anyone's viewpoint but his own.

Although there is value in living life with some rigor, relaxation is just as important. As an adult, I've found that I don't have to tend to my car as if it were an airplane in flight, where any malfunction can kill you if you don't anticipate it in advance and have a contingency plan if things go wrong.

Rick, my oldest brother by just under six years, was extremely deliberate, much more than me, but he was also dogged and practical in ways I never will be. As dad's first born, he was in some ways uniquely capable of handling that impossible role.

Looking back now, the thing I marveled at about Rick, who we called Dick or Dickie till he went away to college, was that he could take a psychic beating from dad, which he most certainly did, get back up off the floor, so to speak, and then just keep working and working till he "*got a good job;*" another of dad's catch phrases for how to live a good life.

"*Get a good job*," was my father's parlance for doing everything with excellence and simplicity at high speed. This was another damn good life-lesson. What I objected to was the pressure, the feeling of oppression, and the contextual void in which we were expected to accomplish excellence in everything we did.

Rick had no problem taking his time, yet somehow, he could adapt to dad's furious pace, too. He was also temperamentally suited to excelling at the kinds of projects my father took on. I just wish pop showed him more appreciation and affection than he did when my oldest brother was a little boy.

My brother Steve, three and a half years my senior, was gifted with great intelligence and a splendid work ethic but could be selfish and sometimes he was cruel to me. Like Rick, Stephen was deliberate and dogged, but he also had a brilliance Rick did not possess.

Although Steve was deeply sensitive, as I was, and like me he had the Moseley temper, he never seemed to let his powerful moods or anger derail his desire to do well at everything he did. He kept his eye on the prize of accomplishing whatever he set out to do, so his anger or moodiness narrowed his focus to carry out whatever task was at hand.

For far too long, I was too self-involved, both as a boy and a man, to give much thought to how my brothers handled their own difficulties dealing with dad.

At any rate, back to kindergarten now, dad got a great picture of my graduation and somehow I shook hands with my principal before he handed me my diploma.

What I learned from this was to avoid getting into an open conflict with my father over something he wanted me to do. If I was clear about anything it was you did not want to be the DIRECT object of my father's rage. I was about to learn this in a big, BIG WAY.

Life Without Training Wheels

As the wrench in dad's hand gripped the lug nut on the first training wheel of my used red bike, backing it off its bolt, I remember watching him in utter futility. *"I can't stop him." "I'm gonna die now and there's nothing I can do about it!"* With every turn of his wrench, I could hear him say, not literally but in my imagination, *"You know how to play. I'm going to teach you how to work."*

"Why the hell does riding a bike have to be a lesson about work, anyway," I puzzled, or at least I would have if I hadn't been petrified.

The world of being a boy and the hazards of becoming a man were about to collide in a way that forever changed me.

In theory, putting my bike on the sharp slope of our driveway, sans training wheels but not sans me, would give me a runny-go and some needed speed. Speed would give me momentum which ought to help my balance, and clearly balance was the key to riding a bike.

All this had a certain logic, but I wasn't a disciplined test pilot, nor was I feeling logical! I was four going on five and I was terrified!

On that overcast and temperate summer morning in 1957, our driveway seemed like Mount Everest to me. To my left, as I stood trembling atop the world's tallest peak, a wall buttressed our front yard. Topped by three tall pine trees, this cinder block partition tapered out, curving left and growing in height until it stood some ten feet high and tied into the north end of our home.

Dad was wearing his weekend project uniform; khakis pants, a white tee shirt and black or cordovan shoes. No doubt I was in knock-off sneakers and shorts, also with a tee shirt, dressed like almost any boy my age. Preschool boys always look the same, somehow, even as styles evolve, and times change.

To this day I don't remember if I actually rode my bike, or not.

When I go back to picture this event, what comes up for me are grey, unfocused images. The sounds I hear are muted, like a slow-motion movie with shouting drawn out at half volume and quarter-speed.

The people present, except for my father, stand as blurred and darkened statues, frozen in time and my memory. As far as I know, mom didn't know, *or more likely she didn't want to know*, what was going on with my father and me. Mother was home, but though physically present, emotionally she was rarely there.

I remember my brothers standing by. I wish I'd asked them for HELP! Maybe they could have gotten dad to give me a break, but they, like me, were intimidated to the point of silence, if not stupor, by his dictates and demanding ways.

Maybe because Rick and Steve were older and could do things I could not, like work right alongside dad doing practical stuff, they existed in a world separate from mine. I was in a world of my own, and when I could avoid working with dad, which in those days I always dreaded, I would go off and play by myself.

I had a special place I'd hide in our tool shed in the back yard. It was cool and dark there and I'd turn the wheelbarrow dad stored there on its side blocking the open doorway and go into the world of my imagination.

My brothers and I weren't really playmates. We only came together as indentured servants when dad needed help around the house, like digging out an extra garage space, which thank God I was too small to do, or laying a patio after pouring a cement base, which I was big enough to handle in a supporting role.

On that occasion dad told me to hold a running hose over his head as he laid flat stones in the unformed cement he'd just poured from our cement mixer. In the sweltering heat that morning, he tied a bandana around his head to keep sweat from running down onto his glasses and clouding his vision. Pop said, *"Hold this hose over my head so I don't die of heatstroke."* And I thought, *"Are you crazy? Wait till its cooler to lay the damn stones. Why do you have to do everything so fast and always RIGHT NOW?"*

Anyhow, back on Mount Everest as dad hoisted me onto my bike, then gave me a gentle push, I shut him out in terror. Afraid of going too fast, terrified at being out of control, I deliberately steered into the wall, cutting the knuckles of my left hand as I tried to slow down using my body as a brake.

It didn't work, and the more I shut dad out, the angrier he got. I'd witnessed dad's fury before, but now it was fully directed at me.

Dad's screaming at me now, making me get back on the bike to go again and again and again. Each time he grabs and shakes me I cower, raging at him from within, yet trying to comply…

"Why are you doing this to me?"

"Why do you want to hurt me?"

"Why don't you care that I'm afraid?"

"Why won't you leave me alone?"

"Leave me alone." **"LEAVE ME ALONE!"**

Every time he shook me, trying to guide me, doing his best to help me get past my fear, but acting like a madman, I pulled more and more inside. In a way I had to deny, it was as if I was returning to Tyson Park and saying again,

"To the last I will grapple with thee!"

Amidst my father's shouts, my brothers and neighbors watched in stunned silence. It felt like the entire world was witnessing my abandonment, failure, and shame. No one knew what to say. They couldn't have stopped my father if they'd tried; nobody could.

At least that's how I saw it then.

Afterwards, we gathered at the kitchen table to eat tuna salad sandwiches laced with diced sweet pickles, or maybe it was the egg salad version that day.

There was a terrible, deafening silence.

I'm sure I was sniveling or maybe I was all cried out by then. I felt battered, numb, and ashamed. Mom said something to ease my pain, but dad, ever responsible to his obligation to toughen me up, said defensively: *"Well, if he's going to be a man, he's got to..."*

I don't recall how he finished the sentence. I didn't give a damn. From that moment till we finished eating it seemed no one uttered a word.

Each of us tried to survive my father's extremities and insanities, in his or her own way. Although we all evolved individual strategies to do so, culling tactics from one another we hoped would protect us from his wrath; none of us escaped unmarked by dad's drives, demons, and demands.

It was all I could do just to survive.

Rick got the worst of it because he was first born. He was stoic, yet so, so sad. My oldest brother seemed forlorn and beat down. Steve fought back, although I don't remember how. It seemed that was a better way to go but I was too afraid of dad to take him on directly. More to the point, I was probably petrified because I wanted to kill him. So, it was from mom that I learned how to handle pop. She followed his commands, was loyal to him even when he was abusive or wrong, and the two of them seemed to get along, so I copied her approach.

My father was never malicious, at least not intentionally so. When he lost his temper with us, it was because he wanted us to be smarter, or faster, or better at *"getting a good job;"* at achieving the ideal outcome of whatever stupid project he had us slaving away at.

Dad was such a titanic force that I never considered how much pain he was in; how much he wanted to help us avoid the horrors he endured growing up but rarely spoke about. Pop's heart was always in the right place, I just couldn't see this. It was all but impossible to see how much he loved us when he went OFF!

The best example of how his rage felt to me was depicted time and again by two actors I always loved, Kirk Douglas and George C. Scott. My father combined the charm and ferocity of both these men and would have given both a run for their money when it came to volcanic behavior.

It was not long after this that I began to say, almost as my default reaction to everything I did, *"So what, who cares,"* trying in my growing shame, futility, and rage to set boundaries that were already crashing down in an avalanche of self-contempt and subconscious, covert vengefulness.

My knuckles healed from this traumatic episode, but the bruised and bloody wounds to my psyche remained for years to come. Many times, in future days I would steer into walls of my own making, in a re-enactment of this pivotal event, and every time;

"To the last I will grapple with thee!"

Yet, amazingly, ironically, the most vividly joyful of my childhood memories, *once I'd learned to ride my bike on my own*, is that of my reckless freedom on two-wheels. Part of me quickly forgot my traumatic initiation on that hellish hill.

I became as fearless as I was bold.

In short order, I felt bullet-proof on my bike, and only the prospect of being put to work, a fate I avoided and grew more and more to hate, would crush my joyful world of play.

I wanted my life to be fun, adventurous, and carefree. When the men in our family were working, I began to imagine I was surrounded by a "force-field" which made me invisible; a protective shield that freed me from their scrutiny and exempted me from the slavishness of dad's projects.

Sometimes this worked. For dad's intense focus would so narrow on the task at hand, he would overlook my playful ways and the obligation he felt to make me into a man.

Rick never seemed to mind that I stayed as far away from the forced labor as I could. For me he had a gentle spirit that I was always drawn to. Steve, however, hated it when I disappeared from the cauldron of dad's projects, often to grab us water, or do anything peripheral to the action, just to get away.

Often I wondered why we couldn't play music while we worked or tell jokes and laugh. Why did work have to be such a pain in the ass?

When I couldn't escape a project, I'd imagine myself at play. Besides riding my bike, playing guns was my favorite pastime. It was great fun to battle friends my age, like my neighbor Scott Norman, and make the sound of rifle fire before toys made those sounds for you. When I got shot, I'd lie down momentarily, then get back up and fight some more. *"You can't do that, I just shot you! You're dead!"* my buddies or I would protest, depending on who had blasted who.

Our standard reply, no matter who had gone down was *"Un-uh, no way, you didn't kill me, you just wounded me!"*

I regret this never-say-die response didn't stick with me as my real life unfolded, but I had much work to do on myself before I could allow such resilience to abide.

Sadly, I never remember playing guns with Rick and Steve. Occasionally, the three of us would wrestle each other in the front yard. Steve would jump on me and rub my face in the lawn, then Rick jumped Steve, pulling him off me, and then I'd jump Rick for jumping onto Steve.

Through all this I always knew my oldest brother loved me and that he would look out for me. Stephen, I wasn't so sure of.

And yet I always loved Steve, too. He was often mean to me but nothing about the way he treated me had the toxicity of my interactions with dad. I never felt the obliterating force from Steve I felt from my father's messianic rage, even though I knew somehow that dad's animus had nothing to do with me.

Why and how I knew all this and how the complexities of love worked in the world of sibling relations reminded me years later of a memorable line from the movie <u>Shakespeare in Love</u>. *"I don't know how things resolve,* the line goes in my memory, *it's a mystery."*

And the ultimate mystery in my life was the interplay of love and hate continually taking place inside me and within my family.

A New Model is Replacing Me and SHE'S A GIRL!?!?!?

1957 had been a tough year. Dad made me bungee jump with my bike off Mount Everest and then on December 19th a new Moseley showed up. To make matters worse, she was a girl.

"Oh, God," I thought, *"I'm being replaced. Shit, they must not want me anymore. "Hum, three boys in a row. I was definitely supposed to be a girl. Hell, Steve was supposed to be a girl! If I'm not perfect now, I'll get kicked out of the family. If that happens, I won't have a place to eat or sleep. Where will I get popsicle money? When will I get to play? Oh, God, does this mean I have to go to* **work**?!?! *How much do gofers make?"*

"God help me if Dad finds out how mad I am at him. God help me if I find out how mad I am at myself."

Such were my subconscious concerns when I first greeted Diane Louise Moseley.

The day mom and dad brought sis home was hot for late December, way too warm for how bundled up she was. Her baby face was nearly beet red when I first laid eyes on my baby sis and I thought, *"Wow, doesn't mama see it's way, way too hot to have her wrapped up in all those blankets?"*

I showed off with apparent delight at our new addition. If I had concerns for my place in the family, AND I DEFINITELY DID, you would never know it as dad filmed this special occasion with his Bell and Howell movie camera.

The character of welcoming big brother to baby sister was one of my earliest acting roles. The dominant feeling I had about Diane was curiosity. I'd never been around a baby girl or any girl for that matter, and she seemed subtly but powerfully different from us boys. I couldn't pinpoint this difference, but the source of my anxiety centered on my shaky status. I didn't take my anxiety out on her, at least not in the first years of our relationship.

To my enduring shame, however, once I got into early adolescence, I terrorized my sister by chasing her with the lawnmower when we were outside and the vacuum cleaner when we found ourselves indoors. The pinnacle of my abuse was when I held the flame of a Bic cigarette lighter to the stem of a can of deodorant and directed its torchy blaze at her, trapping her in the upstairs hall bathroom.

To this day I'm upset at the way I treated her, and I periodically ask her again to forgive me. God bless her sweet heart, for although Diane too has our family temper and tendency towards vengeance, she never bore a grudge at me.

At least she didn't seem to.

Of all my siblings, Diane saw it all; she bore witness to the entire panoply of my parents' behavior and of how we, their progeny, adapted and responded to their good and bad traits. I think one reason she forgave me for terrorizing her was that Diane always saw I was in pain.

Sis and I seemed to have similar trajectories yet separate realities.

In some ways our new family member took pressure off me, almost as if she were my Guardian Angel. This is certainly a role Diane would take on in our relationship as adults.

For now, however, although I felt greater pressure to conform to my father's standards with her arrival, her presence seemed to soften dad, and I was all for that.

On Family Dynamics and Reversals of Fortune

The abandonment and betrayal I felt from Dad with the training-wheel episode became my excuse to go into hiding. Now, however, an equally alienating event occurred at home that sealed my commitment to go so far underground in my family that even I didn't realize the extent of my withdrawal. From this point forward, I was like a secret agent operating behind enemy lines.

What went down now also left me feeling that mom was no more my ally than dad was my champion.

As *"Baby Bobby"* a term of endearment Steve tormented me with, I was always, always, always trying to catch up with both my older brothers. On this particular day I not only caught up, I blew by them, BIG TIME!

Dad had just replaced our kitchen appliances and suddenly we had tons of giant cardboard containers at our disposal. My older brothers, always clever and inventive, decided to break up most of these cartons and make a runway on our steep driveway, keeping the best ones intact so we could race each other down the hill to our giant back yard.

My box, which I dubbed *Alligator I*, turned out to be the fastest of the lot. With every race, probably because I was a lightweight and created less friction, I beat the pants off Rick, Steve, and all comers.

To my amazement, I was now the champion of our entire neighborhood. Not bad for a squirt! Unexpectedly, I had arrived and I was in Hog Heaven. In triumph, I might have crowed a little too much, but I'd never won anything before, so strutting my stuff was understandable.

At long last I was not only a winner but undefeated and unbeatable, too.

"Now this," I reveled, *"is more like it. This is how things OUGHT to be around here!"*

All glory is fleeting and so it was now with my first triumph.

Mom called us inside for lunch and I quickly left our battleground to chow down. If I'd had my wits about me, I would have realized that something was amiss when I found myself eating alone. After all, on those rare occasions when we ate out or even at home, our practice as boys was always to say, *"I get to eat that if you don't want it!"*

As I wolfed down today's egg salad sandwich, eager to get back to my winning ways and wondering where my brothers were, I ambled from the kitchen to the dining room window that overlooked our back yard. There, at the foot of our runway, *Alligator I* was going up in flames!

MOM, MOM, I screamed, ***THEY'RE BURNING MY BOX. THEY'RE BURNING MY BOX!"*** Nothing could have been more devastating but then things got even worse.

Mother didn't lift a finger on my behalf. She didn't say a word to Rick and Steve.

I remember her glancing absent-mindedly at the demise of my golden chariot. She looked out the window in a preoccupied way, but for me her indifference was an unforgivable betrayal. This event, combined with the trauma of the training wheels, put the last nail in the coffin of what would now become my deep withdrawal into myself.

"I hate you! I hate every last one of you! I hate you and I'm gonna get you if it's the last thing I ever do!"

"Why don't I matter? I agonized, *why am I not worth loving, or protecting or being stood up for? Damn this family! Damn me! Damn everything!"*

"To the last I will grapple with thee!"

Then I thought; *"I'll show 'em; I'll become a monster more powerful than the monsters they are! I'll become a monster they can't see!"* Such became my **raison d'etre** before I was five.

I felt hopeless, helpless, powerless, and invisible. Worse still, I became hell-bent to fight these feelings; to eradicate these hated emotions or to die trying. And I realize now that I held my breath as a toddler to obliterate these feelings by trying to obliterate myself.

Worse still, losing *Alligator I* highlighted something about mom that deeply troubled me.

In one sense, I couldn't have had a better mother. Mama made a beautiful, clean, and calm home for all of us. By all conventional standards, we were safe, secure, well-fed, and loved.

But there was something amiss with mom; something off.

Lois Virginia was the first of Dick and Irene Hawk's three children. Born in April of 1926, she kept her family's household from the age of ten because her mother worked long hours in the clothing trade.

Dick was a stern and exacting father. As his first born and only daughter, mom wanted his approval and feared his criticism, which could be both nitpicking and severe. Sometimes she would clean their family home on Chestnut Ridge in Kingsport, Tennessee not once but *twice*, just to make sure it was done right.

My mother's outstanding trait was determination, followed closely by her curiosity about whatever was going on around her and out in the world. But only to a certain point. She had high standards of her own, was honest, frugal, and loyal to a fault. What is more, mom had great endurance plus a naughty fun-loving side dad often quashed, but she also had a deep sense of emptiness.

Like everyone in our family, mom was filled with contradictions.

What puzzled me the most about mama was that she was deeply compassionate yet would shut down if I hugged her for more than a few seconds.

Intimacy was just not her thing.

I hated this part of her because when she froze me out, I felt second-rate.

I know my siblings felt the same way about this part of her.

When I started Kindergarten and elementary school, I also loathed how mom would turn vampire when I got home. I could literally feel her sucking energy from me whenever she asked me how things were are school today.

She struggled with an existential loneliness she seemed ill-equipped to address.

I wish I'd asked her what was wrong; *"why do you need me to fill you up,"* I would have probed. But this part of her creeped me out. It made me want to get away from her and when mom leeched my energy, I did my best to keep a safe distance.

What I hated most about mom is that she would never, ever challenge dad when he went on one of his rampages. She feared for her own welfare if she crossed dad on any family issue. So, when her children came into conflict with him, not one of us could call on mother to stand up on his or her behalf.

The irony here is that mama was tender hearted. There was just something inside her that could not let anyone get too close. Her actions proved how much she loved us but as far as I can tell, and years later my sister Diane told me to my surprise that I was mom's favorite, something remained frozen in her soul.

Perhaps mother's greatest contradiction was that she was a great humanitarian but lacked the human touch. Especially with those closest to her. When it came to motherlove; to the idea of warmth, tenderness, and unconditional acceptance, sometimes it was there, sometimes not, and you never knew which type of mothering to expect.

Once again, I never asked my sibs how they felt about all this, nor did it occur to me to do so.

Hereto, mom's remoteness mirrored a detachment in both of my box-burning brothers.

It's a mystery to me that although I never doubted Rick and Steve loved me, we never deeply bonded, at least not when we were growing up. And it's odd, because I wasn't aware of my desire to be closer to them than I was. Things in our family were just the way they were, none of us had any other frame of reference, and no one ever challenged the self-isolating nature of our family's status quo.

Perhaps I wasn't the only one who felt haunted, alienated, and alone.

My brother Richard was one of the kindest, most soft-spoken, and sweetest people I ever knew. He loved me and was always, always protective of me in ways I wish I felt dad could have been. But I would not describe Rick as warm or easy to know. All his life he was shy and reserved about relating to others with anything like joyful banter or real spontaneity. I believe Richard felt so beat down by dad that he was reluctant to swing out in the world. At the same time, his reserve could not be blamed entirely on how dad treated him. Rick had a guarded constraint all his own.

Sadly, the infamous image of a Holocaust survivor comes to mind when I think on my oldest brother. The well-known film of this prisoner's liberation as he sat on a stretcher with his hands in a praying gesture revealed a person traumatized to the point of paralysis and split between two worlds. In the film he reached out for help but was terrified he would be beaten for doing so.

As an adult, Rick became something of a Renaissance man. In addition to his practical know-how, a trait he shared with dad, Rich loved classical music and was extremely well read, although much of his reading ventured into the sci-fi realm. And when I pondered this and his adult habit of playing solitaire on his computer, it seemed a significant part of him sought escape into a world of his own.

My brother Stephen was something of a loner, too. Two and a half years younger than Rick, he probably had more friends, but neither of my brothers ever brought their buddies home. Steve was self-sufficient yet soulful; self-contained yet charismatic. You found yourself wanting to be with him and to please him. At least I did. So much so, that even though he put me down when we were boys, I've forgotten most of those episodes, and always adored him anyway.

What I most admired about Steve was that he excelled at everything he did. He made things look effortless, but that quality was hard won. He had polio as a child and overcoming that affliction, which lasted most of his formative years, gave him a sense of ambition and resolve only matched by my mother and father.

The most telling physical manifestation of Stephen's challenges was his withered right calf, which also resulted in his shortened right leg. As I understand it, and I could be in error here, a doctor treating Steve's polio cut the tendon of his right Achilles heel. I never learned why, and I don't think Steve did either.

Did being literally hamstringed light a rocket in my brother to excel? I think unquestionably it did.

Stephen was very accomplished early in life; he was a Merit finalist in high school, voted Best All Around in his senior class, was a champion footballer, elected Mr. Brainerd High by his classmates, was offered a full scholarship to Yale, and the girls loved him. But it was only after we became adults that I learned all these achievements didn't boost his self-confidence as much as they should have.

To me he was an amazing person.

Again, *I never asked* him why his early achievements didn't raise his confidence. Perhaps all the things he did compensated for but did not really salve an inner sensitivity that he could not admit to, understand, or sometimes control.

Stephen was deeply emotional but not open. He was also profoundly determined by his habits and patterns, which became entrenched. Like most of us, he bore grudges, too.

As adults we got much closer. My brother reached out to me when he was diagnosed with multiple myeloma in his mid-sixties. Yet even though we were in constant communication from that time forward, Stephen was never as transparent with me as I wish he could have been.

I've used the metaphor of ghostliness to describe my family life in this memoir, and it applies to my sister, too.

Diane, who took my place as the baby of the family, was anything but remote, but she too, was a contradiction. Part of her seemed mute to me, at least when we were growing up. Maybe as the youngest and only girl it was overwhelming for her to witness everything that went on in our family. Maybe, I was mute and projected that trait onto her. Maybe, early on, she didn't have words or sufficient experience to articulate how she felt about our family or how she saw herself.

Sis, however, was no milk-toast. Diane had something to say, and she was going to say it.

When I was eleven and she was six, we got into a fight in the playroom in our home on Missionary Ridge. I punched her in the gut, and she wacked my shin with a two by four construction block. My sister had guts, was not afraid to fight, and was no push over. What is more, she was savvy enough to keep a low profile if speaking up or making a fuss would trigger dad's wrath.

For all these reasons, I was puzzled by Diane's tendency as an adult to pull back from going all-in out in the world. This was not a function of her competence. She became a superb producer for the NBC affiliate in Nashville and she was also successful with projects she produced independently, but Diane suffered from an incredible inner pressure to excel, dad's legacy to her, and this was hard to live with, much less sustain.

My sister seemed to gravitate towards periods of intense, all-out effort at work, and later in areas of her health or her other interests, followed by longer periods of inactivity or even dormancy.

Slow and steady wins the race was not Diane's *modus operandi*. She seemed able to sprint with the best, but at least from my perspective, steady, long-distance running was not her *forte*.

Of course, I tended to withhold myself and still do. Perhaps I'm projecting this onto my brethren and how they went about their business, but even if I am, I still saw this tendency in all my siblings.

With all the angst and drama happening inside everyone in my family, however, my ability to recover from the murder of *Alligator I* was remarkable.

In one moment, I was devastated by monsters and resolved to out-monster them all. In the next, I was back in the thick of things, banging heads with Scott Norman, Joel Cohen, and the rest of my neighborhood buddies.

Sometimes my handicap at being the fledgling of the family saved me, too. My lack of stature worked on occasion to my advantage, although I would never have thought so at the time.

I was standard size for a boy my age. By now, going on age six, I could pretty much keep up with everybody on my bike, but physically there were other things I couldn't handle, like climbing to the top of the tallest pine tree in our front yard.

Rick and Steve were amazing about coming up with things to do, and now they invented the greatest ride ever. It all started when they found a giant pulley Dad stashed in the basement of our home on Brookfield Avenue. The fact that he'd tucked this device away should have been a clue he didn't want it messed with, but their idea for using the pully was too cool for my brothers to consider that.

Atop the wall I'd steered my bike into were three massive pine trees. They rose, it seemed, a thousand-million feet into the clouds. Easily fifteen or twenty feet tall, Rick and Steve decided to climb the tallest tree, pulley in hand, rig a rope from the treetop above and across our infamous driveway, and then tie it off on a very stout tree in our neighbor's yard, far, far below.

Then they found or cut off an old broomstick, slid it through the hook at the bottom of the pulley, and held on for dear life as each one in his turn **FLEW** all the way down to the Flemister's backyard.

"Oh, wow, let me try, let me, let me," I exclaimed, pleading for a boost so I could fly too. But I was too big to carry and too small to climb. *"Forget it runt, if you can't climb, you can't ride,"* was Steve's dismissive reply.

"Shit, I never have any fun," I moped, but suddenly my entire perspective changed.

Just as Rick was in mid-flight, dad came home unexpectedly for lunch and drove right underneath him.

"What the hell are you doing," my angry father screamed as he jumped out of his car. *"Get down from there! That pulley is an exhibit in a lawsuit! I can't leave anything around here without you TWO trying to ruin it!"*

Suddenly being powerless and invisible wasn't all that bad.

CHAPTER II:
Moving to the House on the Hill

As our family grew and Dad became a partner in the law firm of Noone, Moseley and Noone, moving became a practical possibility as well as a necessity. I don't remember much about when or how long we looked for a new home, only that when we found it, it opened up a whole new world to me.

A Change of Venue: 468 North Crest Road

It was after dark. We were coming home from a day of picnicking at Lake Chickamauga. At first, we drove past it. When we backed up to take a look, what we saw at 468 North Crest Road was a large, 4-bedroom home of some 5000 square feet, whatever that meant.

A palace that stood atop Missionary Ridge. It was situated on a slight grade that ran gently downhill from the house's north side, where the screen porch was, to the Sunroom at the south end of the acre and a half sized property. This was the biggest house I'd ever seen. Inside, every room seemed as big as our entire home on Brookfield Ave. Well, not everyone, but the living room, for sure.

Dad bought our new house for $37,500 with a 1% mortgage on a thirty-year note and we moved into our new digs just before Thanksgiving, 1959. This dwelling of light and darker shades of reddish-brown brick became, and always will be, the place I go to in my imagination when I think of HOME.

I was nearly seven years old now.

Except for the enormous distance between the Dining Room and the Sunroom, an expanse that seemed to run the length of a football field, I didn't think too much, one way or another, about our new home. When we moved in, we had so little furniture that you could hear your echo when you shouted out; *"How will we ever fill this castle up..."*

What I most recall about our new digs, which is also what I grew to love about it, was the whistling of the eaves in the fall, winter and sometimes even in early spring.

When the wind came up on Missionary Ridge, the sound our house made in reply was a beautiful, haunting, and unique visitation. I had never heard a house talk before. Many a night, I lay in bed listening to this other-worldly serenade. My brother Steve told me that this sound came from the copper weather stripping that framed the wooden windows of our new abode.

Through years of repainting, these windows would never fully shut, and when the Ridge running wind hit the unsecured and exposed copper stripping, a mournful, wail cried out in varying pitches and volumes according to the force and direction of the breeze. It was the feeling of the sound, not the facts of its origin, that captured me. Just thinking of those unique tones, especially those that haunted our chilly winter nights, takes me back there every time.

Our view of the city of Chattanooga was amazing, too. I didn't admit it back then, of course, simply because it meant so much to dad. It wasn't that I dismissed his dream house come true, I was just preoccupied with my own world. Besides, I could feel it when he fished for affirmation as he waxed poetically about the beauty of our view.

"Yeah, yeah, yeah, OK its cool, but it's not the greatest thing I ever saw. So, stop trying to get me to say it is..."

It really was something though.

Once, many years later when all my siblings were adults with children of their own, Stephen's family was visiting the house on Crest Road. His youngest son, David Patrick brought a friend with him whose name escapes me now. As this little boy took in the view from our home atop Missionary Ridge, he gasped in astonishment viewing the evening lights that illuminated the city of Chattanooga. *"Look,"* he exclaimed, *"diamonds!"*

My Father as a Son

One of my fondest recollections of childhood came from an exchange that passed between Granddaddy Moseley, a big, frail, and gentle man by the time I spent real time with him and his youngest son, my dad.

Grandaddy had come to visit us on Crest Road. It was the early sixties now, and I was somewhere between nine and ten. The patriarch of the Moseley clan, John Alfred Moseley wore light, seersucker clothes and a broad brimmed straw hat. Sometimes, after I got home from school, I'd walk with him when he took his afternoon stroll.

As we ambled along our stretch of Missionary Ridge, I felt like I was walking next to a kinder, gentler version of King Kong. I was astonished by the size of his hands and feet. My paternal grandfather was by now a white-haired man in his seventies, and he had a quiet, humorous, and unassuming intensity.

Over the years, mostly due to "getting religion," a phrase I'd heard but didn't yet understand, Grandaddy had tempered the fire in his belly that came out as fits of temper within his generation of our family.

Once, when John had called on his son Raymond to say a prayer before dinner, my dad came up with this; *"Oh Lord, we thank thee for this meal. We feel indebted to thee for this feed, indeed...* At which point John backhanded dad, knocking him under the sewing machine in the family dining room.

There was a darker episode Pop never spoke about, too. John once went to prison for manslaughter. This was a family secret we were never meant to know, but my cousins, Uncle Paul's kids, told Rick and Steve and I picked it up from them.

The story was that during the Great Depression John was a guard at the Eastman Kodak plant in Kingsport, Tennessee. A former employee showed up drunk at the gate on my grandfather's watch, demanding access to the plant. This fellow persisted and just wouldn't take no for an answer. John wound up punching the drunk, who staggered off, fell headfirst into a puddle, and drowned.

Grandaddy served a year in prison for this.

All this had long since passed. These days my grandfather was a devout Christian, read the Bible daily, and was a gifted carpenter who had built ten churches in various towns in the Smokey Mountains almost all on his own.

My brother Rick told me a story about our grandfather from our days on Brookfield that seemed to jibe with his single-handed construction of the Smokey Mountain church. During the time dad replaced our kitchen appliances there, he realized that he needed to expand the kitchen, too.

Grandaddy Moseley was visiting us at the time and while dad was at work Rick saw grandad use a hacksaw blade to behead every nail securing the outer wall of the kitchen to our Brookfield home. When dad got back home from work, they built a jig together and slid the outer wall away from the body of the house, then framed in the extra space expanding our kitchen.

Grandad had an interesting habit that came from working so much with his hands. He would regularly and meticulously paint cuts on his fingers with mercurochrome. Consequently, he had mostly purple hands.

Inevitably, Dad had a weekend project on and so, as always, there was work to be done. Among today's tasks was securing the railing of the basement stairs at our Crest Road house to its cinder block foundation wall.

There were four or five brackets that locked this banister into that partition. The railing was around fourteen feet long and each bracket, save for the one at the foot of the stairs, was secure.

Dad was stumped over how to seat this last bracket because the hole in the wall was too wide for the bolt that fastened the railing there.

Presented with this problem, grandaddy shrugged his shoulders nonchalantly and said, *"That's easy, son. Just stuff some large gage steel wool in there. When you drive the bolt it'll catch the wool, grip, and hold."* My dad, always the one to come up with ingenious solutions to all manner of challenges, looked at his father in amazement.

I had never seen dad look like this and I never saw him look this way again.

"Would that really work?" my father's face exclaimed, looking like he was my age at the time.

"Watch," said Grandaddy, as he successfully applied his solution to the task at hand.

"Well, I'll be damned," my father's face beamed, as if to say, *"I never would have thought of that."*

It was great to see dad could be just like me.

New Neighborhood, New Life, New School

These next few stories come from my days at Missionary Ridge Elementary School. More like a huge, rambling estate than a modern 1960's style teaching facility, this grand three-story building made mostly of brick was built in 1915. A one-of-a-kind structure that sadly burned to the ground in 1992, it sported massive ground floor windows, oversized, airy rooms and classroom ceilings some twenty feet high with hallway ceilings even higher than that.

*General Douglas MacArthur's father, Arthur, a young officer from Wisconsin, had won the Congressional Medal of Honor at the <u>Battle of Missionary Ridge</u> on November 25, 1863. The 18-year-old MacArthur inspired his regiment during an uncoordinated and spontaneous frontal assault of Union forces against entrenched Confederate soldiers **at the very site of our school**.*

Legend had it that the battle started because Rebel sharpshooters were sniping at the Union forces at the bottom of the Ridge. This enraged the Yankees, who spontaneously and without orders charged up to the crest of the ridge and drove off the confederate forces.

During the charge, the regimental flags of the Union were carried in front, so that every flag-bearer was constantly a target, causing immense casualty among them. MacArthur seized the flag from a fallen comrade and planted it on the crest of Missionary Ridge at a particularly critical moment, shouting "On Wisconsin!" He was brevetted colonel in the Union Army the following year. Only 19 years old at the time, he became nationally recognized as "The Boy Colonel."

There were several large monuments on the school grounds, commemorating the feats of daring-do that had happened there, and folks from all over would come to visit the battle-site. We used to climb all over these monoliths, as other students in the region did, to have pictures made for their school yearbooks.

It's a wonder no one ever fell off a shrine and broke his or her neck. Perhaps the spirits that look over battlefields felt enough harm had come to folks on Missionary Ridge.

My favorite teachers at Ridge school were Mrs. Johnson, who taught third grade and Mrs. Cobble who was my fourth-grade instructor. I enjoyed their classes because I liked them, but I was an indifferent student. The curiosity that marked my earlier childhood seemed to evaporate in proportion to how much I hid from my parents, and I found it hard to engage with any particular subject at school.

At the Ridge I was out of the full-time grip of my parents for the first time, but this change in circumstances didn't open me up. My biggest recollection of these times, other than the stories that follow here, was an epic battle we had during the 1960 Presidential election. Dad was an independent who always voted Republican, so I was in the Nixon camp. One day at recess, a whole bunch of students lined up across from each other, according to their allegiance to Kennedy or

Nixon, forming impromptu skirmish lines. When someone said charge, that's exactly what we did. It's a miracle no one was hurt, but I don't remember a single casualty from this episode.

Starting Over with Charlotte Thurman

Mom was running late, as usual.

The new school in our new neighborhood, which I was attending today for the first time, was deathly quiet. More important, I was deathly afraid. I was repeating first grade, which the authorities had already decided. Looking back now, I think I was a depressed little boy and that impacted my schoolwork. I remember feeling insecure that day, starting at a new school.

By the time Mom got me there, classes had already begun which made me feel even worse.

You could hear a pin drop in the cavernous hallways of Missionary Ridge Elementary. Once Mom learned *from the principal's office* where I was supposed to go, matters got even worse. She left me alone to knock on the door to Mrs. Powell's first grade class.

Some Mom I had.

"What kind of stupid, drunk or brain-dead stork dropped me down this family's chimney anyway!"

I don't remember how I got in the door, but I was seated in the rear of the class, sharing a double-wide desk with a tall, gangly girl who had freckles and wore horn-rimmed glasses. Suddenly, our teacher Mrs. Powell gave us instructions, but I was so embarrassed and anxious that I didn't hear what she told us to do.

"I'm already late. I don't dare ask her to repeat what she just said, I thought, *now what do I do?"*

I looked over at freckle-face, to see what she was writing. Puzzled by what I saw, I copied it down anyway. Then we were told to pass our papers forward.

Suddenly, Mrs. Powell got mad and called ME to the front of the room.

"Oh God, I thought, *what have I done now?"*

I just sleepwalked to her desk in front of everyone. *This is not the beginning I had in mind.* I can see her thin-lipped scowl and her narrow, National Lampoon-like spectacles even now, as in view of the whole class Powell confronted me with two papers. Still not comprehending, she pressed them under my nose.

I had copied Charlotte Thurmond's name on my paper instead of my own.

"What a way to start first grade ALL OVER AGAIN."

I'm not sure what happened next. Maybe my teacher got a ruler and slapped my hand with a *"Don't you ever, ever cheat again,"* love tap, or maybe she just threatened to. I felt like a complete idiot.

"Welcome to your new world, Bozo!"

Mrs. Johnson's Art Prize and the Ice Cream Sandwich

"What a stupid idea," I thought, as Mrs. Johnson, my third-grade instructor explained how our art contest worked; *"Why have an art competition with black construction paper and white chalk? Art is*

supposed to be colorful, isn't it? Why not use purple paper with chalk of assorted colors?"

Then my new teacher said, *"The student with the best drawing will win an ice cream sandwich!"*

"Oh. Boy, all right! Gimmie my stuff, I'm ready to go!"

Unlike Mrs. Powell's class, which had desks set side by side in pairs, and in double rows from front to back, Mrs. Johnson, who had a great big nose but was warm and caring, had all her desks set in a square so everyone could face inward and see each other. *"This is a much better way to teach and learn,"* I judged approvingly.

I was glad Mrs. Johnson was different than the witchy Powell, who'd slapped my hand or threatened to when I went *temporarily insane* by becoming Charlotte Thurmond, a malady that could befall anyone, or so I'd heard on TV.

Mrs. Johnson was fun! She'd get mad quick if anyone sassed her, but she'd laugh out loud with us, too. She was great with people, and I would have hired her and given her a big salary if I had my own company. She smoked as I recall, but I didn't mind that. Mrs. Johnson was real, smart, and down to earth. I liked her.

As I remember, she gave us an hour to create a picture, but I'm sure we had less time than that. The theme Mrs. Johnson gave us was *"coming to school,"* but maybe I recall it that way because that's the kind of picture I made.

Anyway, I drew a picture of a mummy lying underneath the old bridge my parents took to get to the Ridge. On top of the bridge, I drew a car driving south with broad, beaming headlights as it came rolling over the gilded overpass. There was also a smaller, curvy road that snaked under the bridge. It passed right by my mummy, so I put the lower road in my picture, too.

I guess there were twenty-five kids in Mrs. Johnson's class. When she announced I'd won the prize, I was ecstatic. I hadn't won anything since our box races at Brookfield Ave. and unlike then, my pride and joy could not be burned up and obliterated. Better still, I got to keep my drawing and eat my prize, too! And best of all, no one could ever take it away from me.

When I picked out just the right ice cream sandwich and plucked it from the freezer in our school cafeteria, my mouth watered in delightful anticipation. As I strode back to my seat, preening in triumph, the woman at the cash register said,

"Whoa, where do you think you're going?"

"I'm gonna eat my ice cream sandwich," I replied, with a slight tinge of outrage, thinking to myself, *"Who are you to challenge me?!? Haven't you been informed of my victory; don't you know who I am?!?"*

Well, that's fine and dandy, the register lady said, picking up on my lofty disdain with an equally indignant comeback, *but if you want that ice cream sandwich it'll cost you a dime!"*

"This is an outrage, I now silently bristled, *"Just who the hell do you think you are?* I thought, *I won this prize fair and square! Mess with me now and I'll crush you!"*

Slamming my tarnished prize on the counter, but careful not to crush it, I now marched up to the teacher's lunch table in barely contained fury. Normally, I spent most of my energy hiding how volatile I could be. This was the first time the diva side of my personality came out for all to see.

"Mrs. Johnson, they won't give me my prize!"

In my delusion of grandeur, I thought there must have been a big, school-wide announcement that I had won the third-grade art prize. Mrs. Johnson just laughed at my haughtiness, reached into her purse, and handed me a dime for the cashier.

The Sincenset

My first attempt at effective storytelling was also an abject failure at spelling. Spelling, punctuation, and grammar have always been my Achilles heel, and even with spell-check, they probably always will be. What better way to share this with you than to reveal here my first unedited masterwork, written early in the fourth grade when I was nearly ten.

"The Lost Wallet"

One night as I walked down the street, I was pulled into the *allie*. Then I felt a jab at my back. It was blunt and felt like a gun. There, in the misty fog, a low *studdering* voice said, *"Give me the wallet!"* I said *studdering* *"I have no money"* but he would not believe me. *Suddy*, I felt something hit me and I fell but got back up. Earlier I did not *minchen* my *profoshen*. I am a *Sincenset*. Anyway, I saw him *clyming* up a water tower. I would have let him go but inside was a little hall light. It was a red light. Inside the light was a small germ in a tube, which I was trying to find the cause and cure for.

Well, back to the robber.

I knew he would catch the germ's *dezezee*. He was at the top of the water tower. Now suddenly he was red and white and black and blue and all the other colors. Then he turned to stone and fell off and the wallet flew right into my hands. Boy, what a job us *sincets* have. Back to the laboratory.

Dad positively howled with laughter upon reading my story. I was happy it brought him such pleasure, but vaguely aware that his delight had just as much to do with my incompetence as with my talent.

"What the hell, I thought, *I'll take approval however I can get it."*

A Fourth Grade Science Experiment and first time Therapy

Mrs. Cobble was my fourth-grade teacher. Her snow-white hair distinguished her as the oldest teacher at Missionary Ridge. She was gentle but firm with her students in a courtly way. Soft-spoken, but nobody's fool, her combination of grace and savvy reminds me now of Eleanor Roosevelt.

I can't imagine a person better suited to teaching children, then or now.

By this time, I'd graduated to the second floor at the Ridge. No one remarked on this but to me it meant I was moving up in the world.

The most vivid experience I had in fourth grade was my unexpectedly hazardous science experiment. Charged by Mrs. Cobble to come up with something scientific that I could demonstrate to the class, I chose to explain how water evaporated. As I completed this volatile, extremely complicated process to underwhelming applause, I began to break down the materials I used in my presentation.

The first thing I grabbed was my tripod.

Suddenly, my demonstration of evaporation erupted into a scalding clash with CONDUCTION!

My hand felt like a combination of white-hot super glue and silly putty. Stifling the pain with an embarrassment that trumped my physical agony, I winched, but didn't make a sound.

Mrs. Cobble saw all this and became concerned for me.

Shortly after my science experiment, a woman started coming by once or twice a week to take me to a separate room and talk with me. We'd go up to a room somewhere on the third floor, and she'd ask me questions for an hour, or so, and then take me back to class.

This was something new in the world of education; an attempt to address and effectively treat psychological hang-ups that inhibited performance. In retrospect, I believe this was a step in the right direction. The inhibitions it sought to address then have morphed today into an institutional attempt to eliminate not only low performance, but all perceived cultural inequality and victimization.

In my view, the initiatives of Woke culture don't work. Over emphasis on diversity and inclusion derails the educational process for the sake of preventing minorities from having their feelings hurt and shuts down students from risking innovative explorations because they fear being perceived as politically incorrect.

The chief impression I got from my therapy sessions was that I was screwed up. When Dad declined to have me see a psychologist, as the school now recommended, I figured I wasn't worth fixing.

Dad was an ex-fighter pilot in the Navy, however, so he never ignored warning signs. Although he decided not to put me in the hands of experts he deemed crazier than I might or might not be, he now began a campaign to bring me out of my shell.

Pop began with a direct approach to assess what was going on with me and what I needed.

It went down like this;

We had a coal furnace at home. Rick and Steve's job was to remove the clinkers (the waste product of the burnt coal) and take them to the street in heavy metal trash cans. My job was to bring these empty cans back up to the furnace, which I often forgot to do.

I was playing in the side street that fronted our driveway one day when Dad came home from work. I waved to him as he pulled his new maroon Chevy Chevelle coupe into our two-car garage.

It was late fall now and my father was wearing his grey and black herringbone overcoat and a grey Knox hat. *"Hi, Dad"* I said, as he got out of his car, whereupon dad said, *"Son, are you afraid of me?"* The abruptness of his query stopped me in my tracks. No warmup, no chit chat, no preliminaries; he just cut straight to the jugular.

As clear as day, I remember thinking *"UH OH, I'm scared to death of Dad, but how do I tell him, what should I say?"*

What happened now was a short but furious internal debate; the angel on my right shoulder said; *"OK kid, here's your chance! Speak up and tell the truth, the whole truth and nothing but the truth, so help you God."* The devil on my left shoulder said; *"Dummy up! If you tell him you're terrified of him, you're done for. Remember you've sworn to beat this bully in a battle for supremacy. Fess up now and he wins."*

Of course, I wasn't conscious of this point counterpoint at the time, but the truth or consequences time bomb was ticking. I had to say something, so I gulped and semi-whispered *"No."*

In that moment, I secretly hoped the trial lawyer in Dad would smoke me out. Sadly, he accepted my answer and said; *"Then son, why don't you bring up the trash cans?"*

I wish dad dug a little deeper here. He was an expert in cross-examination, a pro at ferreting out the truth. Many times, I've wondered what would have happened if I'd said; *"You bet I'm scared of you, and I'm mad as hell about it!"*

Who knows how things might have changed for me if I'd found the courage to tell my father how I really felt about him? Maybe if I reconsidered my reply and told him the truth, I could've gone in a whole new direction, but I never really considered telling him how I felt about him after this happened.

Oh, how I wish I had.

Sir George Beagle

My father was no quitter and he never quit on me. One of his strategies to bring me out, and it was a good one, was to give me something to love and care for. He was trying to put me in the position of a nurturer.

As it happened, I was watching TV, my favorite means of escape, when my father came upstairs to the playroom the evening of my eleventh birthday. He had a pure-bred beagle puppy in his hands and put it in my lap. I called him Sir George, and he came at the end of a long, unhappy line of dogs and a rabbit that had been my earlier pets.

"Shit, just what I need, another dog!" I thought, as I moped bleakly while George nuzzled me. Georgie was warm, friendly, and soft to the touch. He was the nicest dog I'd ever had. Most of my previous K-9's had been mutts. I really don't remember what became of them, and now, sadly, I was in no frame of mind to love this sweet little beagle who was barely past his puppy stage. It wasn't so much that I mistreated George, as I neglected him. I've always enjoyed dogs, and I've always had good interactions with them, but I just felt loveless and unlovable.

I didn't realize that loving Georgie was possible when I felt so empty and deficient inside. I also didn't realize how angry and hurt I felt all the time. I just didn't have it in me to care for anything, including myself.

I wish I knew then that my pattern of thinking was just digging me deeper into a black hole.

Once more, just like the episode where pop asked me point blank if I was scared of him, I wish I admitted how angry and hurt and ashamed I felt. Blaming pop for my problems helped me evade the simple fact that I had put myself in this state of mind by my own self-condemnation and stubbornness.

Dad was right. My loving George would have been wonderful for both of us.

Everyone liked Sir George and he liked them, too. His friendliness probably got him kidnapped. For when I came home from school one day, he was nowhere to be found. Dad and I talked about what to do to find him and I recall the two of us driving along the Ridge to see if we could rescue him and bring him home, but my heart wasn't in it.

The truth is I never really lifted a finger to rescue him.

Years later, I was living in New York City and doing a role play therapy session utilizing my experience with Georgie. For the first time my remorse and guilt at abandoning my little beagle came up and overwhelmed me.

Sir George Beagle is long gone now. An elder in Dog Heaven, I'm sure, he was more of a joy and comfort to me than I realized. I hope while he was still in this life, he found the love and affection he deserved.

Knowing Georgie, when I see him again, I'll bet he forgives me.

I hope so.

Breathing Room

One thing that usually brightened my childhood was when we visited mom's parents. The Hawk household in Knoxville was half the distance to the Moseley homestead in Kingsport, and we'd often go there while dad flew one weekend a month with the Naval Reserve.

What I liked about grandmother and granddaddy's place was that there was lots of breathing room. I didn't have to DO anything when I was there, there were no weekend projects, no **work** to be done, so when I was there, I always felt I could simply be.

Richard Frank Hawk, my granddad, loved to laugh, enjoy a good story, and kick back and RELAX with a beer. A man of medium height and build with a balding pate, granddaddy's high cheek bones suggested he had some native Indian blood. He had a dry wit, was charming when he chose to be, and he could be disarming. He also had no tolerance for bullshit and didn't suffer fools. My oldest brother, who was named after him, thought Mr. Hawk would have been a helluva gambler.

Now a retired foreman from the Y-12 plant in Oak Ridge, where he had worked on the atomic bomb, Dick Hawk was a gifted and resourceful craftsman. A great teacher with a patient, Socratic style, he'd take my brothers and me through the process of learning a new skill, like shooting his .22 gauge rifle, in a step-by-step fashion that was never hurried.

Unlike dad, granddaddy was always very thorough with his instructions.

He would think out loud, as we went through whatever we were up to. *"What if we did this,* he would say, *"would that work best here? How bout if we did that, what do you think would happen then?"* He always included us in the process and made us feel respected, useful, and valued.

I remember thinking; *"I wish dad could be like this."*

By the time we'd finished a venture with Dick, we felt good about ourselves and the new skills we'd acquired. He showed us love by giving us his time and teaching us how to do things, especially how to think.

Grandmother was always good to me, too, but she was at work all the time. Irene Bishop Hawk was a jobholder in an era in the south when that was rare for a married woman with three children. She loved the independence working afforded her and was devoted to the clothing business. I remember her for her stylish outfits and for how she cried.

Whether we were coming or going grandmother would always tear up. This struck me as odd because whenever we were around, she was always away selling dresses, so how could she get to know us, and if she didn't really know us, how could she miss us?

Except for holidays, and often even then, Irene was rarely home. Then again, the fact that she spent most of her free time with mom and Diane showed my perception of her was probably based on the limited time I spent with her. My sister Diane loved her warm and nurturing ways.

The thing I liked best about grandmother is that she never bossed me around unless I got out of line. Then she'd put her foot down, but mostly she was cool, hip, and unassuming. Irene, like mama, was always up for a new adventure, even though she seemed to be nursing some new malady whenever I saw her. Grandmother showed us love by giving us nice clothes and a 10 or 20-dollar bill on our birthdays or at Christmas.

The Hawk homestead was a two-story, three-bedroom home that my grandfather built as he approached retirement. It had a terra-cotta roof and was situated at the center of a five-acre plot which included a two-car garage, with separate bays barely wide enough to fit one car apiece.

This double garage also had a loft space and there was a separate workshop behind it that overlooked Beaver Creek, a waterway that formed the north, east, and south boundaries of the Hawk homestead. The entrance to the main house faced Solway Road, a highway on the western extreme of the property. The Hawk's place was large and rambling with trees lining the creek and an orchard on site. It was a great place to run, play and explore.

Dick built his dream home with the help of his two sons and my father. Construction was nearing completion, and granddaddy was facing the house from top to bottom with a sectioned veneer called perma-stone, when a nosy passer-by pulled into the driveway.

Apparently, my dad and Mr. Hawk strongly agreed on at least one point; *"Never bother a man while he's working; especially by asking stupid questions."*

Seeing that the perma-stone was being laid from the gutter down, this intruder, a middle-aged lady with a pompous manner, looked up at my granddaddy and said; *"I say, how do you keep that stonework up?"* Never one to suffer fools, Dick curtly replied, *"Helium."* Then he turned his back to her and got back to work.

My grandfather was a reformed wild man. A unique brand of hellion who could only have been bred in the south. He was over his heavy drinking and skirt chasing by the time I came along, but what remained of his wild days was a raw vitality that his meticulous nature kept in harness like a turbocharged Ferrari. Whatever the speed limit was in these pre-interstate highway days, I'll bet Dick's standard driving pace was twenty miles per hour faster than whatever was posted.

Dad always worried about us riding with granddad because he'd once been such a lead-footed hell-raiser. What pop didn't realize is that his grandchildren brought out Dick's protective side. Granddad never drove over sixty with one of us in his car.

Looking back now, I see my grandfather made a deliberate effort to keep himself in check whenever he was with his grandkids. Of course, it didn't always work. One day, when we went to a lawn and garden store on Kingston Pike, someone boxed us in. Granddaddy, who was blind in one eye, started muttering a spicy litany at the stupid idiot who blocked our exit.

As he struggled to extricate us from the parking lot, hearing this side of him made me laugh. Still, I never saw him lose his temper outright. Dick Hawk had an unmistakable edge but when my brothers and sister were around it always showed up as wry, knowing, and understated humor, with a touch of cynicism.

Thanks to grandmother, the rooms at Hawk Haven were abundantly appointed, each with a style all its own. The only thing I found disconcerting was the stairway to the upstairs bedrooms. It had no railing. When I was little, I was always afraid of falling off those stairs.

It seemed like most of our time was spent in the basement, which was part den and part storage area. There was also a large kitchen that comprised at least half of this subterranean space.

The only fixed rule at the Hawk house was that Saturday night at 8pm you'd be watching *The Lawrence Welk Show* on the telly or nothing at all. I thought Lawrence Welk sucked and very much preferred *The Saturday Night Movie*, but there were plenty of other things to do that made this one bummer easy to take in stride.

For example, there was granddaddy's twenty-two rifle, the one he'd taught me and my brothers how to shoot. There was sneaking a sip of his beer while he was underneath his car changing the oil. (*It was awful, but I'm sure he left it on the front fender of his yellow and white Studebaker just so I could try it*).

I also loved the musty smell of the attic-like space above his garage. That's where he stored his now cobwebbed pipes after he quit smoking cold turkey just before I was born. Other than shooting acorns in the creek, which was my favorite thing to do at the Hawk's, I don't remember what I did with granddaddy. What I recall in rich detail, however, are the stories I heard about him.

Once, my grandmother's car broke down when she was away from home. When Irene complained at what she'd been charged to replace her Buick's timing belt, Dick got so mad he drove forty miles from Kingsport to Morristown, where the breakdown happened, to beat up the mechanic who ripped her off.

All this took place near the end of World War II when gas rationing was still in effect. Dick got one weekend off a month. In that time, he had to drive from Oak Ridge where he worked on an electro-magnetic process to harvest U-235 for the atom bomb, to the Hawk family home on Chestnut Ridge in Kingsport, and then back again. This was nearly a three-hundred mile round trip on old, two-lane roads. Add to that the trip to Morristown, and you can see how angry he was.

I guess we got our temper from both sides of the family.

Just as he arrived at the scene of the crime, Dick saw a state trooper in the waiting area of the repair shop having a coke. Now unable to speak with his fists, he walked up to the apparent proprietor and said, *"You own this place?"*

When the mechanic nodded yes, my granddaddy tore into him with a verbal tongue-lashing demanding where the hell he got off, charging Mrs. Hawk triple what the repair was worth. *"Well, I'm just starting over,* said the chastised cheat, *I just got back from Germany and the war."*

Unsatisfied but constrained by the presence of the trooper who was now enjoying the show, Dick shot back, *"Well, it's too goddamn bad the Krauts didn't shoot you down for the no-good dog you are!"* Then granddaddy left, got back in his car, and drove a couple of blocks, steaming at the gills and still in need of physical satisfaction.

Torn by what to do next, Dick saw a palette of bricks next to a nearby Baptist church that was under construction. When he looked back and saw the trooper leave, grandad got out of his car, picked up a brick, drove back by the mechanic's repair shop, and threw it through the big picture window at the front of the thieving bastard's business.

All and all, I think that mechanic got off light.

My grandfather loved dogs. He bought a pair of Airedales and dubbed them Jack and Jill. When Jack got killed chasing cars on Solway Road, Mr. Hawk built a zip line for Jill, which kept her a safe distance from the deadly highway. She still had plenty of room to roam the big front and side yards and could even go round back to drink from Beaver Creek or sit in her doghouse.

One day a man named George stopped by for a visit. He had worked with Granddad at Y-12 before Dick retired. George was driving a new Plymouth station wagon and he clearly wanted to show it off. He chitchatted with Dick, who was busy spading his potato patch, and fished for a compliment on his new wheels. After a few minutes of inane talk George asked Dick, *"Say, where are your two Airedales?"* Apparently, Airedale Jill was nowhere to be seen.

George's query about the dogs gave granddaddy just the opening he needed. Continuing to work while he deliberately ignored the shiny new Plymouth, granddaddy said;

"Well, George, it's a sad thing. Ole Jack got killed chasing a car in the road and Jill took it awful hard."

"Oh, that's too bad," said George.

"Yeah, it got so bad Jill needed some therapy to get through it all," Dick went on.

"Therapy...? How'd that work?"

"Well, her shrink got her to counting cars and trucks to get her mind off her loss and she was making progress for a while, but that's all over now."

"What in the world went wrong, Dick?"

"These goddamn new station-wagons came along, and she didn't know if they were cars or trucks. Confused her so bad she had a nervous breakdown!"

George turned three shades of red, took off in his slandered vehicle, scattering the gravel in Dick's driveway as he went, and never again bothered grandaddy when he was working.

This next story was the result of an auto accident granddad had in his front yard. Solway Road made a long straightaway that passed in front of the Hawk's place, but it was only a two-lane highway with not much of a shoulder on either side of the pavement.

Granddaddy drove home at the front of what became a protracted line of traffic as he waited for oncoming vehicles to pass so he could pull into his driveway. Just as Dick began his left-hand turn, some impatient jackass tried to pass him at high speed on his right side and clipped the rear end of grandad's hunchbacked 544 Volvo, knocking his car some sixty feet into his front yard.

Dick got a pinched nerve in his neck from this collision, resulting in some terrible, recurring headaches. One day when he got one of these mind-benders, granddad couldn't read the dosage of the medication he was supposed to take. He reasoned that if some medicine was good, more was better, so he took most of the bottle, and blinded himself in his right eye.

But all this is just the background to my favorite story about R.F. Hawk.

One day when Dick got yet another headache, he phoned his youngest son, my uncle Larry and asked him to come over right away.

"Dad, what's wrong," Larry asked as soon as he got there.

Dick said, *"Larry, go out into the shop and get my rubber mallet."*

"Why?"

"Because I want you to hit me on the back of the head with it just as hard as you can."

"Hell, Dad, you're crazy," Larry protested, *"if I do that, I could kill you."*

Without missing a beat Dick said, *"I'd rather be dead than have this goddamn headache!"*

Larry did as he was told. When Dick came to, he was fine.

I had some of my best and most memorable moments at the Hawk homestead. I recall lying awake long after bedtime, just to hear cars drive by. Like the ghostly whistling of the eves on Missionary Ridge, the sound of vehicles passing Dick and Irene's place was a unique and lush experience.

The highway fronting my grandparent's home ran straight and true for some three or four miles. Hawk Haven, my nickname for their place, was situated about a mile west of where this stretch of road began. Beginning with the faintest murmur, a single car would make its presence felt it seemed as far away as China. Slowly but steadily, the rumble of its engine would build, louder and louder in a progressively rich vibrato, creeping closer and closer at speed, till it roared by with a distinctive whoosh, waxing and waning in an instant, as the sound of its passing vanished back into the night.

Single cars were the best. The melody and light of their night passage far and away trumped the sound and sight of cars passing by day. Even now, my memory of that exquisite hum, always unique in tone to the size, shape and speed of the passing traveler, combined with the ever-changing shadows their headlights formed on the ceiling of my room, taps the tuning fork of my heart.

Such were the delights of the nighttime on Solway Road.

A Close Call

In my experience, older siblings dump their suppressed anger on whoever is next down their family's line. Steve did this with me and I did it with Diane. For my part, I felt like a complete disappointment and failure. The pattern this took in infancy was my breath-holding.

My self-hatred evolved as half-hearted attempts at school and displaced rage that manifested as neglect of my pets or mistreating my baby sister. It was only later that I realized my not-so-subtle self-destruction expressed self-condemnation and revenge to punish Dad.

I used to chase sis with our running lawn mower when we were outside and our vacuum cleaner when we were inside the house. She probably felt she had no place to hide. Even now, I'm shocked at the brutality of my displaced rage.

The unjustified wrath I foisted on my sister came close to tragedy one weekend we were in Knoxville. Dad was in Marieta, Georgia flying in the Naval Reserve. As it happened, I was playing in grandaddy's Hawk's shop, who was also elsewhere at the time.

Dick Hawk's workspace was as meticulously laid out as my dad's shop was a chaotic mess. Everything had its place, and I loved the combined smell of oil, grease and gas that permeated his masculine haven. At the rear of his workshop, grandaddy built a door which opened out to a small platform, two feet square, overlooking Beaver Creek. This perch is where we shot his .22 rifle at acorns floating in the estuary that bound his property on three sides.

As I gazed up from the shop floor where I was playing that day, I spied my grandfather's rifle in its rack, far above and opposite his workbench. It was upside down with a cleaning rod rammed down the barrel and the bolt action was open.

"Hum," I pondered. I stood up, took the rifle from its rack, removed the ramrod, and closed the bolt. Then I removed the safety on the gun, just as Grandaddy had taught me. Diane was playing in the gravel just outside the shop. I took dead aim at her head and nearly pulled the trigger when I heard a voice inside me say;

"You're not supposed to point a gun at someone."

I lowered the rifle, aiming to the left of my sister and pulled the trigger. I can still feel the gun kick and the pop of the bullet as it exploded in the gravel right next to her.

Diane's head snapped around, locking eyes with mine. Stunned, I stammered, *"I just threw a rock at you."* <u>LIKE HELL YOU DID,</u> she silently screamed, as the sound and smell of blue-grey smoke oozing from the gun's barrel confirmed my lie. Before I could say another word, sis bolted towards the house, screaming bloody murder and I was in hot water for the rest of the weekend.

Mom never told dad or grandaddy what happened because they would both have killed me had they found out. And the truth is I would have beat them to the punch, because if I'd shot Diane, I'd have found the cartridges to the gun and turned it on myself.

To this day, whenever I get the chance, if I'm around kids who are playing with toy guns or being supervised firing real weapons, I always tell them this story.

"Never, ever point a real firearm at anyone."

This episode came so close to tragedy that over the years I deeply pondered what was playing out with me, my sister and in our family at this time. My fear of being replaced by Diane had not happened. If anything, her existence softened our family life and she brought out dad's sensitive side. Although sis's presence tenderized my dad it probably threatened mom, who I think was insecure about Diane's effect on pop and where that left her in his affections.

My mom and sister seemed to have a cool to semi-distant relationship. One day when Diane was around sixteen or so, though perhaps it was later than that, she told me mother had never taught her how to apply make-up. I took this to mean that there must be some sort of jealousy between them.

My sister had grown up a tom-boy. If any competition existed between these two, I reckoned it was mom's issue, not Diane's. If anything, my sister seemed to identify with dad's viewpoint on things. She was temperamentally and intellectually aligned with dad in a way mom was not. But I never saw any emotional competition between the two of them for dad's affections.

It would be easy to conclude that I hated Diane, but I never did. I hated myself and took it out on her.

My baby sister had an openness I did not. I guess I had too much to hide. When sis fell in love with Barbra Streisand and sang full out imagining she too was a world class singer, I was the one who was jealous because I couldn't sing myself.

I was too bottled up in myself.

I resented Diane's freedom to sing in front of our congregation at Brainerd Presbyterian Church. Given my way of being then, there was just no way I could ever experience that kind of liberating joy. I was too invested in revenge and too frightened to admit the truth of this to myself or anyone else.

I suppose my adult assessment of our family life comes down to this; sis was struggling with the same things all my siblings grappled with; *how to survive in a home with a rage-a-holic father and a caring yet conflicted, insecure, and withdrawn mother.*

When I think of Diane, I see her eyes. I see her silently bearing witness to all the pain in our household and I see her struggling, as I did, to sort it all out. If anything, she was more vulnerable than I was because of her gender. I had no idea the dynamics she was dealing with because emotionally, I think my father sought comfort from her that mother didn't have the capacity to give.

Diane never shut down that I could see and although mom loved and cared for us, she was simply unavailable beyond providing us with the basics you would expect from any decent parent.

Sadly, as with most things we experienced individually or together, we never spoke of our struggles as siblings. Each of us seemed to exist alone. Each of us in his or her way was simply trying to survive.

I love you; I hate you-What the Hell do you do with Girls?

One day, a friend called to clue me in on the latest thing; everyone was gonna start classes after school in "Social Dance." *"You gotta be kidding,* I blurted out. *"What the hell is Social Dance?... No way..."*

For kids my age, now twelve; the mystery of sex was dawning. Soon it would be time to face the music with girls and the mystery of the goddess' body, mind, and spirit.

"Oh, God, I thought, *I feel weird enough as it is, now I have to deal with girls???"*

Still, you had to do what you had to do; I didn't want to add **social outcast** to my overstuffed resume of inadequacies but taking dance classes didn't help.

Learning the Fox Trot was like trying to defuse an internal bomb that moved like an awkward manakin (*me*) in harness with an unpredictable explosive device (*her*) but doing so in a suave (*what's that?*) and at a refined (*and what's that?*) distance.

It's no wonder dancing felt artificial and awful to me.

The music from my time like the Beach Boys or the Beatles didn't remotely match the ancient stuff we were being taught anyway. What the hell kind of music matched the fox trot? Maybe early Sinatra but even Frank was getting long in the tooth by 1965. The girls smelled good, which I liked, but I didn't connect with what we were being taught or with anyone I was interested in or drawn to.

At least, not quite.

Susan Edwards was the youngest of three sisters and, as I think about it, she was kinda short but sexy, too. She took dance classes with the rest of us, which were taught in packages of four or six and I was attracted to her. Susan, however, didn't feel drawn to me. You can always tell. Not that I had any idea yet what you "did" with girls, anyway.

Nancy, Judy, and Susan Edwards lived about a mile north of us on Missionary Ridge. From time to time, Mrs. Edwards would give me rides to elementary school and later to Brainerd Junior High. Sometimes, in turn, Mom would pick up the Edwards sisters for the same purpose, depending on our mother's schedules and who needed help ferrying their kids to or from school.

As my crush on Susan developed, I guess from dancing with her, I felt the power of sex for the first time. I didn't know yet what was going on with me because the physical symptoms of arousal hadn't quite hit me yet. I guess the phrase "romantic longing" best describes what was coming up for me. This new experience of "the feminine mystique" was something beyond my understanding.

My buddies, of course, could tell I was sweet on Sue. One day during lunch at school they teased me about her unmercifully. We were now in sixth grade, our last year at Missionary Ridge, and as I came up to class from the cafeteria, there in the hallway was Susan.

Feeling pushed, pulled, confused and thoroughly out of my depth I blurted out *"I hate you."*

On mornings when Mrs. Edwards would pick me up for school, I'd wait in our living room or out on the front steps, looking for their car. The red taillights of their tan, 63' Chevy Impala strike me as memorable even now. No doubt, their red glare cautioned I was about to be exposed to an alien and exotic universe beyond my capacity to grasp or control.

Getting into the Edward's Chevy was like entering another world. The inner sanctum of this goddess chariot felt like a cross between a perfume factory and a harem.

Talk about another planet.

Each sister was at pains to distinguish herself from her siblings. Nancy, the oldest, had her platinum hair rolled under and up in a Barbie Doll dome. It looked like a lacquered beehive. She was in high school and epitomized the virginal Southern Belle.

Judy, the next oldest, went with a more natural hairstyle that turned out and up at the bottom. She had a vaguely rebellious air; I came to learn was sometimes the M. O. of a middle child.

Susan, like her mom, was stout. She was always quiet when they gave me a ride, probably because of my outburst at school. Still, though she didn't engage at all with me there was something I really liked about her. For sure, I thought she had a great ass.

I was still completely unaware of the roots of my attraction to the Edwards' youngest daughter, though she had some similarities to my mom, but I really didn't know much about sex or what you did when you had sex.

As I moved into middle school now, other girls registered on my nascent radar, so nothing ever came of my crush on Susan. Still my encounter with the Edwards girls was my first exposure to the mysteries of the feminine universe. My sap was rising. It took its time coming to a boil, but I could feel ominous, powerful, life-altering changes were stirring.

Changing Classes

It was both my blessing and burden to feel things deeply and intensely, and as all adolescents do, I made much more of everything than was good for me.

My biggest worry, going from elementary to junior high school, was that I'd forget which class to go to when the bell rang for us to switch classrooms. I excelled at making mountains out of molehills. Regrettably, this was a tendency I took a long time to get past. Back in high school, however, it pained me to my very core.

Adolescence sucked.

At Brainerd Junior, I met a girl named Carla Davis. I guess Carla was supposed to be a girl because her father was named Carl. Anyhow, Carla was tomboyish and loads of freckled face fun! She had a great laugh, and she was warm, real, and very down to earth. Somehow, with Ms. Davis in the picture, if only temporarily, I came out of my shell. Maybe because I just met her in Junior High, I felt freer around her than I ever had felt around girls before. Feeling my oats now, I became uncharacteristically bold, brash, and cocky courting Carla.

Ironically, Susan Edwards had a party in the basement of her house, and several of us first time couple wannabes showed up to make out. All Carla and I did was kiss, but we did it a lot and it felt good.

After this low-key bash, the Davis's middle daughter became my girl.

The only problem was that once I won her, I had no idea what to do with her, so I did nothing with her at all!

It was like; *"OK, that's over and done, what's next?"*

By the time I realized I needed to pay attention to Carla and cultivate our bond it was too late. Chip Bell, a classmate I didn't really know or like, snaked Carla from me because I ignored her.

I was so embarrassed and ashamed when I realized what I'd done, or rather NOT done, that I went into social isolation till I finished college!

So much for adolescent extremes and overreactions.

Even now, I can't believe I made this sort of isolating mountain out of such an inexperienced, unforced molehill. Writing about this episode in my young life, so many years now after the fact, makes me want to scream at myself to have made ANY other choice. At this early stage of my journey, however, I was so absorbed in my anxiety, I didn't have a clue about how to relate to myself or anybody else.

I suppose the truth is I've always tended to isolate. I had buddies in high school and college, but they were football teammates I really didn't see outside practice or our high school games and in college I joined an anti-social social fraternity, Chi Phi.

The only high school chum I had was an odd ball, like me, Mark Lawrence. We identified with each other's alienation, like a pair of Holden Caulfields. After our friendship formed at Brainerd High, we lost touch till I saw him at our 40th Reunion.

I did better with my brothers at the Phi Delta Chapter of Chi Phi at UT in Knoxville, and I dated some in college, but during those years I never seemed to develop an even fairly normal relationship with a woman who I could call my girlfriend.

I've had a lifelong friendship with Jimbo Hash, my fraternity brother from my days at the University of Tennessee, and he like me, is a person most folks might see as eccentric, but other than Jimbo, I didn't keep in touch with any other Chi Phi's, with the exception of my actual brothers Rick and Steve, with whom I formed a triple legacy as Chi fees.

Hitting My First Golf Shot

As I saw his golf ball rise, flying straight for me, I was transfixed. I was watching the great Arnold Palmer hit a tee shot on TV, and seeing it fly almost directly at the camera opened me to a desire I didn't know I had.

The yearning to fly!

Golf has always been more than a stick and ball game to me. I had a powerful, instinctive, and immediate reaction to it. What excited me was the idea that I could generate flight from my own mind, body, and spirit. That I could tack through nature like a sailor in all kinds of weather, using only my own resources. The playing ground of a golf course was the largest of any sport, and the game had a majesty that was acted out on a colossal scale.

Now, thirteen, I was hooked on golf from the start.

As it happened, no one was home but me the afternoon Arnold Palmer hit that drive. I ran down to the basement where Steve had a set of golf clubs in a red plaid bag he got at Sears & Roebuck, grabbed it, and rushed out to the lowest level of our two-tiered backyard.

"Hit it like Arnie," I thought, as I teed up a ball to give it a smash. Throwing my body and soul into my first effort, my first drive sliced into the Moore's' house on the back side of our property with a loud WACK. Luckily, I didn't damage the asbestos siding of their happily vacant home.

"Try again!" My second and third drives did the same.

"SHIT, try again!"

Then it happened.

On my fourth try, slashing at the ball with the flat planed, forceful action of Arnold Palmer, I nailed a drive that flew straight and true over and beyond the Price's, the Drake's, the Chapman's backyards, and deep into the woods behind the Green's house.

To my mind, heart, and spirit, it flew clear to the North Pole!

Then and there, I was forever possessed.

The fusion of mind, body, and spirit that golf demands *does it for me*. Playing golf well is all about self-mastery. Although I often come up short in this regard it's making the effort that makes the game worthwhile for me. This was true that day in 1965 and it's still true today.

I remember the first drive I hit in the first round of golf I ever played. Anxious to see the ball soar, I came out of my swing and topped it on the par 4 first hole at Concord Golf Club in Chattanooga. It took me till the fourteenth hole to hit a good drive but that one solid shot brought me back to try and improve the next round, and the next, and the next.

The true magic of the royal and ancient game is that you can love it and be more or less successful, but you can never truly master it. When you play well, the feeling inside your body is a fusion of all your senses and resources that's incomparable to any other sporting endeavor I've experienced.

There is no fruit as sweet as forbidden fruit, and no love like unrequited love. Golf, then, becomes a quest for a sort of Holy Grail of personal self-possession and power; an endless pursuit of that fleeting fusion of mind, body and spirit that is illusive to capture, but feels effortless when you play your best.

The knowledge that you're capable of stringing together a couple of solid shots, then a few good rounds or seasons as you improve, or a respectable golfing career depending on your level of talent and devotion, brings you back to the game again and again. Like having great sex., when you play great golf, you think to yourself; *"this is who I really am; this is me and how I was meant to be."*

For those of us who are true golfers, at whatever level we play, so shall it always be.

Golf was the first activity I encountered that felt like it was entirely my own. I still acted out my pattern of self-interference when I played but something about the game touched my heart and soul. Although it's just another stick and ball game, golf would become a vehicle for my growth and transformation that transcended making birdies or bogeys. The game would be a friend to me time and again over the years to come.

CHAPTER III:
Broadening My Horizons

My First Awakening

I accepted Christ as my savior for a week when I turned eleven, but it didn't take. At least not in a conventional sense. Dad had tried along with Jesus to save me from myself, but neither one of them pried me open. A higher power somewhere, somehow was watching over me, however, for I now began the slow, start, stop, and start again process of emerging from my well-polished and deeply unconscious shell.

The vehicle that jump-started my transformation was an unforgettable trip to the Mediterranean and the middle east in June of 1966. It was a three-week affair, and now at thirteen going on fourteen, it was a time in my life where three weeks felt like an eternity to me. In that time we traveled from Chattanooga to Atlanta, then on to Boston, Milan, Rome, Cairo, Jerusalem, Tel Aviv, Beirut, Damascus, Athens and finally to Paris.

Our first stop was in Boston via Atlanta, where we spent some time with Dad's older brother, my kooky Uncle Alf, and his family. As characters go, Alf was an anomaly. Movie star handsome and very bright yet somehow off-the-wall, he had an iron-clad constitution and work ethic that was the Moseley family blessing/curse, but my uncle was obsessed with sex. He absolutely reveled in telling one blue story after another, delighting in how uncomfortable this made everyone around him feel.

Maybe Alf saw himself as a crusader against prudery, but I felt sorry for his wife Ellen and their three children. Somehow, he seemed to damage everything and everyone he touched. I might have my complaints about my father, but compared to Alf, I counted myself lucky to have the dad I did.

As I've already related, pop was tough, but he was never capricious or malicious. He was always out to help us help ourselves; always about making us strong and smart in ways that empowered us and gave us command of our lives. Papa seemed to understand that the only way a person could master the life's ups and downs was to come at things from a place of self-mastery.

Growing up, my absolute favorite memory of dad repeated in the winter year after year. At the foot of the basement stairs where grandaddy had fastened the railing using the steel wool, I watched dad finish buttoning his herringbone topcoat. His hat and scarf were in place, and nothing was askew. When he exited our basement door, got in his car, and began his day, my father exemplified a man who had his shit together.

Regrettably, the man flying us to Italy showed nothing like pop's self-mastery. Milan was our first stop to refuel before flying on to Rome. It should have been a welcome escape from Boston and Uncle Alf's weird ways, but we nearly didn't make it. When we got over Italy's financial and fashion center the pilot of our *Alitalia* Boeing 707 put the plane into what Dad said afterwards was a full-power stall.

In a matter of seconds, we dropped several thousand feet, compressing my cheekbones as well as my other cheeks deep into my spine. Then our so-called pilot, if you could call him that, nearly tore the wheels off our plane when we touched down, necessitating a four-hour delay while we waited for a replacement.

Rome

The Eternal City was aptly named and well worth the hazards we endured getting there. In a word, it was **spectacular**. Famous cities, especially ancient ones, ooze the ambience of their special history. Freud, as many sensitive people are, was famously afraid to visit Rome because of its lineage and powerful psychic energy. I came alive in Rome as I had never been before. Better still, it was in Rome I started to *feel* alive, too.

I was fascinated by history and this center point of antiquity captured my imagination.

Situated atop the famous Spanish Steps, our base of operations was the Hotel Del la Ville and the weather that balmy June was sublime. For the most part, we took prearranged tour buses to see the city with onboard tour guides. Our first stop was the Pantheon. Next to the Trevi Fountain, where we threw a coin or two into its bubbling water for good luck, I marveled at how the ceiling of that building with a hole in its roof had stayed intact for centuries.

What I liked about Rome was the continuity of its architecture. Every building of note placed golden Rome at the center point of ancient times. Throughout the city there seemed to be nothing that jarred my eye. It stood in positive counterpoint to my least favorite city, Washington DC, where egomaniacal architects garishly foisted their viewpoints, designing a polyglot of government buildings overstating their ego's need *to be seen.*

Often, our mode of transportation was a giant FIAT bus. The traffic in Rome was amazing to behold. It was a real madhouse, but I only saw one mishap, despite what seemed the improvisational style of everyone there who drove a motorcycle, car, or bus. The key to navigating the streets seemed to be the signals drivers of all types would flash with their turn-indicators *to show the direction they intended to go.*

I became convinced, though I didn't have the guts to test my theory, that at rush hour I could walk unharmed in a straight line amidst the gaggle of cars, buses and scooters flying between the Forum and the Colosseum, if only I stayed absolutely true to my course without hesitation or deviation.

Mom was involved in the only accident I saw. Our giant tour bus had forward and aft doors, and as she entered the bus from the rear, a motor coach of equal size cut too close and caught our vehicle's open door, wedging it between the two behemoths. The departing bus screeched to a halt, whereupon its driver and ours launched into a Montague vs. Capulet-like brouhaha.

This rigamarole brought mama to tears, but once the drivers saw no real harm was done, the exiting driver backed up just enough to refold our rear door on its hinges, and with a slight adjustment both vehicles were freed to move on.

The only thing I didn't like about Rome was all the damned Basilicas we were compelled to visit. It seemed all our various tour guides would drone, *"Now this, of course, is the famous Basilica Grandolfo,"* or *"Here we have the legendary Basilica Perugia,"* or *"Here is the world-renowned Basilica De Boyardee."*

After a while, I was ready to convert to Judaism.

On the other hand, I loved the Forum, where Dad, the doctors Nelson and Waters, and our pastor, Fred Woodward acted out the murder of Julius Caesar as a photo op. When we got to the Catacombs, I thought they were kinda creepy, but also kinda cool.

What I remembered most besides the architecture and history was the people and the pasta. The interior courtyard of our hotel served as a restaurant where we took most of our meals. As the youngest member of our group, the waiters there dubbed me *Robertino*. Like the super starchy pasta we were served, the name stuck. For the next thirty years, many in my family considered this handle my *nom de guerre*.

A night or two before we left for Cairo, the second stop on our three-week trip, Steve and I, who roomed together throughout the journey, stayed up telling family stories. We would laugh, then fart, then laugh and fart some more.

Perhaps, in some mystical way, this behavior stopped-up our toilet. I called down to the front desk the next morning to get some *assistanza* and the management sent a housekeeper to our room. She spoke Italian only and I was stuck with English, so I used sign-language to communicate.

Pulling on an imaginary chain (we had a chain-toilet) and then gesturing *nada* to illustrate no flushing occurred. Steve roared with laughter at my pantomime, but I felt I conveyed our problem and bridged the language gap admirably.

The following day, when we returned from our morning tour, our commode was back up (or rather back down) and fully operational.

The day after our toilet got fixed, I came across the housekeeper who rescued us and tried to show all was well by tugging again on an imaginary chain, and then with a smile gesturing thumbs up.

The poor woman just shrugged her shoulders, muttering something in Italian, and walked away.

Cairo

When the hatch opened, cuing us to deplane our flight to Cairo, a blast of hot, stifling air slapped my face like a hairdryer on steroids. The blow furnace climate in the land of the Pharaohs was worlds apart from the lush gardens and the cool, ornate basilicas of Rome. The desert seemed intent on sucking all the oxygen from the air. Egypt was vastly different from Italy.

Apart from a few palm trees, our entire drive from the airport to downtown was surrounded by desert. We stayed at the fashionable Hilton, but there was another incredible hotel in Giza, the home of Egypt's most famous pyramids, and I wished we'd been booked there instead.

The Giza resort had a covered portico surrounding the main structure. It was festooned with mini palm trees, comfortable rocking chairs and outdoor ceiling fans that labored to ease the heat. At the Hilton, we had a high-rise view of Cairo and the Nile, and our room had its own balcony, but there was a pervasive odor from the cleaning products the hotel used that made me want to puke.

I never got used to that awful, inexplicable smell.

In Rome, the variety of tastes had been memorable, but here the variance of smells stood out. There was a plethora of intense perfumes in the city markets. They delighted the nose if heavy fragrances were to your taste but failed to mask the odor of standing water in back street puddles that had been sitting there since the time of Ramses II. These little patches were like tiny fetid swamps.

In contrast to the covered backstreet bazaars throughout the Egyptian capital, giant boulevards created a sense of luxurious space as we moved about Egypt's capital city, now in the Arabian Nights version of our latest tour bus.

Another oddity here was the lack of drawbridges. If a vessel sailing the Nile needed to pass under a bridge, and its sail was too tall, the crew would simply fold it down on a hinge rigged at the bottom of the mast.

As we toured the city, our oversized motor coach would often park along a wide throughfare, then we'd foray into the interior of whatever neighborhood we were visiting to sample the wide variety of offerings in Cairo's never-ending shops. At almost every stop, the backstreet smell of putrid standing water was worse than the disinfectant they used at the Hilton.

Once I got wise to this, I avoided back street bazaars.

Of course, puddle-hopping aside, all this was a new and compelling world for me. As in Rome, I was always first in line, soaking up whatever historical site we visited with an unfettered desire to fully absorb everything I was being exposed to. This delighted my father, though he said nothing, for fear I'd shut down just to spite him.

Still, I maintained an ability to periodically piss him off.

When it came time for the obligatory group photo of everyone posed in front of the Sphinx, and sitting astride a camel, I mounted a horse. *"I'll be damned if you're gonna come three thousand miles to the pyramids, just to get you picture made sitting on a goddamn nag,"* Dad growled, as he quickly found a camel that would match my thirteen-year-old stature, and semi-flung me on top of it. This episode aside, I pretty much steered clear of any other conflicts with Pop because I was so enthusiastic about my daily discoveries.

Of all the sites, the most impressive was the Great Pyramid at Giza. The largest Egyptian pyramid, it served as the tomb of pharaoh Khufu who ruled during the Fourth Dynasty of the Old Kingdom, whenever that was. Built over a period of about 27 years in the early 26th century BC, it was and today still is the oldest of the Seven Wonders of the Ancient World, and the only one that's remained relatively intact.

Originally standing 481 feet high, the Great Pyramid was the world's tallest human-made structure for 3,800 years. Over time, its smooth white outer casing of limestone disappeared. What we saw in 1966, and what is seen today, is the underlying core structure, which lowered the pyramid's height nearly thirty feet.

I mention these details only because my brother Steve, at the time nearly seventeen, was determined to race the Egyptian champion, a small, wiry fellow, to the top of Khufu's tomb. Sadly, Dad put the kabala on this match race. The last thing he needed was for one of his sons to break a leg in the middle of the trip of a lifetime.

Thinking back on it all, my habitual preoccupation with **what's wrong with me** was blissfully absent the entire trip. This is not to say that Stephen and I didn't get into some grief, for boys will always be boys, but that didn't happen till I nearly got us murdered in Jerusalem.

Jerusalem

The first stage of our visit to Jerusalem was spent on the Arab side of that then divided city. Steve hooked up with Ann Corley, a girl his age, who had come on the trip with her mother June, and older sister, Julia. Steve and Ann went out one night and met two shopkeepers named Simon and Amon who sold him a beautiful scimitar with a scabbard accented with silver. Not long after, I bought a rifle from them that also had silver imbedded in its stock.

At first, I was pissed when dad made me return the rifle. Only when I was randomly selected as the first in our party to cross from Arab to Israeli Jerusalem, did I realize pop was right. This wasteland between Arab and Israeli Jerusalem was horribly real. The last thing I needed was to carry a rifle as I tip-toed through such a hellish battle zone.

Unfortunately, over the course of the next few days I got diarrhea. This forced me to miss some cool places like the Garden of Gethsemane. While I was convalescing from King Tut's Revenge, Steve was having a blast with Ann and seeing what he could get away with. One day, he tried facing the Wailing Wall, something that only Jews would do to pray there. The rub here was that the Wailing Wall was currently on the Arab side of Jerusalem. If you faced the wall directly, you could get shot. Dad, ever ready to protect us from ourselves, saw what my older brother was up to. He pulled Stephen away from the wall before he got himself killed.

Incapacitated as I was, I got fed up hearing prayers to Mecca broadcast on the worst speakers ever, FIVE TIMES A DAY!

While Steve was taking a shower, having just returned from another site I was missing out on, a noonday prayer started up AGAIN. I'd had enough. As soon as it stopped, I made up some Muslim-like lingo and started my own prayer to Mecca. Stephen laughed when he saw what I was doing and joined in on the fun.

My beleaguered father, who heard our loud and potentially deadly serenade in the hotel lobby, seven floors below, flew up to our room in a flash and grabbed us both by the ears. Steve was barely out of the shower and had a towel wrapped around his waist.

"Are you two crazy, Dad exclaimed, *these people will cut your throats for mocking their religion!"* Stephen got dressed in record time

and pop took us out into the city for a couple of hours, hoping no one else saw or heard us.

I suppose episodes like this underscore the old saying: *Sons are meant to trouble their fathers.*

Tel Aviv

There was an austerity about Israel, mixed with a powerful sense of community, enterprise, and mobilization. This was a country on a constant war-footing. A feeling of frugality abounded here, too. Like most of the people we dealt with, even the food was simple and direct, and all our meals were dominated by vegetable *crudites*.

Our big, hulking escort, a man named Wolf, was more like a boxing promotor or political officer than a tour guide. The Israelis were the least sentimental and the most pragmatic of all the people we encountered on our trip.

The sense of mobilization I sensed proved to be wise on their part, as one year later the Jewish state fought and won the Six-Day War.

The best thing about Israel, as far as the thirteen-year-old in me was concerned, was floating on my back in the Dead Sea. It was the first and last time I was able to do anything but a dead man's float. Steve had the same problem. Our bodies were too dense for either one of us to float on our backs.

I suppose this is a trivial thing to celebrate, but it also speaks to how simple things can bring children endless delight.

The impression I had of Israel is that the Jewish people were completely absorbed with the here and now. Tradition is important there; it always has been and always will be, but as far as I saw in 1966, and as far as I can see today, of all the nations in the middle east, Israel remains the most contemporary in pragmatism and consciousness.

Of all the people we interacted with on our journey, the Israelis lived most in the moment.

Beirut

The most westernized place we visited was Beirut. Things seemed to work like clockwork there. Our tour guide called this happening city *"The Hollywood of the Near East."*

It's ironic, then, that such a vibrant metropolis could fall into such despair. By the mid-80's this Lebanese playground had been so devastated by civil war I could barely recognize it as the hip city I first encountered as a boy.

I remember a photograph of Beirut featuring a Ferris-wheel near the Mediterranean Sea. Years later, around 1985 or 86, I saw a photo of this landmark standing amidst the smoking ruins of this once beautiful coastal resort.

I felt sad for the people who had to endure such madness.

Seeing the devastation here also reminded me of the conclusion I came to when I crossed over from Arab to Israeli Jerusalem; if I lived amidst such generational madness, I wouldn't try to change it because the animosity in the region was so intrenched.

I'd save every Lebanese pound I could and find a place to move where I could live in peace.

Damascus

I'm unaware of any sacred ground I violated during our stay in Egypt, but the Pharoah's Revenge struck me for a second time on a one-day bus ride from Beirut to Damascus. Terrified I'd shit my pants, I flexed my butt cheeks hard every time our bus hit a pothole in the road.

It was a bumpy ride.

Once we arrived, I remember rushing to the public men's room close by our bus stop. There were no urinals or stalls, just a ledge. This was not a problem if you were doing number one. If you were doing number two, however, balance became your primary concern because you had to hang your ass over the ledge just far enough, *but not too far*, or you'd wind up quite literally swimming in shit.

My most vivid memory of Damascus, other than my desperate attempt to stay balanced, was an excavation of one of its ancient gates. The dig was a good twenty-five feet deep. What struck me then and sticks with me today is that civilizations worldwide have been built layer by layer *on top of each other*.

This realization somehow brought new meaning to the phrase, buried alive, but it also resonates with me like this; we all stand on the shoulders of the psychic and emotional history of our ancestors.

Until we acknowledge and address that history, we seem condemned to repeat it.

Athens and Santorini

What struck me most about Greece was its brilliant, *painter's* light. It also seemed there was marble, marble everywhere. The pastries in Athens were fantastic, too.

Steve and I noticed and commented on the fact that there seemed to be a lot of high-level gatherings of military folks going on at the time of our visit. For some reason, I recall seeing a Greek general pull up to our hotel, being driven in a black 1954 Cadilliac.

There was a coup in Greece in 1967, the year after our visit to Athens.

I'll bet all the generals we saw were planning that coup when we saw them gathered at our hotel.

One day we took a daylong ocean cruise to Santorini, an island in the Aegean Sea. There's a picture in our family photo album of me riding a donkey from the harbor there up to the main church situated high above the Bay.

When we got to the church, vendors had laid out their wares. They were virtually identical to the keepsakes and trinkets we saw in Athens and everywhere else we went in Greece.

Grandaddy Hawk didn't come with us when our tour ship docked. He'd had enough of sightseeing by then. He stayed aboard our vessel, who's name I've now long forgotten, and hung out on deck having a Heineken beer.

I don't like beer and never really have, but I wish I'd joined him.

Paris

By the time we got to the City of Light, I just wanted to go home.

When we arrived at the room in our hotel Steve and I both puzzled at the fact that our twin beds were puffed up like two oversized eclairs. The top of each bed seemed so precipitous that I thought if I wasn't top dead center on the mattress, I'd tip off one side or the other and fall to the floor.

Luckily, once you situated yourself on the true top of the bed, it seemed to collapse straight down, enfolding you on all sides.

Paris was grey and coolish for much of our time there.

We made the obligatory rounds of various shops, whose proprietors' like everywhere else we'd been, probably kicked-back to our guides a percentage of whatever we spent.

My favorite sites were Napoleon's tomb, the Louvre Museum, and the Eifel Tower, hardly an original list of sites. Strangely, I have almost no memory of Sacra Coeur or Notre Dame.

At Napoleon's Tomb I was struck by dark color of his casket and how it seemed to clash with its surroundings. The French probably thought the lighter color marble of the building complimented the shade of marble used in the casement of the emperor's remains.

The Louvre Museum was massive, of course, but it was the sculpture of Winged Victory and Da Vinci's Mona Lisa that stood out to me there. Winged Victory was situated on a staircase all by itself. Mona seemed to be a much smaller painting than I imagined it would be.

I was surprised by the almost dark orange color of the metal used to build the Eiffel Tower. At least that's how I remember it although I'm told the iron used in the tower is actually black.

The last night we were in Paris we were scheduled to go to the Follies Bergère. Mom felt I was too young to see the show, but dad disagreed. Pop said, *"If you're going, he's going,"* and there's no way mom was going to miss out on this or any other part of our trip.

At the show's finale, a four-person carousel descended from the ceiling passing right in front of my seat in the balcony. Four gorgeous women clad only in G-strings and feathers sat on this merry-go-round right in front of thirteen-year-old me.

I was actually half asleep when this happened, and I couldn't have cared less. If anything, this just confirmed my homesickness.

On June 28th, Steve celebrated his 17th birthday with a one-candle rum cake and both of us bought some dark blue paisley ties with matching handkerchiefs to mark the occasion.

Nothing in Paris thrilled me as much as seeing the lights of Chattanooga as our final flight from Atlanta brought us home.

You Can't Go Home Again

Things were different when I got back home because I'd changed. After my voyage to the Mediterranean and the middle east I became more interested in life, more alive. When the Six Day War dominated the news the next summer, I was glued to the TV. I felt connected to the ground being contested. I got involved for a change. As he addressed the world at the U.N. on Israel's behalf, I remember how elegant and erudite Aba Eban was. I would never have been interested in things like this before my trip. My schoolwork seemed to improve too, but all too soon, I got back to my self-inhibiting ways. Still, now opened, I could never close-up again, at least not as tightly as I was pre-trip.

As my adolescence progressed, my sensory awareness became intense. I wasn't conscious of this but the salt-pills I took before football practice and the layered smells of accumulated sweat in our locker room at Brainerd Junior affected me more deeply than I realized. I don't know why I went out for the football team except that Steve played ball and so it seemed natural to follow his lead. It was just something one did, I guess. I had become a copycat, adopting mom's way of being to survive dad, and now going down the same road as Steve with football. I remember at my first practice in seventh grade we were told to line up as running backs or linemen. Steve had been a lineman so you can guess the group I went with.

At school, I recall the feel of my oxford cloth, button down Gant shirts and how important it was to wear them with khaki pants and Bass Weegun loafers. If I wore a light yellow or blue shirt, I had to have matching socks. This was the unofficial uniform of my youth. Today, when I recall the smell of the leather uppers of my weeguns and how hard they were to break in, I'm transported back to my early teens. These sense memories evoke my moods and memories of those times.

My Secret Garden

What's happening to me? I wondered, as I became much more interested in playing with myself than I did in continuing to read the Victorian sex novel I'd pinched from the drawer of dad's bedside table. Back now from the middle east for a couple of months, the blossoming triggered by the trip now included my sexual awakening.

By this time, I had experienced quite a few erections and even a few nocturnal emissions but was still clueless about what all this meant. All I knew in this moment was that what I was doing to myself was beginning to feel much better than reading! Indeed, and the better it felt, the more I intended to pursue this delightful new sensation.

"Whoa, WHoa, WHOA, KABOOM! Oh, my God, what just happened, I puzzled in amazed and dizzy delight; *and what an ugly, smelly mess this is and who the hell cares cause that felt GOOOODDDD!"*

Now I quickly became the latest clone of Holden Caufield, as I looked for every possible opportunity to DO IT again, and again, and AGAIN! Why I couldn't make the leap to get back in the game with girls was beyond me, for now the evident rewards of sharing such pleasures with the opposite sex was worth the risk of crashing and burning with even the homeliest object of my desire.

My favorite venue for masturbation became our upstairs hall bathroom and shower. Dad, inevitably, caught on to my new obsession. He knew, as I was fast coming to realize, that I was into something now that would be no passing fancy. My father never drove me to Brainerd Junior in those days. He hadn't taken me to school since my days at elementary school, so I should have known something was up when he made it clear at breakfast one morning that he would drive me to school today.

We weren't in his car two-minutes when he lowered the boom on me;

"It's come to my attention what you've been doing lately," he began.

"Oh, shit, I'm busted," I thought.

...and I want you to know, right now, he continued, *that if you don't stop it, I'll kill you."*

"Surely, he didn't say that, I've thought, in review of this episode, but that's exactly how I **heard** it.

Of course, once I'd opened the door to my sexuality, I couldn't and wouldn't stop. Consulting with my brothers might have helped me here but that never occurred to me. My sexuality was private, and of course, very, very personal. I felt too exposed and too embarrassed to approach Rick or Steve about what was happening to me and my body.

Once more, this was an instance that could have brought me closer to my brothers, but as per normal I, like everyone else in our family, tended to work things out on my own.

Warming Up with Darlene

In eighth grade, my second year at Brainerd Junior and a year into my self-imposed social isolation, I was in my second season of playing football. The gridiron gave me some kind of involvement outside of school and a way to direct my energies that went beyond my activities in the upstairs bathroom.

The worst part of school, other than how shut down I felt, was math.

Mrs. Wagner taught Algebra, one of my worst subjects, but among Rick and Steve's best. For me, math just seemed too abstract. I was struggling to make sense of life and myself as it was; I didn't see any value in mastering a system that seemed irrelevant to my day to day concerns.

Nevertheless, I heard from mom about the split between my performance at school and the superior grades my older brothers got, seemingly in every conceivable subject, across the board.

"But your brothers are so good at math, why aren't you?"

At BJHS, most of the classrooms were identical with five or six rows of single half-desks. You slid in from the opening on the left side of the desktop and there was a storage area for your stuff under the seat.

Wagner's class was on the second floor and just above the constantly humming, resin smelling woodshop. My desk was one row shy of the windows that overlooked the shop and further out onto our combined baseball and football field.

I sat at the third desk from the front. A girl named Darlene sat at the desk right behind me. Darlene had black, medium length hair that flipped out and up at the bottom and she was pretty in an offbeat way. She seemed older than her age, or maybe somehow more world weary, with a guarded fragility. Darlene had a tough veneer and ran with a rebellious crowd. We didn't really live in the same worlds, but self-obsessed though I was, I noticed she often wore nylons with a run or a snag. This left me with the impression that her circumstances, like her wardrobe, were less prosperous than she would like and less fortunate than my own.

Today, Mrs. Wagner, who on her best days was not of this world, was lost in her deepest Algebraic space. Bored, I thoughtlessly reached back behind my desk and rubbed Darlene's calf with my open palm. Naturally, she swatted my hand away, which only encouraged me to make another pass, only this time higher up. Again, she slapped my hand, but I noticed she didn't make a sound.

Suddenly, Mrs. Wagner became my ally, for I realized my prey wouldn't say a word for fear of having to explain what was happening between us. This freed me to have my way and I crossed the line from assault to battery. Today this would be labeled sexual harassment, which it clearly was, but at the time and perhaps unfairly, I put it in the category of feeling my oats.

Now I ran my hand up beyond the top of Darlene's stocking and felt the heat and softness of her naked inner thigh. Whether it was my imagination or her subtle swoon, I felt her body shudder, then soften. Now in a delightful quandary as to how to proceed, a bell rang, ending the class and breaking the moment.

This episode charged me up, taking me beyond playful teasing, although I didn't get aroused. I could have gotten in big time trouble for this prank, but I didn't. Neither did I pursue things with Darlene. I like to think now that she got turned on, though she never spoke to me about this episode or anything else.

As an adult, it's occurred to me now that there was another possibility, however. I may well have traumatized Darlene in a way that caused her more pain than she already had. I was just fourteen now, and I saw this experience as a prank. I hope she didn't feel damaged by me and if she did, I regret it.

As it turned out, this episode became another excruciatingly slow step to my further sexual awakening.

Acne

I don't quite remember when my face first broke out. Probably because I'd like to forget it ever happened. I might not have had an extreme case of what the British call spots, but when I hit puberty, my face seemed to irrupt with the worst case of zits in human history.

At least that's how it felt to me.

I still recall the smell of Clearasil, feel the painful swelling, and within that the pinpoint pain of areas more acutely afflicted than other blemishes on my face. I yearned for some divine dispensation that would purge this poison from my body forever.

From seventh to tenth grade, I struggled with acne and the shame and pain I felt with this new affliction just worsened my alienation.

Combined with the fact that now I was wearing dental braces, too, I felt totally gross and horribly awkward.

My broken face seemed to encapsulate my struggle with adolescence. The toughest part of this time was that I had no real-life experience; nothing to give me some perspective or faith that this was just a passing phase.

It felt like my face would be a road map of hell FOREVER!

Thankfully, by the time I got to be a junior in high school my zits seemed to settle down if not fully disappear.

What amazes me now is how the pain of it all comes back to me. It feels as raw and awful as when I went through it. I hated this difficult passage and never really want to think about it again. Often, there are redeeming sides of a bad experience, but I can't think of one good thing about my exploding face.

Thank God, I got past it.

Considering how evocative this episode still is, maybe I'll never get past it.

Maybe you just move on, or maybe you just try.

Civil and Uncivil Protest

I was in serious need of a mentor. Right around the time of my pseudo-dalliance with Darlene, I found a spiritual guide in John Sullivan. Mr. Sullivan taught science and P.E. He also coached the Brainerd Junior linemen, while our head football coach, Randy Gutschal, handled the Bomber running backs.

Coach Sullivan was tough but gentle in a masculine way. I thought of him as sort of a velvet hammer. He was a short, squat, and powerful man, who challenged and supported me in ways that brought out my best. He was the first mentor I responded to free of passive aggressive, covert defiance.

Coach believed in me and helped me believe in myself.

When I screwed up a block playing football, he'd deal with it in a way that made me want to improve. In this way, we built up a bond of trust, affection, and support. I played my heart out for him.

Nobody's perfect.

John Sullivan had a full-bore Irish temper. He didn't suffer fools or bullshit from anyone. One day he slapped the face of a student who was acting up in Homeroom and got suspended for it. At lunch, the day after his suspension, a hundred members of our student body staged a walkout to support him.

Although our protest made local headlines, it had broader significance. Heretofore, actions of this type were unheard of in our community. Conformity and complacency were the rule not the exception in the Chattanooga of 1967. My piers and I were asleep to the social and political issues of the day, unlike the rest of the country, but this wasn't a protest of the war in Vietnam, it was personal. John Sullivan was a significant person in our lives.

Political correctness or student rights weren't on anyone's radar in those days. Integration and the busing that came with it started in 1967, the same year as the Sullivan walkout, but this was accepted, if not entirely welcomed, by both the white and black establishment of Chattanooga.

Whatever people's private feelings were, the law demanded change. Authority was trusted and respected, so no public protests occurred. Picket lines, walkouts, and sit-ins, at least for the most part, just weren't our way of doing things.

Personally, I didn't think much about integration, one way or another. At fourteen, I was just too self-involved. I had no problem going to school with black kids or other children of color. I tended to relate to people as people. I responded to an individual's personality. I was color-blind and felt kinship with anyone who shared my experience.

Larry Wade, for instance, was a black kid my age and we were tight. We were football teammates, which accounted for the kinship we felt, and he was our star running back. Larry scored 84 points for the season our last year at Brainerd Junior, and we won the city championship. Outside of practice, we didn't hang out but Larry, who was small in stature but had a great heart, was a good and trusted friend. Ours was a quiet, almost unspoken affection.

My oldest brother's peers, who like him graduated from high school in the early to mid-60's, marched naively into the morass of Vietnam. Of everyone in our family, Rick was the most likely bound for Nam. Then, during his days in ROTC, it was discovered he had epilepsy.

Steve, not quite three years younger than Rick, was in a group who protested the war more forcefully, but their dissent was slow to take root in the conservative, traditional south.

When a lottery was established to decide who would serve and who would not, Steve and I were lucky to get higher numbers that protected us from the draft.

For the most part, southerners of that time trusted our societal structures and political institutions. We had too much faith in our politicians, as what went on with Vietnam and later with Watergate would make plain.

Truth be told, however, if we didn't deal with, know about, or feel connected to the inequalities of our time, it was because we didn't want to know. In the early to mid-60's personal and private affairs were kept separate from public and political concerns. This mindset allowed JFK and countless politicos to keep their mistresses and who knows what else from public scrutiny. The duplicities surrounding Nam and Watergate alerted us all to the need to get more directly involved in social policy.

In any case, at this mundane, local level, our walkout for Coach Sullivan was more an expression of loyalty than a reflection of a budding social conscience. It was an issue of proper conduct and the right use of discipline vs. the affection many of us had for a good and effective teacher. Image and social media did not yet dominate public life as they do today.

Although several kids walked out just for fun, the uncharacteristic activism of the rest of us resulted in his reinstatement and eventually Mr. Sullivan became a principle at Northside Junior High.

I was still asleep to playing an active role in my own governance, but I was happy Coach got a break. He was a good man and helped me begin to believe in myself.

Standing up to a Bully

Corporal punishment is frowned upon today, but say what you will, Coach Sullivan's approach to discipline helped me and many others become better, stronger people, and by extension more effective, constructive citizens.

Occasionally, for instance, Sullivan had us strap on boxing gloves in P.E. He'd pair us up and we'd have at each other in the tiny locker room beneath the school's gym. Some frowned on this, but I saw many boys learn to stand up for themselves in these one-round, three-minute mini boxing matches. Duking it out had the potential to raise your confidence and self-esteem, or at the very least help you to access where you fit on that spectrum.

Everyone was expected to have a go in these casual matches, though Mr. Sullivan was anything but casual about who he matched. And I think it speaks to the effectiveness of his strategy that no one ever broke ranks to complain about our pugilistic melees.

I always got a little scared on boxing days. I only weighed 127 pounds and I wasn't all that strong, but I learned it was OK to be afraid.

Teaching us to face our fears and toughen up was what Coach had in mind.

One day, I got paired to duke it out with Joe McCroskey. McCroskey was a fat-ass, a bully, and an asshole. We'd been friends at one time but had gone in opposite directions. Joe went the chain smoking, street tough, bad boy route and I went in the clean-cut, jock direction.

McCroskey was always riding me, goading me, and putting me down. I didn't openly react to him but anger and resentment at him had been building up inside me for months. I was anxious about our match because he was bigger than me. I didn't know if I could take him. But win or lose, I knew the time had come to stand up to him and that ours would be a battle royal.

The moment coach blew the whistle, we were all over each other. Forget boxing, this was a slug fest from start to finish. Joe outweighed me by thirty pounds, and he was strong, but he was also fat and out of shape. As we pummeled each other I got the sense that I was fighting for all the jocks, and he for all the malcontents. We went at each other savagely till neither one of us had the strength to raise his glove and *BOY DID IT FEEL GOOD!*

When I sensed the end was near, I wanted to throw the last punch. Just as blubber boy rose from bending over to catch his breath, I caught him with an exhausted haymaker, but I got my last shot, and he couldn't answer.

Joe McCroskey never dissed me again.

As he took off my gloves while I caught my breath, my mentor winked at me and smiled.

A Dead Volvo and a Violation

One summer's day when I was fourteen, my brother Steve was driving home when the carburetor on his hunchbacked 544 Volvo caught fire. Less than fifty yards from our house the engine stalled. As he sprinted home for a fire extinguisher, the flame spread. When Stephen found our basement door locked, he realized he'd left his keys in the car. Desperate now to save his ride, he rushed to the kitchen door, but it too was locked. Steve pounded for someone to let him in, but mom was on the phone, oblivious to his cries.

By the time she heard Steve's screams, his Volvo was toast.

After the insurance adjuster wrote off the corpse, he sent a tow truck to cart off the wreck. I don't remember this driver's name, but I helped him hook up Steve's dead vehicle and he offered me a job on the spot.

Ever mindful of bringing me out of myself, dad thought this was a good idea, so I went to work towing wrecks to my new employer's junk yard. As we drove from one wrecked car to hook up another, we started smoking his Parliament cigarettes and talking about sex.

Little did I know I was being groomed.

One day, we hauled another totaled vehicle back to his shop and before I knew it, my boss *went down on me!* The compliance I had adopted as a tactic to survive my father had so come to dominate my behavior that I didn't even try to fight this bastard off. I just let him have his way. Physically, I was hard as a rock, but emotionally I was checked out. Despite his intense efforts I didn't climax. All I remember about being raped was the smell of the man's greasy hair.

When I told dad I didn't want to work for this guy anymore, pop sensed something had happened, but I clammed up. I just buried the shame and violation I felt because I didn't know how to deal with it.

Although I didn't want to dwell on what happened to me, or on what might happen to others if I revealed what went down, I probably feared the manslaughter conviction that haunted dad's family of origin, might now befall my family if I cut dad loose on the coward who raped me. Deep down, I probably wanted to kill him, myself.

Years later, when I was nearly forty, I was doing a spiritual workshop with a meditation group. We were instructed to pick a partner with whom to share an experience of grief we'd never revealed before.

I chose the biggest, broadest, stoutest woman in our group.

Subconsciously, I knew it was time to deal with the man with the greasy hair. I also knew I needed someone strong to embrace me as my pain and shame over this ancient violation erupted in anguished grief.

Then something startling and unexpected came up that blindsided me.

I was stunned to discover that while I made goofy faces and feigned delight at her arrival, what I actually felt the day mom and dad brought my baby sister, Diane, home from the hospital was abject terror. I was petrified that if I wasn't perfect now, I would be abandoned.

How this deeper denial was evoked by my revelation about being raped, escaped me.

Perhaps I abandoned myself when Diane was born, as I did when this predatory bastard took advantage of me. I became even more compliant in my family so I wouldn't be rejected. With the rapist, I stuffed my feelings of violation because I feared dad would do something to him that landed my father in jail.

The Kimball Case

In the spring of 1967, dad was hired by one of several insurance companies to contest the *accidental* death of Dr. John Kimball in federal court. On the surface, Kimball was a respected gynecologist in his mid-forties. He owned a thriving women's hospital, had a socially prominent family, and one of his sons was a cadet at West Point.

Kimball's family contended that while cleaning his Remington shotgun it slipped in his hands. It was loaded, and when it fell to his thickly carpeted bedroom floor it fired, blowing most of the good Doctor's head off.

From his viewpoint as a defense attorney, if the jury found this death was accidental, dad's client and seven other defendants would have to pay a sixteen-million-dollar claim.

Preparing for trial, dad canvassed drug stores throughout the Chattanooga area. In this pre-HIPAA era, he discovered Kimball had fifteen sources to get Percodan, an opioid combining oxycodone and aspirin. An oral form of morphine, Percodan was highly addictive, and produced significant withdrawal symptoms if a user abruptly stopped taking it.

The likelihood that regular use of Percodan could cause personality changes and delusions was indisputable. What is more, the drug required stronger and stronger doses to be effective. Dad theorized that Kimball became hooked on the drug and risked losing his license and destroying his practice if he was found out.

The insurance claims at issue provided double-indemnity payouts in case of accidental death. Kimball bought several of these policies during the last year of his life. The night of his death, his body was taken across state lines to Georgia, where it was cremated. The blood-stained carpet in his bedroom was stripped and replaced and the room was repainted *before dawn the next day.*

More damning, still, the coroner's testimony and photographs of the death scene showed that Kimball's personal medical file was sitting on his dresser. That file, clearly identified in the photos, was a record an inch and a half thick. Like the carpet and other physical evidence, it too, had disappeared.

Dad's strong suit as a trial lawyer was preparation. He made several trips to the Remington Company in Rochester, New York where Kimball's shotgun was manufactured. Pop got to where he could break down the model involved, and then put it back together again while blindfolded.

The questions at the crux of the case were; *did Kimball have cause to do himself in and could the gun have been accidentally discharged?*

The night of her husband's death, Mrs. Kimball testified the two of them were watching *Gunsmoke* on TV, when John said; *"I've had enough of this"* and went into their bedroom. When the shotgun discharged, she said she saw John's body fall, but didn't go to him. Instead, she phoned their neighbor, Dr. Baker, who came over right away. It was Mert Baker who discovered the doctor's dead body. Kimball's wife didn't enter their bedroom till after her husband's remains were taken away.

Jack Chambliss, dad's co-counsel for the defense, got the deceased's medical partner to testify that he had taken away Kimball's key to the drug dispensary where they practiced because John Kimball had become addicted to Percodan.

Now dad had to deal with the shotgun.

Luckily, Diane and I got out of school to watch much of the trial, which was being covered by all the Chattanooga newspapers. The Kimball's lawyer called a gunsmith as an expert. His name was Stagmeyer, and pop now had him on cross-examination. To the best of my recall, their interaction went something like this;

"Mr. Stagmeyer," dad began, "can you identify the gun you examined?"

"Yes, it's sitting there on the exhibit table."

Dad picked up the shotgun and handed it to the expert witness.

"Would you show the jury how to cock it?"

Stagmeyer cocked the shotgun.

"Now, sir, what would you say the floor of this courtroom is made of?"

"I don't know, looks like marble to me."

"Please hold the shotgun upright out over the edge of the witness stand."

The witness did so.

"How far above the floor is the butt end of this gun?"

"Around three feet,"

"Drop the gun."

When the shotgun hit the floor, it made a crack so loud, members of the jury jumped in their seats. Dad picked up the Remington and put it into Stagmeyer's hands.

"Did it fire?"

"I don't know."

"Pull the trigger."

When the hammer fell, the jury crossed their arms as one, then sat back in their chairs.

If the shotgun hadn't discharged from hitting a marble floor from a height of three feet, it surely hadn't done so when dropped onto a carpeted bedroom floor. Pop then asked two more questions to seal the deal;

"Were you ever able to make this gun fire accidentally?"

"No, sir."

"In your expert opinion, what would you have to do to make that happen?"

"Jimmy the trigger without fully cocking it."

Kimball's lawyer objected to this speculation, but the jury had made up its mind.

Judge Frank Wilson called a recess for lunch. When papa joined our family to grab a bite, I said; *"Dad, what would you have done if the hammer dropped?"* My hero said, *"Son, I'd a shit."*

Years later, pop told me that he had broken down that model so many times that he was certain it could never fire by accident. Moreover, dad's law partner at the time, Roger Noone, told him that he knew Stagmeyer and assured him that the gunsmith would never lie under oath.

The verdict of the jury was John Kimball's death wasn't accidental.

Captain Kirk and Being a Champion

If dad had triumphed yet again in the courtroom, I was a champion by my own standards and officially, only once. When I was fourteen, I played right offensive guard and left defensive tackle for the Brainerd Junior High Bombers. That year, 1967, we played Northside Junior for the Hamilton County Football Championship. We won 48 to 28 and capped off an undefeated season with a record of 7-0.

Kirk Spencer was my quarterback.

He was also our team Captain and although I didn't know it then, my ideal. Most of all he was my friend.

Even before we got to high school, which would be next year, I was certain Kirk was going places. He was industrious and accomplished, yet humble and down to earth. This made the fact that we shared that championship even more special to me.

Kirk wore number 10 on our red jerseys with white numerals and I wore 65. I remember the Chattanooga Free-Press ran a photo showing both of us coming in to tackle a Northside running back in that Championship game.

Both Kirk and I were shy. Darlene would doubtlessly disagree, but the Spencer's only son and I were slow to deal with the opposite sex. We'd often sit at lunch together on our own while other boys would table hop, teasing and flirting with the best-looking, most popular girls.

Because Kirk and I were teammates, he'd hang with me, despite his desire to chat up the girls, too. In time, my quarterback developed an on again off again relationship with a girl named Terry Moore. He struggled, if more successfully than I had with Carla Davis, to do the girlfriend thing.

Looking back, watching Kirk and Terry try again and again to get together should have been a clue that it was OK to re-up with Carla, or at least to take a shot at getting back in the game, but I didn't.

At any rate, it seemed Terry and Kirk broke up then made up, over and over again. Terry had a great body but an underdeveloped brain. She also had a baby doll voice unique to bratty southern girls and the tone of her twang just made me want to swat her. I admit I was jealous of her and couldn't compete with her feminine charms, but it always seemed to me she was more trouble than she was worth.

Kirk's outstanding trait was discipline. Before weight-training and physical conditioning were mandatory for ballers, he was doing both. Often, he'd get up early and run before school. No one did that back then. He just seemed to have the freedom to go for things in ways I didn't. I was completely confident Kirk would become a college football star, and maybe someday play in the NFL.

Everyone knew Kirk was the apple of his father's eye.

On Friday afternoon May 24, 1968, my buddy laid a towel on his driveway like we all did in those days so he could work on his tan. By the time his dad pulled into that drive his only son had fallen asleep. Bill Spencer, they said, was looking to avoid some children playing in the street when he got home.

He never saw his boy.

Kirk David Spencer held on for a day and a half. I heard his chest had been crushed.

I never went to see him. I couldn't bear to.

It took more than thirty years for me to fully own the grief and guilt I felt about abandoning my quarterback. I felt I left him on the battlefield to die alone. I also felt an enduring loss that periodically overwhelms me now more than fifty years after Kirk died.

I should have sucked it up. I should have gone to him.

I hope my quarterback forgives me.

Losing Kirk was my first experience of tragedy.

I will never forget Bill Spencer's wail of grief as he collapsed at the service for his beloved boy. He had to be carried from the chapel at Cumberland Presbyterian Church.

After Kirk's memorial service, his family took him home to be buried in their family plot in Roanoke, Virginia. A year after that they moved to South Carolina, or so I heard.

We all understood why.

Naked Bait

One of the funniest things that ever happened to me, although it was scary at the time, came on the heels of Kirk's passing. Dad wasn't home, and my brothers were at Camp Cherokee, or maybe it was Camp Ocoee, with the Boy Scouts.

After doing chores in the yard all day, I'd just slipped into some gloriously hot water in mom and dad's big bathtub. *"Ah, this is just what I NEED,"* I sighed as the liquid elixir began to loosen me up.

Just as I began to doze and dream, mom knocked loudly on the bathroom door.

"What is it?," I groused.

"Son, there's something in the pantry. Come out and see what it is..."

"Aw, mom, I just got in the tub."

"Honey, please, mother replied, *your brothers aren't home, and Diane is afraid."*

"Diane's afraid, my ass; you're the chicken shit," I silently retorted. *"OK, wait a minute,"* I said, as I wrapped a thin towel around my dripping waist.

The pantry was on the far side of the kitchen next to the rear end of the house. The instant I set my soggy foot into the kitchen, I saw Diane perched on a countertop, pointing to the pantry. Almost simultaneously, I heard some jars break on the pantry floor. Fully attentive now, I crept back to the brown plastic accordion-like curtain that enclosed our canned and "put up" goods, opening it as quietly as possible.

"*Jesus Christ,*" I silently screamed, disbelieving my eyes. At the end of four giant jars of Jiff Super Chunk peanut butter set side by side, I saw a whiskered snout with sharp, pointed teeth. At the other end, a mile away, was a serpentine tail.

"*Shit, this is the biggest rat in history! What do I do?*"

Steve had that Arab scimitar from our middle east trip up in the closet of his bedroom. I tiptoed away on the QT, then sprinted upstairs. "*Always have a backup,*" I heard dad's voice in my head, so along with the sword, I grabbed a baseball bat standing next to his golf clubs.

"*What is it, what do you see?*" mother pleaded, now hiding behind the dining room door with my sister. "*You don't want to know, stay out of the kitchen,*" I barked, not thinking to dry off or put some clothes on.

When I got back downstairs, I shut the doors to mom and dad's bedroom, then to the basement and the dining room, sealing off the kitchen from entire house.

"*Whatever happens, don't let him bite you,*" was my last thought as once more I eked open the pantry door.

The giant was still there.

Using the butt end of the bat, I toppled the second jar of Jiff, exposing the ample trunk of this behemoth. Luckily, my adversary didn't stir.

"*I'll run him through with the sword,* I resolved, *then beat his head in with the bat. It's an ugly job and it'll be an awful mess, but I'll make Diane clean it up, after all, I'm risking rabies to save her!*"

Steeled to my course, I thrust the blade, pinning the monster against the wall! NOT! The antique scimitar, brittle from lack of use, broke at my stab, and biggie rat, reacting to my attack, leapt from his perch to chow down on me!

As the rodent from hell went for me, I jumped back, slipping on the puddle my towel had made underfoot, and fell. *"Holy fucking shit, he's gonna eat me,"* I thought, using what remained of the sword and my bat to fend off the frenzied rodent.

God knows what mom and Diane were thinking as I scrambled to get a safe distance and reform my attack.

Running to the other side of the room now, I threw off my booby-trapping towel, leaped up naked on the kitchen table, then grabbed a table chair to use like a lion tamer.

"Please, God, don't let him get my feet," I prayed, as I jumped from my perch, thrusting my bat and parrying my rival's aggressive counters with the chair. *"What I need is an elephant gun,"* I fantasized, when suddenly I connected with my bat, crushing my opponent's head against the baseboard of the kitchen sink.

"God, what a mess," I thought, as I franticly beat the invader's head to a grisly pulp.

Once I knew the intruder was dead, I called for mom to bring me some shoes and pants. *Are you alright,"* she asked, as she passed my clothes through the partially open dining room door. *"Yeah, yeah, I'm OK,"* I lied, trying to calm down as I put on my jeans.

Once dressed, I wedged the bat under my dead foe's middle and picked him up. He weighed a ton. I hauled his carcass outside and threw it into the woods that fronted our house on Missionary Ridge.

Now mom's hero, when dad got home that night, I told him with warrior pride how I'd saved the day.

Dad started laughing at my blow-by-blow description...

"Son, you didn't kill a rat, you killed a possum. He probably came up into the pantry from the old coal bin. I'm proud you protected your mother and sister, but all you had to do was say Shoo. He probably would have scrambled back wherever he came from."

"Boy, don't I feel like an asshole," I sighed, deflated but still somewhat elated.

It was odd to feel like a hero and an idiot at the same time.

High School Daze

These next four stories concern my High School days up until I left home for college in the fall of 1971. Slowly, but surely, I began to individuate, although my complaint defiance retarded that process to a snail's pace. I started to grow up some, exploring life philosophies that made sense to me. As I began to get past cloning my father, I realized I was unconventional and a free-thinker. During this period, I got laid for the first time and then went away to college. As I returned to the city of my birth, I had the vague awareness that I just might find a way of being more suited to my actual temperament and move past getting my father's approval or suffering too much from his criticism..

Meeting My Shadow and Discovering the Stars

One day when I was a junior, I found myself in the Brainerd High library. There were some books on sale near the checkout counter and I was drawn to a paperback entitled *Dracula*. On the cover of this classic horror novel, a genre I avoided because I didn't like to be scared, was the frightening face of a seeming man with an aquiline nose and slightly visible fangs where his upper cuspid teeth should be.

For some reason, I bought this Dell paperback, marked down from a quarter, for a single dime.

I was terrified of the Count from the start.

My brother Stephen, who I thought was bulletproof but had demons of his own, was haunted by Frankenstein, but the Transylvanian Count was my shadowy self-projection of choice.

Steve had a recurring dream that Frankenstein was coming after him. My brother would take one step and the big lummox would match him. The only problem was that zipper neck had a bigger stride than Steve, so with every step the monster got closer to catching my big brother and chewing him up.

For me, Frankenstein was a clumsy oaf. I could outrun and out-maneuver him, so he didn't bother me at all. Throw a fish to the Creature of the Black Lagoon, and he'd be as happy as a clam. I felt the same about the Wolfman. For the price of a dog bone, I was sure any werewolf would leave me alone.

But Dracula was quite another matter.

He could become mist and slide through the narrowest crack, and once he had you, you were worse than dead. You were eternally damned!

On the upside, he seemed to have a way with women. He could have any girl he liked. He could also live forever. If you could get used to sleeping in a coffin and drinking people's blood, (which I supposed was a vampire's equivalent to having sex) you were guaranteed an eternity of new beginnings and fresh flesh. I also liked the fact that he had the strength of twenty men.

The upshot is that I identified with Bram Stoker's Count. What frightened me was this literary image of my anger, incarnate. Cleaving back to the burning of *Alligator I*, and my vow to become an undetectable demon more monstrous than the ghouls in my family, it's no wonder I was freaked out by my Transylvanian doppelganger.

Considering my childhood, what put me on tilt with the Count was that he was the living, breathing embodiment (well maybe not breathing) of my most damned and damning self. He was my worst nightmare and at the same time the expression of my shadow self's desire for power and dominance.

All and all, to me, he was more than real.

Fifteen years later, I would begin to explore the Dracula within me by writing a play based on Bram Stoker's novel, but with a metaphysical, redemptive twist.

Along this same time, I became interested in Astrology. I didn't associate the study of the Cosmos with vampires but was intrigued by this wisdom tradition's ability to deepen my understanding of myself and other people. What fascinated me about the art/science of the stars was the intentionality it expressed. In time, I began to feel astrology helped me connect with my spiritual core and to gain a greater understanding of my contradictions and the sorts of pursuits that were right for me.

The study of the stars implied self-connection was not only possible but that I could use what I learned about myself to live a life that suited me.

I first began to study the stars in high school. Over the years, I got deeper and deeper into the subject and the more I studied it, the more relevant it became. Astrology has a spiritual dimension that aligns with what I've always felt was true about being and doing.

My notion of spirituality has always canted towards reincarnation, karma, and the idea that we should live in harmony with the natural world. This just makes sense to me. The idea that we get one shot at life, and only one, is and always has been a ridiculous concept to me.

I feel that you and I select our family before we're born; that our family has common themes that every family member works on, and that we reincarnate as many times as necessary to sort out our personal and familial issues.

Anger has always been an issue with the Moseley's. In time, I would come to believe that my father's rage had deeper roots than his experience of the Great Depression. I believe volatility has been a central challenge for my entire family for many lifetimes. I also feel that with time and effort, my family members and I are meant to source the passion in our anger to get to a deeper understanding of who we are and what we care about.

This memoir and the stories that comprise it are an expression of my desire to live a more self-aware, inclusive, and constructive life. I want my passion to take me to a deeper, wiser way of being and doing.

The more I learned about astrology, the more directed and focused I became. In time, it helped me understand why becoming an actor was important to me, and then later, why I needed to move beyond living a performer's life.

But I'm getting ahead of myself. My days as an actor and everything related to that experience comes later in these narratives.

Saved by Southern Belle

While I was beginning to ponder my fate from a metaphysical viewpoint, mom and dad went to Mexico City to attend one of the many Bar Association conferences dad frequented to drum up business. In the meantime, Diane and I were left in the care of a kindly widow we knew from church named Mrs. Deakins.

As a new driver, now sixteen, I was permitted to drive the family Volvo, but only at day with Diane aboard, only to her or my school, and then directly back home.

In no time, I was driving all over the place, day and night.

This Saturday evening, I was out and about with my buddy, Eric Mease. We'd just crested a steep roadway called Cabin Lane. Take a right at the top of this hill and it was less than a mile to our house.

Regrettably, I took a left.

"Running the Ridge" was driving like a bat out of hell down the narrow, winding road where we lived. I'd seen my brother Steve do this many times, but each time as a passenger only.

Peddle to the metal and southbound now, I barely negotiated the hairpin turn just north of the Anderson's house. Doing 60 in a 35 mph zone, I lost it, hitting one of the hundreds of 5" x 5" concrete boundary posts that fronted the entire length of Missionary Ridge. The impact was so hard my knee dented the chrome liner of the air-conditioner that sat just below the car's dashboard.

Its frame bent by the collision; our family station wagon was a total wreck.

Staring at the top of the black steering wheel, just after I wiped out, I couldn't believe I'd put myself into such hot water.

Mercifully, no one was injured, and the dead Volvo was towed away. When I got up the next morning to check our garage, just in case I'd had a nightmare, I saw nothing but empty space.

Then it hit me; *"When dad gets home, there's gonna be hell to pay.* And in the ten days until that happened, all I could do was contemplate the various forms my execution might take.

Dr. Bill Lemon, a radiologist, and our great family friend got word of my accident from Mrs. Deakins. He called me to discuss strategy. My intention was to man-up, meet mom and dad at the airport when they returned, and fess-up.

Bill Lemon advised me as my physician, to let him meet my parents, instead. He figured I needed a buffer, and he was right. So, I stayed home to await the consequences of my fuck-up.

"Oh, look, there's the Lemons," mom said in delight, as my parents arrived at the airport.

"At one am Monday morning?" dad came back, *"Something's wrong."*

Doc Lemon, God bless him, did double-duty as my doctor and my lawyer that night. Driving home from the airport, doc said to dad, *"Ray, your youngest son had a mishap. You've got some scrap metal on your hands, but you need to be thankful your boy is OK."*

I stayed up to meet my parents. Once we said goodbye and thanks to the Lemons, all pop said was, *"It's late, son. Let's talk about what happened tomorrow."*

CLOCKING the GOOSE

By the next afternoon, dad had gone to the junk yard to see the evidence. We'd just had dinner when he began to set me up for the kill. Instinctively, I now referenced everything I'd ever heard about surviving a cross-examination in a capital case.

"Never volunteer anything," I'd heard pop say a thousand times. I also called on my memory of his tells. When dad was about to lose it, he'd start readjusting the frames of his glasses. Watching for this like the half-Hawk I was, our conversation went something like this;

"So, tell me about your adventure."

"I was driving with Eric, and we were headed south towards Shallowford Road.

"Driving with Eric. What time was it?

"About 9 pm Saturday night."

"Saturday night. How fast were you going?

"Thirty-five."

"Thirty-five?"

"Yes, sir."

"I saw the car today. Are you sure you were driving thirty-five?"

"Well..."

"Our wrecked station wagon now bends in two places. I don't buy you were doing thirty-five?"

"Well, maybe I was going..."

"In the first place, there's no way you were doing under sixty, you had no business being out at night, and Eric had no right to be in the car!"

Suddenly, the phone rang. Mom and Diane, anticipating dad's eruption, had retreated to the Sunroom on the far side of the house. Mom picked up the extension. Steve was on the line. According to my sister, mom chatted him up a for a moment till my brother gently cut her off and said,

"Mom, if dad's home, could you get him on the line?"

Mom called out for dad to get on the phone, *"Stephen's calling,"* she said.

"Hello," came dad's distracted voice, as he picked up from the kitchen.

"Mom, dad, I just called to tell you I've eloped."

"Jesus Christ, Almighty," dad exclaimed, twisting his glasses into a pretzel while mom's cheery greeting fell into a mortified stupor.

Dad sat on a chair next to the kitchen cabinet where the telephone was, putting his head in his hands.

From that instant, my father never said another word to me about the Volvo. He didn't ground me, didn't yell at me, didn't do anything at all.

All four of us children, each in turn, got in trouble from time to time. Often, we'd complain to mom about how dad treated us. When we'd ask mama why papa was so exacting she'd just say, *"Well I don't know; your father is a good man, and he loves you."* Then each of us in his or her turn would retort, *"But he acts like he wants to disown me, or something."*

"Oh, honey, mom replied, *sometimes he wishes he didn't have any children, at all."*

My First Time

It was now May 1971. As a high school graduation present dad took me back to Rome, the site of my first awakening five years before. Pop also invited his older brother, my Uncle Paul, and my football teammate, David King.

David's nickname among his peers was W.T. Bass. It was not a flattering appellation, but a backhanded rap laid on him by teammates who thought, as I did, that he had a big mouth, literally and figuratively. David wasn't' shy, had no problem going after whatever he wanted, and could be overbearing.

In fairness to W.T., his father, Big Jack King, was a minister, so it was only right to give him some leeway as a preacher's son. I got the distinct impression that dad wished I was more like David, who was our senior class President while I was an enigmatic and peripheral specter at school, ever refining my alienation.

The trip to Rome was sponsored by UT, dad's alma mater, and was a ten-day journey. As I recall there were about twenty-five in our party. Among us, there was a girl making the trip with her mother. She was the only one in our entire group the same age as David and me.

Susan O. Wilson, God knows what the O stood for, was slim but sexy in a sort of reformed hippy/waif kinda way. Reformed isn't quite the right word to describe her. I got the feeling her mom had "cleaned her up" to make her more conventionally presentable.

Susan wore thinned rimmed glasses that gave her a naughty librarian look. She was low key and well behaved but clearly had a rebellious streak. Susan also had an experienced, knowing look, and was attracted to me.

I was now 18 with no dating experience and had the fresh-faced look of the virgin I was. For sure, David and Susan were more experienced in the sexual arena than I was.

Our accommodation in Rome was the Hotel Boston. David and I went out exploring the moment we arrived. Being an expert on the Eternal City based on the single week I spent there at thirteen, I led us into the night and quickly got us lost. God knows where we were when two guys in a Fiat pulled up and offered us a ride to a bar.

"Well, I don't know about goin to a bar, but can you drop us at the Hotel Boston," my President inquired as he jumped straight into the backseat. *Are you out of your mind? We don't know who the hell these guys are or what they're up to,* I silently protested, but not to be outdone by my confident teammate, I jumped in too. Sure enough after we rode a block or two the Romeo sitting shotgun turned to us and said; *"How'd you like to get a nice Italian blow-job?"*

Oh, shit, I wondered, *here we go.*

Suddenly we pulled to the side of the road, were ushered to a downstairs bar, and were introduced to a pair of ladies who took us to a private area with a couple of separate booths in a back room.

OK, asshole, you're the one that got us into this mess, I fumed, ignoring my complicity in what I now saw as an unattractive opportunity to bust my cherry, *now what are you gonna do to get us out of this?* As I waited for W.T. to make the next move, the brunette I'd been paired with, who wasn't as good-looking as David's blonde, took my hand and tried to make small talk.

Just as my hooker asked me to order a bottle of Champaigne, David spoke up from the pitch-black void and said, *"Hey Bob, you got any money?" "Nah, I'm broke,"* I replied. Immediately my girl's touch went cold, and she let go of me. Who knows, maybe we should have gone for it, but all I wanted to do was high-tail it out of there and that's exactly what we did.

Back on the street now, we ran into a mechanic whose repair shop was open late. We quickly communicated that we were lost, showed him our room key with the hotel's address. Our hotel was just up the street and around the corner from the bar we'd just escaped.

After we'd been in Rome several days, a portion of our group took a brief trip south to Pompei. Dad and Uncle Paul stayed in Rome while David and I, along with Susan and her mom went on the day trip which also included a stop at Capri.

I guess sex was in the air, because when we got to Pompei our guide asked all the women in our party to exit the room we'd just entered. He then unlocked a metal box on the wall that revealed a Roman soldier wearing a harness to support his cock, a phallus that was the size of a great white shark. Only one woman from our party peaked to see what was going on. It was Susan. She saw what the Centurion was packing, smiled, and looked straight at ME!?!

I wish I could report we made mad, passionate love that night to the sound of the crashing waves of Capri's Blue Grotto, but it wasn't until we got back to Rome that I began to act on the signals I was getting from young Ms. Wilson.

Looking back, lots of boys and girls began their sexual lives when going overseas. If you were lucky enough to travel, relatively few tourists knew each other prior to these trips. Erotic encounters had a built-in time limit, and since you didn't have to deal with your reputation being overseas, it was easier to let go. You knew there was little likelihood of getting entangled in complications.

Nevertheless, I didn't spend time alone with Susan till she asked me if I'd like to go for a walk two nights before we flew home.

As we took off on our own for the first time, I guess I was a little nervous. I was more greyhound than human, taking strides like a Tennessee walking horse.

Susan slowed me down, then took my hand.

Now taking human strides, we passed the Hotel Del la Ville, site of my first visit to the Eternal City, then beyond the top of the Spanish Steps, and entered the Borgese Gardens. We spied a bench under a beautiful water clock there and decided to sit and talk awhile.

It was a beautiful, temperate Roman night and we had the park all to ourselves. I don't remember how we got into it but in no time we were kissing. A woman in the mood has an unmistakable softness, combined with a subtle and spidery allure that enfolds you. As we warmed to each other, and it didn't take long, the kissing got hot, and I started to explore Susan's body.

I touched her breasts and she swooned. I caressed her ass and she gasped. I slid my hand inside her and she completely melted down. *WHAT THE HELL DO I DO NOW?* The prospect of having sex then and there was imminent, but I'd never had sex anywhere. The risk of getting caught and jailed when the only lawyer I knew in Rome was dad, and he didn't speak Italian, gave me pause. Picking up on my reluctance, and for reasons of her own, Susan also sensed the circumstance of our immediate situation made intercourse unadvisable.

We paused. Then we came up with a plan.

Having cloned my father completely by now, I could predict his every thought and action. We all attended a farewell party in the hotel bar the next evening, during which I said my goodbyes and good nights and went up to my room. Like clockwork dad called me as I knew he would to say good night. I said I was tired, was turning in, and told him I'd see him in the morning. W.T. was aware and supportive of what I was up to and vacated our room to give me time alone with Susan.

With all this in place by prearrangement, I snuck down through the bowels of the hotel to the kitchen, a place I'd never been before. Inspired at the prospect of my first ever conquest, I navigated in pitch black darkness from the kitchen to the bar. There, my willing paramour awaited me with open arms.

Bringing her back the way I came, we went back up to my room. *Now what*, I thought. *"Do you want to take a shower?"* I said, *"No,"* came Susan's calm and clearly more knowledgeable reply. *"Come here,"* she said.

From my royal blue cuff-linked shirt to the tie and suit I was wearing, to the sensation of her lips, and her naked skin pressing my own, I still remember the smell, taste, and feel of everything that passed between us. Susan was a seasoned, slow hand. She took me step by step through an elegant ritual of undressing her. Then, as she stood naked before me like Botticelli's Venus, she slowly undressed me.

Now wearing my open shirt and nothing else, my lover sat on the bedside and took me in her mouth. *Whoa, wow, WHOA!* I groaned and almost swooned. After a brief eternity, where she brought me to the very edge, she laid down and had me tend to her as she'd just tended to me.

Then the moment came to ease insider her.

It felt as good, easy, and natural as falling off a log and we took an eternity to pleasure each other as time stopped for me as it never had before.

After we both finished everything was a blur. Now I knew what the O in Susan's name stood for; OH MY GOD!

As we returned home the next day, I was in a semi-numb reverie. *So, this is the secret of life*, I thought.

I still don't know why I never called or wrote to Susan. I still remember the address she gave me; 124 Balboa Circle, Oak Ridge, Tennessee. Perhaps there's something deep down in my soul that keeps me alone, despite my desire for an enduring partner. There are deep parts of me that remain a mystery to me, despite my efforts to fully know myself.

Still, despite all my quirks and contradictions, I happily remember my first time in the Eternal City. I hope her memory of our time together warms Susan, too.

CHAPTER IV:
Fleeting First Steps On my Own

The Last Time in Your Life No One Expects Anything of You

When I enrolled as a first-year student at the University of Tennessee, I didn't realize the freedom that was now available to me. Returning to the city of my birth, I could re-invent myself. In college, no one knew who I thought I was or cared about who I'd been up till now. I was entering a world ostensibly designed to test and develop my mind and my ability to re-create myself according to my vision of who I could become.

Regrettably, the world of academia today has changed from a place of free, full and boundary breaking exploration, (at least in the humanities) to a culture where conforming to politically correct social agendas stifles students' willingness to risk unconventional behavior and stretch their possibilities. As I see it, the Woke movement is counterproductive to the main mission of our universities. Apparently, the mere risk of offending a minority group puts handcuffs on anything new and different that might have wide-spread positive effects merely because it might ruffle someone's feathers.

As I have throughout these narratives, I cite movies to illustrate my viewpoint. Here, 1976's <u>Marathon Man</u> comes to mind. Although this film only peripherally touches the academic world, (Dustin Hoffman's character Babe is a graduate student at Columbia), there's a line of dialogue from another character that sums up the way college used to be. Christian Szell, the villain of the piece, says to Babe,

"I envy you your school days. Enjoy them fully. It's the last time in your life no one expects anything of you."

Of course, college in my day wasn't free of expectation, but those expectancies were about getting good grades as a measure of the development of one's mind, not about thinking approved of thoughts. Higher education was also free of the economic consequences that pressure people into making compromises they don't really want to make. Although this is largely still the case, today the hazard is how social pressures overshadow intellectual risk-taking and rigor. As a student focusing on liberal arts at UT in the 1970's I wasn't burdened with woke-think. Moreover, I had a very real opportunity to create myself free of self-interference.

The View from Rocky Top

I remember a marvelous moment I had as a freshman at UT. It was a bright, temperate, and beautiful autumn day in 1972. I found myself in the valley where the massive Neyland Stadium was situated. I hiked partway up what we called "the Hill," just west of Neyland, then sat down on the grassy knoll overlooking the open end of the horseshoe stadium, Shields-Watkins football field, and the better part of the general campus. Looking down from what seemed a semi-divine perch, I watched all the people go by.

As I sat there, I could feel the possibilities of my new beginning. I marveled at the beehive of stories that were evolving in the person of everyone I saw. I felt on top of the world; at one with the promise of this vibrant new setting.

I didn't really know anyone at school yet, but I had a genuine personal bond at the Chi Phi, or what grandaddy Hawk called, the *Hi-Fi* Fraternity house. My brother Steve had joined Chi Phi at UNC at Chapel Hill. He'd left the Tar Heel state and was now paying his own way through school at UT. Financially, Stephen was on his own. I got the impression this was because he told dad that he'd rather make his own decisions, good or bad, than accept money from pop with strings attached.

For my part, I was playing follow the leader again.

My first quarter at school, I spent as much time at the frat house as I did in class and my dorm room combined. Sam Smith, a senior classman in our chapter, called me "Moochie" because I was bumming cigarettes all the time. What he was saying to me was that once my grades were posted, (a condition dad put on my joining the fraternity) it would be time for me to pay for all the privileges and activities that I was now enjoying *gratis* and in advance. When my grades came through, I got dad's blessing via his check and pledged.

Bill Eldridge was assigned by the chapter to be my big brother. Eldridge was from Jacksonville, Florida and although he majored in Engineering, at heart he was a mad scientist. Bill, much like my grandaddy Hawk, had a great dry wit.

One night, just for fun, he took me to a computer center deep in the bowels of Neyland Stadium to play some games. In those days, there were only three computer games available; *Star Trek, U-Boat Kommander* and a program called *LEM*. We stayed there late into the night playing every possible variation of each game until we got bored.

That's when we really had some fun.

In *Star Trek* the game began with a print-out that read; *"Klingon vessel sighted, what are your orders, captain?"* Just for fun I keyed in *"Self-Destruct,"* blowing the USS Enterprise to hell and gone. The programmer anticipated my bone-head order. After Damage Control spelled out the extent of the devastation, the program said *"What the hell did you do that for? You just destroyed a damn fine starship!"*

Not to be outdone, I went to the next game to see how I could wreak more havoc. In *U-Boat Kommander* I let the destroyers escorting an allied convoy close in on the Nazi submarine I commanded till they were in point blank range. Once they surrounded me and were all set to blow me out of the water, I surrendered. When the program asked me for my sword and flag, I fired my forward and aft torpedoes, sinking three allied vessels. My reward? The Fuhrer sent me to the Russian Front for disobeying orders. *What bullshit*, I thought. *The real Fuhrer would have given me a Knight's Cross with Oak leaf clusters!*

LEM was the abbreviation for the Lunar module that *NASA* used to land on the moon. The object of LEM was to successfully land on the lunar surface. My most successful effort rebounded fifteen feet in the air before it settled down. I guess the program thought I'd like to try again. It gave me my initial altitude, heading and air speed, for another attempt. I inverted the LEM and hit full thrusters. At impact I was doing 600 mph and blew a crater in the Moon 15 miles wide!

All in all, my higher education was getting off to a great start!

One of my favorite college recollections happened every third weekend of October in 1972 and 1974. That's when we'd stay up all night roasting a pig as Tennessee hosted Alabama in our annual football rivalry.

Our Vols would play Bear Bryant's Bama straight up for three-quarters, then they'd kick our ass in the final stanza and win the game going away. To this day, I have never SEEN the Vols beat Bama in a football game.

The intent of roasting a pig was to have a celebratory feast commemorating **our** victory. Hope springs eternal and every other year we roasted a new piggy, hoping that this would be the home game vs. the Tide we finally won.

The process began by digging a pit in the side yard of our chapter house. The key to a tender pork loin was to baste Porky in Jack Daniels Old No. 7 all through the night. Around 11 am the next morning, the real drinking began. By game time at 2 pm we were trashed. Insanity is doing the same damn thing repeatedly, expecting a different result. Eventually, we accepted that the third Saturday in October would be more of a wake than a joyful celebration.

For weeks after we lost to Bama, anyone who dropped by our chapter house at 124 Lake Avenue was welcome to chow down on all the pork they liked, which we kept in a black garbage bag in the kitchen fridge.

It's a miracle no one died of trichinosis.

One highlight of my first year was the mandatory pledge trip Steve Barlew and I took to the University of Virginia. The two of us made up the smallest pledge class in our chapter's history.

We drove my 1964 Rambler, which was having alternator problems and decided to grab proof of our trip right away, then drive home ASAP. We figured the shorter the trip the less chance my car had to breakdown. Once we arrived in Charlottesville, we found two possible targets; Edgar Allan Poe's blanket, which decorated his former rooms in The Quad at the center of the UVA campus, or a brass plaque, also nearby, which commemorated the founding of Pi Kappa Alpha fraternity.

Wary that the ghost of Poe would lay waste to my balky alternator, we decided to rip off the Pike plaque.

A formal dance was happening in the area where the tablet was located. Our prize was screwed into a wall next to a sidewalk where couples constantly passed by going to or leaving the party. Some bushes close by provided us with cover and we hid there any time a couple walked by. Once each pair passed, we'd jump out and work on the four giant screws that secured the heavy brass plaque to the wall.

After playing hide and seek several times, we realized that the screws were much longer than we anticipated, and our attempted theft was taking forever to pull off.

Finally, we said to hell with it and continued our efforts while a couple or two passed us by. Apparently, these folks were so engrossed in each other they didn't see us. At last, we liberated the plaque, ran with it to my car, and immediately set out for Knoxville.

As I recall, I drove us straight through to K-town. Nearly home, I briefly nodded off with Barlew asleep in the back seat and only avoided colliding with a railway bridge when the road's gravel shoulder jolted me awake.

We duly presented our trophy at our usual chapter meeting on Monday evening. Only then did we learn that Chi Phi's national president got word of our exploit and called to see if we'd really absconded with the sacred heirloom.

Wanting to enjoy our prize a bit longer, we denied all knowledge of the theft.

Unfortunately, one of our little sisters was dating a Pike at the time. She ratted us out. The Pikes sent over a swat team to reclaim our prize while we were competing in an inter-fraternity track meet, and that was that.

Oh, yes and then there was school.

I was an above average student but little more. Despite my tendency to hold myself back, my desire to know things deeply, all evidence to the contrary, continued to develop. I was drawn to subjects like philosophy.

There was a newspaper joke posted outside the Philosophy Department located in the Liberal Arts Administration Building at the center of the campus. It was a spin-off of Descartes's famous statement in the form of two ducks floating in a pond. One duck said to the other; *"I quack, therefore I am."* I read this to mean; *while I breathe, I hope*, the Latin motto at St. Andrews in Scotland.

Despite my shenanigans at school, I was looking for a sense of mission and purpose. Regrettably, in all my time at UT, only two experiences inspired my full interest and participation.

The first was a survey course in Western Art. I was fascinated with how art in any era reflected the culture of that period. I don't remember my instructor's name, or the year I took her course, but I recall she was an elegant middle-aged woman, and I had a crush on her.

Our final exam was to identify paintings we'd studied in class via projected slides of those works. The only slide I missed was *Nude descending a Staircase* by Marcel Duchamp, which, of course, is the only title I remember now.

In my era, the best example I recall about the role a student's expectations played in their education came from an interaction my eventual sister-in-law, Brenda Gilliam, had with Dr. Dwight Van de Vate, a philosophy professor who taught both of us in a class whose title I also don't remember. At that time, we were on a quarter system and at the beginning of each cycle, the professor asked new students why they took his class and what their expectations were.

All of us answered his query to the best of our ability and Brenda was the last to respond.

Brenda said, *"I have no idea why I took this course and no expectations; that's why I took the course; to find out why and what would come of it..."*

Dr. Van de Vate replied, *"But for you, I would sleep tonight."*

Magic and Mastery at Augusta National

If I ever needed a lesson in concentration and skill, how to apply it, and the rewards of self-mastery, I could've found no better example what I saw at the Master's golf tournament in 1972.

By a stroke of good luck, I took my brother Steve's place when he dropped out of going at the last minute. Although I forget why he couldn't make it, I felt incredibly lucky to have this chance to see the best players in the world ply their trade.

My fraternity brother, Larry Mansfield, had two clubhouse passes for the last two rounds that year. Larry, who was from Atlanta, had attended the Masters all his life.

Not only was I attending the first major golf tournament of 1972, but this was also the first tournament I'd ever been to. I was thrilled beyond words. To make things even more exciting, Jack Nicklaus, my hero, was leading the field after the first two rounds and was in position to tie Arnold Palmer, my other golfing hero, by winning four Masters titles apiece.

CLOCKING the GOOSE

The first thing I noticed about Augusta, besides Magnolia Lane and its famous cupola-topped clubhouse, was how hilly the National was. TV didn't convey the extremity of its slopes.

From its apex at the level of the first and tenth teeing grounds, the course virtually drops into a valley. Built on the site of a former nursery, the history of the golf course is well documented, yet to see the beauty of the place in person was very, very special.

Bobby Jones, the founder of the club, had died the previous December. His loss was palpable and the golf course itself had suffered a difficult winter. Poa annua, a pesky weed, had infested several greens and made them bumpy and unpredictable to putt.

Truthfully, these playing conditions were of little interest to me. I was dazzled by the beauty of Augusta National and in awe of the golfing gods who were gathered there.

By acclamation, Jack Nicklaus was the greatest player in the world and to this day he remains golf's most prolific major champion. The first time I saw Jack was at the driving range where competitors warmed-up and sometimes practiced after their rounds. I'd positioned myself on the front row at the range and I'll be damned if the man himself didn't stop dead in front of me to begin his warm-up for Saturday's third round.

I was mesmerized. I couldn't believe my good fortune. The by God Golden Bear was warming up right in front of me.

Starting with the laces on his white, tassel-free golf shoes I absorbed everything he did. I watched him pull a club from his green and white MacGregor golf bag, wedge it in the crook of his elbows and behind his back and then rotate his body to loosen up. As he began to hit soft wedge shots, I watched his feet, ankles, knees, thighs, waist, arms and shoulders, as he worked his way up to hitting the longest clubs in his bag.

What was compelling about Nicklaus was his bright blue-grey eyes and his confident presence. Now 32, he had the look of eagles. His tanned and tempered confidence was the quintessence of relaxed yet focused intensity. This was a man who thrived in the furnace of major championship pressure, and everyone who knew anything about golf knew that Jack never, ever beat himself. He had the most predatory focus of any athlete I've ever seen.

Once Jack warmed up and left the practice ground to tee off, I followed him for a few holes, then bounced around and watched some of the other greats who were playing that year.

Arnold Palmer was built like a bull. His brash, blunt force swing was unconventional, but polished, rhythmic and powerful. Arnie's action was an expression of the force of his will and his *"go for broke/never say die"* attitude. Nicklaus's famous upright move was deliberate and highly disciplined, like the man himself. Tom Weiskopf's swing had a beautiful fluidity with an unmistakable majesty. Ironically, Weiskopf himself, given his stature and the regality of his swing, was thin skinned with a brittle pride. He was more than slightly vain and a little remote. Tom was easy to admire but not easy to warm up to.

Of all the players competing, only Nicklaus and Weiskopf could generate a uniquely high ball flight, producing shots that soared it seemed to the Pearly Gates, momentarily suspend in midair, and then descend to terra firma like what columnist Dan Jenkins called *a butterfly with sore feet.*

All the players had distinctive swings but every one of them also had a silky-smooth tempo.

Two shots in the tournament stand out in my memory. Nicklaus made both of them.

Jack's opening tee shot on Saturday was slightly pulled. I was lucky to be on the left side of the fairway and I got about six feet from him as he played his second into the green. At that time, Nicklaus had a signature move that began his swing. Almost simultaneously he would trigger his backswing by extending and firming up his arms, then cock his head to the right to free up his move away from the ball.

What astounded me was his focus. His concentration had the density of a black hole. The seven-iron he put on the green was never going anywhere but exactly where he intended it to go.

His other memorable shot was his second on the tenth hole. Jack pushed his drive into the trees to the right of the fairway. As he lined up his escape from the pine straw that carpeted his lie, I witnessed once more his massive concentration as he played a shot that towered through the trees, hit, and held the green.

Nicklaus wasn't at his best that Sunday, but the combination of his course management, tough course conditions, and the fact that no one made a run at him, won him his fourth green jacket with a score of two over par, 74.

Such was my first and most memorable exposure to major championship golf. There's no question in my mind that if I'd had the talent, the game, and the inner fortitude to play golf at the highest level, I would have chosen professional golf as my career. Its demand for power, precision, and self-mastery were inspirational to me.

Although I adore the game and always will, my talents and abilities lay elsewhere but the characteristics that made for a fine golf game, especially self-mastery, went a long way in helping me to understand the qualities that would be most important to me in whatever field I made my life's work.

Going Door to Door

After my first year at UT, I followed in Steve's footsteps again. Just as with football and Chi Phi, I made up my mind to sell books like he had because I thought it would be a cool experience. The Bible publishers, Southwestern Company, had recruiters on campus and Jack Roddy signed me up for the summer of 1972. *"Who knows,* I pondered, *I might have one of those traveling salesman flings with a sexy girl."*

Southwestern's door-to-door sales scheme was your basic pyramid. I was to get customer orders throughout the summer, buy my books wholesale based on those orders, deliver them at retail and keep the profit. Roddy got a cut of my income and Graham Swafford, my field manager, got a piece, too.

On my way to Nashville to get a few days training before the summer sales season, my 64' Rambler overheated. I pulled into a gas station to investigate and when I opened the radiator cap a bit too much, I got doused with some super-hot water. *"Some fucking cooling system,"* I thought, flashing back to my science experiment in Mrs. Cobble's class. Luckily, I was more embarrassed than hurt, but my tennis shorts were ruined.

Once our sales training was complete, we paired-up to save on expenses. My roommate, Phil Colquitt, was a friend of my field manager and he was a piece of work. Born and raised in South Pittsburgh, Tennessee, Phil sported eternally rosy cheeks, longish platinum hair, and a smooth baby face that suggested innocence but belied his bitchy side.

A doppelganger for the Keeble Cookie Elf, Philip was almost always good company and sometimes hilarious, but he had one terrible habit. The second our alarm clock went off every morning Phil said, *"SHIT!"*

This is not how I wanted to greet my day.

To make matters worse, being from South Pittsburgh, it took my roommate three minutes to say a single word! As I was to discover years later when I trained as an actor, we southerner's turn vowel sounds into diphthongs, merging two vowel sounds into one, so Phil's "Shit" sounded more like *"SHEEUUHHTTUH!*

Another unique visitation like the whistling of the eaves, this sound did not intrigue but annoyed me. Worse still, *"SHEEUUHHTTUH* was always followed with *"BAABUH,* (a Philism for Bob) *wahtuh are wee gonnuh dew tudei?"*

Given his linguistic style, I'll never understand how Phil sold more books than me that summer.

He also had a unique way of saying yes and no. Yes, was s*chnay* and *ish-schnay* meant no. Schnay and ish-schnay had added meanings, too. Schnay meant great, that's very very good. Ish-schnay meant *"sheeuuhhttuh, that sucks."*

Experience had taught Southwestern to send their summer sales crews a fair distance from home. That way, you were less inclined to throw in the towel when you wanted to quit. We were assigned to southern Ohio in the Cincinnati area and our first territory was northeast of Cincy in the sleepy little town of Loveland.

I got off to a good start, but soon hit a lull. Then, one Saturday morning, I got a jolt.

I was working in a new subdivision selling reference books. New subdivisions weren't fertile territory even though they were loaded with school age kids. I was batting zero this morning and it was so hot outside, I felt like my constantly overheating Rambler.

I knocked on the door of the twentieth house in a row that looked slightly different from but was just a duplicate of every other home in that neighborhood. Virtually all these houses were air-conditioned. Whether I made a sale or not, I was hoping for an invitation to come in just to cool off.

Normally, to soften the abruptness of being confronted with a stranger, I turned my back to the door so I could feign surprise or preoccupation when the occupant answered their door bell. I followed this protocol and heard a little voice say *"hello."* When I turned around I saw a boy and girl of five or six. He was in his underwear, and she was wearing a dress.

"Is your mom home?" I asked.

"Uh huh," said the boy.

"Could you go get her for me?"

"OK," he replied and off he went.

"I'm Mary. What's your name?" asked the little girl.

"My name is Bob."

Now little Mary inquired in rapid succession, *"What do you do? How'd you get here? Do you do this every day? How can you be out here when it's so HOT? It's supposed to be 100 today..."*

I was in no mood to deal with this, so ignoring her questions, I said, *"Can you go see where your Mommy is?"*

What Mary wanted, and God knows what she needed, was just a little attention. I wish I'd given her just that because she ignored my request to find her mom and said, *"Look,"* **simultaneously walking out onto the front walkway and lifting her dress to reveal her completely naked torso!**

"Jesus Christ, kid, are you trying to get me jailed as a pervert," I silently screamed, now giving her my total focus in hopes she'd lower her dress. **Then, at the worst possible time, her mom appeared at the door.** *"Oh, God, I'm dead. This woman is gonna scream to high heaven and I'll be tarred and feathered, for sure!"*

But now came another surprise.

Mary's mom was smashed on sleeping pills. She didn't see her naked daughter on display and even invited me to come in out of the heat and take a seat in her living room.

Fortune favors the oblivious, I guess.

Almost at once, I went into my sales pitch when I should have sized up this impossible situation and moved on.

I had been taught to nod my head as I showed my books. If you could get your prospect to nod back in affirmation, your chances of making a sale improved because, at least in theory, it was hard to say NO when you'd been nodding yes through an entire pitch.

Mary's mom was so far gone, the only thing I should have tried to sell her was a mattress. As I continued to nod and she mirrored me back, her groggy nod got larger and more pronounced till she tipped her head too far and she fell off her chair.

I burst out laughing and said, *"thanks for your time. Good luck. See ya later."*

And that's as close as I ever got to getting thrown in jail.

Comebacks, Chocolate-Chip Cookies and a Big Scare

I saw 53 movies during my first stint selling books, mostly during work hours. Lack of discipline and getting into some negative patterns did me in. I wound up making thirty bucks for the entire summer. Phil made $600 and my Rambler blew up.

All this plus the embarrassment of calling dad to tow me home from Horse Cave, Kentucky, where the head gasket of my car disintegrated, made me so angry I returned one more summer to get it right.

Wise to the pitfalls I'd experienced in Ohio, this time I worked hard and smart when I was assigned to the Winston-Salem, Greensboro area in North Carolina. There were still highs and lows, but it felt good to have a strong resolve and some experience.

This time I made around $1500 for my efforts. Not much of a profit, really, but it was 5000 % more that I made the year before and that wasn't bad.

One afternoon I was making a pitch to a family with the biggest black cat I'd ever seen. More like a baby panther, this feline weighed around forty pounds. As I was doing my thing, he jumped on my lap, nearly breaking my legs. From my lap he started moving up my torso. I kept pitching as his size and weight caused me to pull back till I was almost lying prone. The family was intrigued that I could keep pitching while all this was happening.

They either bought some books from me because they were impressed by my commitment or to forestall me from suing them for feline assault.

Steve Allen and Bob Elliot took over from Phil as my roommates, who had the sense to quit after last summer, and my new buddies would cut loose with me from time to time, just to blow off steam. Steve and I were doing pretty well sales wise, so we decided to take a weekend of and fly to Atlanta for some fun.

We went to the Greensboro airport and made up some cock and bull story about my mom being sick. We were so convincing that Delta literally stopped a plane that had left its gate so we could get on board. When we got to Hotlanta, we hit bars and strip joints galore and had the time of our lives.

Elliot, who was nearly the spitting image of my future brother-in-law, David Crabtree, got plastered with me one night. We staggered out to the parking lot of whatever establishment we were patronizing and did a drunken wedding march up and over the top of a Volkswagen Carman Ghia.

Despite such unforgivable and destructive acts, we were otherwise law-abiding citizens and successful salesmen.

As far as I know, though we gave it our best shot, there were no women abandoned by us to raise unexpected and unwanted children in the Carolina piedmont.

By far, the best thing that happened that summer of 73' was the $300 in commissions I scored on a Tuesday I'll never forget. Some days you just get a gut feeling that something special is going to happen. This was one of those days.

I sold so many books that I ran out of the supply I kept in the trunk of my car. Driving back to my apartment I got a flat but somehow knew I should deal with it after hours. So, I hitched a ride the rest of the way to my place, got some more merchandise, taxied back to my car, put them in the trunk, and then got back to working my territory. I was still hot, and I sold out my resupply, too.

By the time I stopped working and put on my spare tire, I'd had my biggest day ever. I felt like I'd pitched every game of the World Series and won them all in one afternoon.

By far the worst thing that happened that summer was when mom collapsed at the post office in Chattanooga right after she mailed me some chocolate chip cookies. I think my brother Steve called me with this news and I rushed home from Carolina to be with mama.

The doctor said my mother had a meningioma; a tumor outside her brain that was golf-ball size and was putting debilitating but not fatal pressure on her frontal lobes.

I will never forget the site that greeted Stephen and I when we went to the ICU after her surgery. At that time, and I hope things have improved now for the better, anyone who had brain surgery had to sleep on a bed of ice for 24 hours afterwards because their entire body would swell up like a bloated corpse.

I kept my composure and didn't let on how freaked out I was to see her, but mom's head looked like she was an Egyptian Priestess in full head-dress. Her cranium had swollen so much she looked like the Queen of the Nile!

Mom had been lucky. Her tumor was outside her brain. After a couple of months of recovery, she got much better, and I realized how lucky I was that both my parents were healthy for most of their lives. I also resolved to never again make up any bullshit about having a sick relative just so I could get away to have some play time.

My Late Drop

A few months after my last summer selling books door to door, I confronted an unusual academic challenge that would test every facet of my creativity. It would be nice to say this concerned getting my PHD, but it involved dropping a class I hated after the drop deadline had passed.

This proved to be a challenge worthy of the ingenuity of a grandaddy Hawk, and it actually involved his son, my Uncle Dick, without who's help I'd never have pulled it off. What's more, this ruse gave me a foretaste of what would prove to be my profession for several years to come.

I was a history major at UT. At the time I was taking a course in Ancient Rome as well as a class on U.S. Foreign Policy. Dr. Bing and Dr. Utley, the professors teaching these two courses, just happened to share office space. I presumed they knew each other fairly well.

From my viewpoint, Bing was bizarre. He sported a goat-tee which made him look like a Persian King and I thought he was living in the wrong millennium. As I saw it, Dr. Bing shouldn't be teaching about Rome, he should've been a hot dog vendor at the Coliseum. His lectures were monotonous and uninspiring. Dr. Utley, my foreign relations professor, was a good instructor. He was arrogant and a know-it-all, but he was also entertaining. His lectures were insightful and thought-provoking.

Bing gave us the option of taking a midterm that would account for thirty-five per cent of our final grade. We were also to write a final paper comparing and contrasting the rise and fall of the Republic and the Empire of Rome. Given the fact that I loved the Eternal City and lost my virginity there I was looking forward to Bing's class, but once I got into it all I wanted was out.

I passed on taking the mid-term, then tried to write a serviceable final paper but got my first experience of writer's block. Unfortunately, I'd stuffed myself with Nodose so I sat at my typewriter all night long trying to write an analysis that wouldn't come. When I heard the birds chirping the next morning along with the buzz of my electric typewriter, I knew I was in trouble.

What to do?

Getting out of a course after the deadline required permission from my department (History) for a late drop. Now my task was to orchestrate a plausible excuse.

First, I set up a meeting with a Dr. Johnson to plead my case. Johnson was a history professor I'd never met. Then I made up a cock and bull tale to indicate I'd experienced unusual stress which prevented me from applying myself fully to the Rome course.

Since I declined to take the mid-term, I needed an explanation for this, too. I relocated grandaddy Hawk, who had recently been diagnosed with cancer, from Knoxville to Kingsport. I felt guilty about this but rationalized that I was making all the hospital visits I claimed, they were just right off campus, not two-hundred miles roundtrip for each visit.

If grandaddy found out what I was doing, I hoped he'd get a kick out of my dodge.

Next, I arranged to put myself in the hospital the entire week before my final paper was due. Here I consulted with my Uncle Dick, who was a dentist and gave me the greatest doctor's note ever saying I'd been admitted to Fort Sanders hospital for oral surgery. My malady was acute Alviosis, whatever the hell that was.

Once I had all this documented I was ready for my *"woe is me"* scene with the unknown Dr. Johnson.

Rexall had a drug store on Cumberland Avenue, better known to UT students as the Strip. I bought a box of cotton there, stuffed it in my mouth till I looked like a Pinata, then presented myself at the Liberal Arts Advising Center for my date with destiny.

Working for a condition of fatigue, as a professional actor would term it, my debut as a thespian was upon me. Arriving on time and confident in my preparation, I was unnerved to find that Dr. Johnson was out, and Dr. Utley was in.

Yes, that Dr. Utley

"Moseley, do you really want me to hear your case?" said my suspicious foreign relations prof. As wanly as I could muster, I said, *"yes, sir."*

Thank God I'd prepared. Utley wrote down every detail of my chronology. For some reason, he didn't cross-exam me on my attendance to his class and how that jibbed with my phony timeline, because that might have blown my entire subterfuge.

When I was done, my dubious professor slid a notepad in front of me. All my lies were written down for my review. *"Sign here at the bottom if all these facts are true..."*

"Fuck it," I said to myself as I feebly signed the damning document.

"Come with me," Dr. Utley now commanded, as we exited the cubby-hole where he'd interviewed me, and went out to the lobby. Feigning a semi-gamey limp (an impromptu addition to my characterization I threw in that had nothing to do with oral surgery) I followed him.

"Oh, Jesus, I thought *I'm done for. Dad will kill me. I'll be expelled. God, help me!*

Utley knew exactly what I was up to, or so I thought, but I think he admired my inventiveness and attention to detail. Opening the top drawer of the reception desk, he pulled out a late-drop form and said, *"what is your social security number?"*

In my only slip up, I robustly blurted out *"412-49-4267."*

"Here," he said, handing me the form after taking an eternity to fill it out. *"Take this to the computer center across campus and they'll drop the course for you."*

Convinced that Utley was following me to see if I was faking, I almost shuffled across campus till I got my drop. Even though it was unforgivable to relocate grandaddy for my nefarious purposes, I'm sure he would have got a kick out of my well staged obfuscation.

In the immediate aftermath of this episode, I felt great about getting over on the system. Soon enough, however, I would learn my real problem was how I was getting over on myself.

Riffraff

Although I didn't associate getting over on myself with being bought off my dad, I discovered this was true shortly after my late-drop. I was home on a break from school when I got into a stand-off with him in defense of Diane.

My sister's Junior prom was coming up and she wanted to stay out past the traditional midnight curfew dad had established for all his children over the years. Apparently, he thought she would turn into a pumpkin if she stayed up past the stroke of twelve. Diane was appealing for an extension to one am, but dad was having none of it.

"Only Riffraff stays out all night, my father pontificated. Unhappy with dad's decree, sis went off somewhere to ponder her next move, so I waited till she left. Then I said, *"That's bullshit, dad, I've been out all night and I'm not Riffraff."*

Dad fixed my gaze with silent thunder. In my imagination he said, *"I own you, boy. You've been bought and paid for. Go against me now and I'll cut you off, you spineless bitch!"*

This was true, at least from my father's viewpoint.

For years I had followed dad's wishes because I wanted his love, but that love came in the form of his money, so I accepted it as such. The consequences of my sellout now rubbed my face in my own weakness via the combination of betrayal and contempt I saw in his face.

Cut to the quick by my father's stare, I wanted to rip his throat out for confronting me with my spineless conformity. My shame and rage threw me into a fight or flight mode. I bolted from the kitchen where our confrontation took place, and literally ran upstairs and into my bedroom closet.

Mother, knowing some pain deep in my soul had been ripped open, and perhaps sensing the pain of her own complicity in abandoning herself and her children to get along with dad, ran after me as I tried to escape the reckoning that was upon me.

She did her best to comfort me as I started laughing and crying at the same time. I was just completely undone. I wish I could say this event prompted me to change my ways, but it didn't. For years, I'd abandoned myself, my gut, my viewpoint, and my very sense of self, just to get along with my insecure, controlling, and tyrannical father. Self-betrayal had become my way of life. The cost of cloning my father to survive him had absented me from my own life.

Sadly, it would take several more years for me to truly face all this and do something about it.

Losing Grandaddy Hawk

Back in 1949, the year my brother Stephen was born, grandaddy Hawk was working late one night shaping the molding he was using in the living room of the retirement home he was building on Solway Road. Working on an electric molding machine, his hand slipped, and he pushed his thumb straight into the device's three-blade lathe. He was cut pretty badly and a piece of the cutting blade broke-off, imbedding in the boney joint of his right thumb. Dick had the thumb sown up but did nothing to remove the metal in his hand.

One afternoon, now twenty-five years later in the spring of 1974, his son, my Uncle Dick, dropped by his parent's Solway place to say hello. When his namesake told him he'd been having on again, off again trouble with the same thumb, my uncle took grandad straight to the doctor. Tests were done, and grandaddy was told he had cancer and that his thumb would have to be removed.

Six-months later, my grandad was lying in UT hospital. I didn't know his condition was terminal, just that he was ill, and tonight it was my turn to watch over him. I'd never developed the close relationship with my grandfather that my brother's had because I was a toddler when we moved to Chattanooga. But the man who sat me on his knee when I was a chubby little kid and made me belly laugh with his stories was as special to me as anyone I've ever known.

As the afternoon of January 22, 1975, moved into the night, grandad's lungs filled with fluid, and he became delusional. He would come in and out of consciousness, drifting periodically into conversations with random phantoms in interactions that took place years before and that spanned decades. He was trying to resolve old issues and relationships, but I had no idea who he was talking to or where he was going in his mind. I felt helpless and powerless to comfort him and this freaked me out.

It was late night now, and grandad needed help getting to the bathroom. I was nodding off and there were a few times we didn't make it to the toilet. Suddenly I had an overwhelming and irrepressible impulse to laugh. I immediately recognized this as hysteria and did my best to stifle it, but I couldn't. I prayed that grandaddy wouldn't hear me or feel shamed by my reaction to his ramblings. Somehow, we made it through to the morning and I left the hospital exhausted and numb.

Richard Frank Hawk died later that afternoon.

I went back to the Chi Phi house where I was living at the time but was out when word came from the hospital. Joe Fannon, my fraternity brother, got the call and when he told me that grandad had passed, I couldn't believe it.

I still don't.

In a sense, my grandad hadn't gone and never will be. There are certain people who have been so vivid and present in my life that, dead or alive, I always feel they're with me. Call me delusional but that's how I'll always feel about grandaddy Hawk.

I never missed him. Not once. I know he's with me, just as he was the day I was born, and he always will be.

A Glimpse of the Future

Having the space at school to be frivolous, and to both succeed and fail, was very valuable to me. I had come to UT from a family where I felt I had to be perfect; a culture that demanded I conform to its rigid rules and regulations.

I'd rebelled against dad's way of being in my passive aggressive way, but I still knew no other way of being.

One of the good things that came from making up and then playing the role I invented in my late drop episode is that I became genuinely interested in acting for the first time, so I took a Drama in Literature course.

Later was better than never, and now I was beginning to explore alternatives to defying or complying with my father's point of view.

My teaching assistant in this course was Leanne Kressin. She recognized my deep need for expression and encouraged me to open up. Leanne had me read a poem by John Dunne, and although I don't remember its title now, this was a pivotal moment for me.

Something about using drama as a vehicle for self-expression connected me to the next part of my journey.

I remember Leanne had wonderfully mobile features which she used years later with great success doing commercials in New York City. Here and now, however, she served as a mirror, a messenger, and a guide. Her support and encouragement and her way of being made it safe for me to open up and risk myself in ways I didn't know I could.

What my future sister-in-law Brenda had sparked in Dr. Van de Vate, Ms. Kressin now evoked in me; *"But for you,* I might well have said to Leanne, *I would sleep tonight."*

Not long after my drama in literature class was done, we had a party at the Chi Phi house and I did a whole spate of impressions of all my fraternity brothers and of the chapter's little sisters, too. I captured everyone's idiosyncrasies and then reduced them to a few telling looks or gestures.

It was all great fun.

I got to express myself by imitating them yet was able to maintain my privacy as I took on their characteristics. I didn't know it at the time, but this started the next phase of my spiritual awakening. Still the prospect of becoming a professional actor, or even the thought of it, petrified me.

Graduation to a Future Uncertain

Although I graduated from UT with a B.A. in History on December 12, 1975, it was not a cause for celebration. I didn't know who I was, what I felt, or what I wanted to become.

I told myself that I wanted to be a lawyer but that was just something I said. The truth is I was a cipher, so obsessed with survival I'd subsumed whoever I really was by copycatting my father or doing whatever my brothers did because I had no idea how to be my own person. I was scared to death to step out into life on my own.

I moved back home and began to agonize about what I would do with my life and who I would become.

For some years, I'd periodically worked for my father as he prepared his cases for trial. There would be a car wreck or a plane crash and when he was hired, usually to defend a manufacturer, I'd track down witnesses and take their statements.

More often than not, this was a stopgap strategy of dad's to protect his client. I got good at getting people to say things that did just that. If during trial, a witness changed their story in a way that hurt whoever dad was representing, he could take out the statement they made to me and if necessary, discredit them with the jury.

I tried to make this a full-time job, but it wasn't. In the meantime, I did some work for Vandsco Advertising, an outdoor billboard ad company, that was a client of my father's law firm. I don't remember what I did there, but their young president liked it and he offered me a job which I accepted as his administrative assistant.

Using this new job to save money, I began acting in local theater productions and planning to move to New York to study and pursue acting professionally.

Other Worlds, Other Possibilities: My Acting Days and the Women in my Life

Just as going off to college opened a whole new world, now that I had my degree in History, another universe emerged. I'd experienced movies and theater as a spectator but never as a creator. In short order, I became interested in and then pursued acting as a profession. In a way this world of story-telling was an extension of my joyful days of play, but it was also an intriguing and exotic new territory to experience and explore.

In many ways, I'd never been anything but an actor, assuming the role I felt was safest and most pleasing in my family. But now I would learn there was more to acting than getting over on others to survive them. At its core, acting was about emotional and spiritual truth. Like many, I'd grown up hearing my friends say, "I'm a great actor; I can lie about anything." As these next stories reveal, great acting involved creating a persona to survive the world, something we all do, but it also went much deeper; it illuminated the reality beneath the masks we wear.

Just as acting would add a completely new dimension to my life, so too would my experience of women. As I moved into adulthood, the wounds of my youth would color the choices I made and determine the kinds of women I was drawn to. It may be cliché to say that I was attracted to women who reflected my mother's character, but as I examined my relationships, my mother's fear of intimacy often showed up in my own behavior or in the conduct of the women in my life.

You Want to Be What? My Introduction to Acting

Noel Coward introduced me to the theater, but it took me eight months to accept his invitation. I agonized all that time before doing my first audition. *"Does wanting to be an actor mean I'm gay,"* I thought. I was astounded at this concern and by other conflicts that were coming up for me as I took my first baby steps as a thespian.

The cipher in me was looking for another role to play, any role to avoid being the person I actually was. My inner dialogue was *"I don't know who I am, so let me find someone else to be."* And, of course, surprise, surprise, when I finally got to an audition, I was cast by a gay director who wanted to get into my pants.

He wasn't successful but just as I anticipated the director requested a private session with me not long after we began rehearsals. He said he wanted to show me how to walk on stage, *but I would have to be nude to do the exercise.* "EXERCISE, MY ASS," I thought. Nevertheless, I bucked up in our private session just to stir him up. I wanted to torture him because he was crossing the line.

My theatrical debut was as an Italian water-skiing gigolo in <u>Come into the Garden Maude</u>, a witty but vapid piece of fluff written by Coward in his final years. As the lights came up on my first-ever scene, I felt a giant hand reach into my chest and squeeze the hell out of my heart. My over-stressed organ bulged at its top and bottom ends as if it were about to explode.

It was at this time that I first heard the term, *"work on yourself."* Gradually, over the next year or so, I lived with my parents, worked my Man-Friday job at Vandsco, and did theater at night. After *Maude* closed, I went on to play roles in <u>Oliver</u> then in <u>The Lion in Winter</u> and after that in a stage adaptation of Faulkner's "As I Lay Dying" entitled *Journey to Jefferson*.

In the meantime, I started working out, running, doing vocal exercises and everything else I could think of to *"work on myself."*

In this day and age, *working on yourself* is a concept that gets lots of play. What it means to me is becoming more open, self-aware, and intentional in ways that liberate success producing action. In the context of performing, this is done in a variety of ways, from working through emotional blocks, to challenging yourself in a wide variety of roles that test and expand your acting chops.

As was my habit with whatever interested me, I went about reading everything I could about acting, too, trying to cram a PHD level education into a part-time pursuit, while I made time to work 9 to 5 and then rehearse and perform whenever I got the opportunity. My intention was to save as much money as possible and move to New York City where I could get the professional training I needed to become a working actor.

As the time came closer to my planned departure, I had to prepare audition material for the acting schools I was interested in attending. Jim Spence was an assistant Professor in the Theater Department at UTC, the Chattanooga branch of our state university system, and he encouraged me to work up a piece from Georg Buchner's Woyzec.

Essentially, this was the story of an insane character, Woyzec, who fell in love with a prostitute, murdered her in a paranoid, jealous rage, and then drowned himself.

When I first read the piece it seemed strange to me, but I took it on faith that Jim knew what he was doing so I prepared to perform it as best I could.

Robert Moseley

Ignorance is bliss. Although it can set you up for a fall, being unaware can also make you available for things an experienced actor would know to avoid. Only someone who had no idea what he was doing would have attempted the piece I did from <u>Woyzec</u>, and that's exactly why it worked.

CHAPTER V:
Life and Love in The Big Apple

Circle in the Square

It was now July 1977. I'd come to New York City and was on time for my audition but late in the game. As usual, I'd dragged my feet, not by minutes but by months, and there were few remaining places in the Professional Workshop at Circle in the Square. Circle had started as a small theater in Greenwich Village in the late 50's and was now a full-fledged Broadway house, with a full-time training program for actors based on a university M.F.A. model.

Johnnie Klontz was an assistant to Mary Kearny Levinstein, the Managing Director of the program at that time, and he auditioned me for one of three remaining spots.

The school asked me to present two pieces.

I began by rushing onstage being chased by an imaginary mob, then embraced my invisible dead lover, who laid before me on the shoreline of a lake, stabbed and strangled by my hand, cooed and scolded her imaginary carcass, at which point I heard an angry mob closing in on me, then dropped her body to search for and find the knife I'd killed her with, then threw it out into the lake, but fearful now it would be found, waded out and somehow found it and chucked even further out, and topped all this off by drowning myself on the bare rehearsal room floor.

As I bowed my head to indicate my first piece was complete, the look on Johnnie's was priceless. *"OK,"* he said, doing his best to hide what he thought of my mad display.

"Do you have something else for me?" he half-whispered.

Merely attempting the *Woyzec* piece I'd just done was impossible, not to mentioned ill-advised, but since I was blissfully ignorant of this, I somehow pulled it off.

Now I played Andrei from Chekov's *Three Sisters*. It was a blissfully short and straightforward bit, where my character told his sisters he was perfectly alright with their father, and absolutely wasn't, but although I identified more with this second piece, it was *Woyzeck* that got me accepted at Circle.

I only attempted the *Woyzec* once more at Stella Adler's summer school. By now, nearly a year later, I knew it was a performance piece, and not audition material. Auditions were about sketching with craft and talent, not eating the theater whole. The little knowledge I'd acquired by now had become dangerous to my presentation. This time, I crashed and burned, as I should have at Circle.

My inner voice told me as much before I did this audition, but I hadn't yet learned to ***listen*** to it.

Once our first-year class assembled, I realized that all of us were very different types. This made sense. The wider variety of actors, the more chance we had to succeed, and this would up the Professional Workshops reputation which at that time was only a couple of years old.

What didn't make sense to me was where I fit in.

This was an amazing new world for me. I was walking on frightening, exciting and untrod new ground. No one in my family, nor anyone I'd ever known, had attempted to become an actor. All I had going for me was a year of performing in my hometown. I'd never taken a class in acting, nor had any formal training. Up till now, I'd simply learned as much as I could by reading, watching and from my limited experience performing.

The upshot of all this is that by the time Christmas break came, I was so desperate to get the acting thing down that I'd lost my sense of humor.

Adding to the pressure I felt was the fact that most of my peers had degrees in theater, which didn't mean a damn thing, but I didn't know that. What is more, I was the only southerner in my class and therefore the only student who spoke with an accent.

On that score, I learned that as a Tennessean, I turned vowels into diphthongs (two vowel sounds uttered as one) and vice versa. This gave my speech a combination of drawl and twang that made me the object of fun or derision, depending on how insecure my critics were.

For my part, I developed a chip on my shoulder about my speech and erased my *"regionalism,"* and with it something of my essential self, by the end of my first year at Circle.

The foremost enemy of fine acting is being uptight. It's OK to be terrified as long as you're open and relax into it. The key is to be present; to just be wherever you are without imposing anything on your state of being. Some say tension is talent but until you let yourself be, including everything you dislike feeling or being as a person, you can't really let go, and letting go is a major step to becoming a fine actor.

This is especially true of any kind of tension. You gotta go through it to get past it.

Often, the first thing that happens when an actor becomes truly expressive is that they offload a ton of rage. Once that surface level of pain releases, you've popped the cork on your talent and the real work of building your game and your *"instrument"* can begin.

Your instrument is simply your voice, which involves speech, diction, and the quality and range of your speaking, your body, and how facile you are expressing yourself, your sensory awareness and suggestibility, and your overall sensitivity and expressiveness.

Developing all this takes the time it takes, and everyone has their own pace and rhythm, so it's best not to rush this process, which of course, is what all inexperienced actors do.

I was well-stocked in the rage department, with twenty plus years of suppressed shame and pain, not to mention my karmic *mishigas,* and I was ready to BLOW. The vehicle for releasing what my teachers dubbed my *energies* was Scene Study. We had a variety of supporting classes in movement, voice and diction, stage combat, and sensory techniques, all of which contributed to our overall ability to play any part, but the rubber met the road when we applied everything we were learning to characters in scenes.

I was trained to put myself in the position of the role I played; to use my actual emotions as they occurred in the given circumstances of the character, the scene, and the play, and then to maintain a disciplined spontaneity and openness within the confines of the actor's craft.

Opening myself up, becoming spontaneous, then enduring and harnessing the clash of my conflicting emotions and contradictory inner impulses made my evolving work compelling. Or so I was told. I learned that acting was not about being a good liar, though sometimes that could be useful, but rather involved surrendering my heart, body, and soul to the character I was playing.

I was the character. I stood as a proxy to the given circumstances of whatever role I played in the larger context of the playwright's intentions and/or the director's aims.

Effective acting required me to be emotionally reactive and subjective while at the same time I became emotionally objective and selective as an artist. First, I had to unlock my passion and then harness and apply it with the precision of a surgeon.

As I began to build up my acting chops, I developed a great love of the craft. It appealed to my need for deep self-knowledge and self-mastery. It fed and extended my self-involvement and challenged me at every level of my being, good and bad. I got off attempting to master the illusive and elegant balance between having full access to my inner ferocity and maintaining the relaxation, self-possession and selectivity great acting demanded.

My new world was also composed of a colorful cast of characters.

Nikolas Konstantin Athanasios Psacharoupoulos VII, or Nikos for short, was the founder and Artistic Director of the Williamstown Theater Festival. He was celebrated for directing large plays on a grand, operatic scale. Nikos was hip, tough, irascible, and he'd stop a scene in a heartbeat if we were faking or disconnected. Being disconnected meant being out of touch with our feelings or out of sync with our actions.

Conversely, being in touch with our emotions energized us and made us believable, but this was basic and fundamental. There was much more to acting than knowing how you felt and being true to the moment. He taught us that emotion was rocket fuel, but you didn't let your feelings drive your rocket. You had to master your feelings and then be selective in what you expressed and how you expressed it. *"Passion without technique is embarrassing,* he said, *and technique without passion is boring."*

Nikos was the Big Kahuna at Circle and if you did well, you'd be invited to apprentice at Williamstown over the summer. Students lived in fear of his wrath but for some reason he left me alone. I sometimes wondered at this for very few of us we spared his ire. Looking back, I think he saw I was fragile, yet strong and volatile, too. His instinct was to go easier on me because he knew I was hard on myself, and he also knew I respected and would meet his standards.

I had a real appetite for the work that took me past my old withholding behavior. I always worked hard and usually with positive effect, so he let me find my own way.

From the Mad Greek of Williamstown, I also learned that making good theater wasn't about *being nice.* It involved tapping into, containing, and mastering my primordial inner savage: just my cup of tea. Nikos was not an openly sentimental man and in many ways he was a tough son-of-a-bitch, but writing about him now all these years later, I miss him. In a world of illusion, duplicity, and bullshit, he was authentically theatrical. He was the real deal and say what you will of his methods, he toughened us up for the gauntlet of life in the professional theater.

Theresa Hayden taught us technique. A native of Nashville, she'd lived most of her sixty odd years in the Big Apple. She was distant, sharp-eyed, and mostly impenetrable. At once unbearably sensitive and unreachably remote, she was rumored to be a lesbian. Her sexual orientation meant nothing to me, but I noticed she had a palpable gift for pissing off the women in my class.

Terry immediately recognized my hunger for expression and my appetite for the work. From her I learned to create sensory realities that would occupy, concentrate, and relax me. This work was done separately from but in partnership with my character work. It gave me a compelling life independent of the words I spoke, and it helped me create real behavior that complemented my work on say a limp or a lisp, thereby rounding out my characterizations.

Michael Kahn, like Nikos, was a successful working director. He was also a fine teacher and excelled at conveying the fundamentals of acting. Kahn had great, grounding clarity about how to build a performance and he gave us solid steppingstones to accomplish exactly that. Working with Michael we learned Stanislavski's famous language of acting; intentions, actions, objectives and the beats or transitions within scenes.

In their role as teachers, Nikos was more instinctive and a "fixer" of scenes. His gut feeling for authentic human behavior and his commitment to keep the work real, even when we worked on non-realistic material, was unparalleled. Combined with Michael's Design Engineer approach, emphasizing the essential building blocks of craft, their different talents made them a terrific teaching tandem.

Larry Moss, who would later teach Oscar winners Helen Hunt and Hillary Swank, applied psychotherapeutic insights to stagecraft. He was clear that we couldn't play something if we couldn't personally "live it;" that our range as performers was circumscribed by our limitations as people, and that to fulfill our potential we had to liberate ourselves from our personal hangups.

Larry had a wonderful, infectious enthusiasm that brought people out. He came to Circle my second year there and taught a musical theater class. Singing was of less than zero interest to me, but it was exactly what I needed to flesh out my game as a performer and as a person. The openness singing required absolutely terrified me. I could deal with pain and angst all day, but the openness, freedom, and vulnerability, not to mention the joy of singing, froze and freaked me out.

Sadly, I never did well singing because the joy of it conflicted fundamentally with my fear of being open and alive in that way.

Marge Phillips and Yasmine, her Scottish terrier, were two low-key but fabulous characters at the professional workshop. Marge taught speech and diction and was of the old English school. She had great stories and an impish, dry wit that reminded me of grandaddy Hawk. She was a radiant beauty now in her sixties and positively glowed with an inner intensity. The giveaway to her passionate nature was her amazing, blazing eyes. It was her style and poise that inspired me to get my speech to a place where I could play Shakespeare and play it well.

I never got to know Marge as well as I would have liked, and I'm sure I was the lesser for it.

Wila Kahn and Nora Peterson-Kasarda were our movement instructors. Wila taught traditional and stylized movement to be used in period dramas and Nora taught us jazz dance. B.H. Barry rounded out our faculty and was our stage fight master.

The only thing missing from Circle's approach at that time was some instruction in how to unify all the different elements we were being taught into a cohesive whole. What I didn't fully realize at the time is that as an artist I had to sort out for myself my own best way of working, so putting it all together was really on me.

What sticks with me after all these years is that the basis of our training was this: what makes a play, film or musical work is the committed partnership of talented colleagues who are creative and courageous. That *collaboration* inevitably works best when players channel their sensitivities, be they demonic or divine, into working as a team in service of the playwright or director's vision.

Invariably, the best work in any medium comes from talent, trust, commitment, and creative cooperation. Likewise, when a project goes south, it almost always reflects the presence of an everyman for him or herself attitude.

Breakthrough on My Birthday

The afternoon of Tuesday, December 13, 1977, the day after my 25th birthday, it all came to a head for me. Desperate to be successful as a craftsman, if not as a professional actor, (a reality it would take me more than a dozen more years to admit), I was in the exquisite and unenviable place of being primed to either rocket up into the firmament with a liberated self-expression or implode on the launch pad of my self-sabotaged creativity.

Push had come to shove. I was at the make-or-break point. Either my defenses and denials would dominate me, or I would crack open my soul, and make use of all that shit and all the rest of me, utilizing my whole humanity in my performing.

The trigger point of this heavyweight fight between my denial and my expression was sensory work.

Today, six of us were doing an exercise in the basement of the old Martinique Hotel. All of us were sitting in metal folding chairs when Terry Hayden instructed us to "work for a place." Our task was to focus

100% of our attention on creating and maintaining the sensory elements of a physical location of our choice.

After the exercise was over, I learned that everyone who worked before me created a beach setting. That seemed like a pretty good idea because the Apple had just been hit by a blizzard and there was a foot of snow outside. For some reason, however, I worked for taking a shower in the bathroom of my ratty old apartment at the time.

Breaking through to real expression requires deep relaxation. More importantly, you must get so involved in the present moment that your deepest defenses ease up and stand down.

I was the last to work. As the five people before me went in turn, every one of them had emotional breakthroughs. Time and again, I came out of my shower, intrigued by the frenzied feelings erupting in the room. Time and again, by force of will and discipline, I got back in my shower and refocused on my place. Out, then back in, out, then back in, with each repetition I went deeper and deeper into the sights, smells, sounds, and sensations of my slightly moldy bathtub and the shower I was taking in my mind.

Finally, it was my turn.

I was so relaxed, so in the moment, I couldn't anticipate anything. I couldn't distract myself with comparisons or expectations or any other damn thing. I was open. I was defenseless. Then Terry Hayden said, *"begin the words of a monologue."*

I did the Chekov piece from *Three Sisters* I'd auditioned with to get into Circle.

BOOM! A white thunderbolt literally exploded from the center of my forehead like a rifle-shot. Instantly I was in a raging, roaring typhoon. My creative expression irrupted in a wailing cyclone of pain and grief as Terry, shouting through the wind, rain, and waves of emotion that were overwhelming me, ordered me to connect this mass of emotion to the vowels and consonants of the words of my monologue.

"Connect your feelings to the words! Connect your feelings to the words! Connect your feelings to the words!" She repeated again and again. *"Stretch the words out, extend the vowels and consonants! Play with the sound! Extend it! Pitch it up! Pitch it down! Play with the sound!"*

I was discovering enormous emotion exists in vowels and consonants and as each new wave of emotion hit me like a body-slam, I stretched out each word as fully as I could, connecting my primordial feelings to my speech; to the language of the piece.

Laughing and crying at the same time, by the time the multiple tidal waves in me passed, I almost laid on my metal chair, completely spent. To this day, it was the most cathartic moment I ever experienced. As a couple of my classmates embraced me, making sure I was OK, Terry said, *"You just did fifteen years of work."*

I'm not sure what she meant but I think she was telling me that this is how I must work as an actor. That my task was to connect with my inner being and unify that experience with the language of whatever role I played. All this, and that her *fifteen years* comment suggested I'd made a major leap in unleashing and applying my talent.

God, what an experience. Jeez, what a lesson.

The Pigeon and the Nazi

Somewhere around the time I erupted in Terry's technique class, I had a powerful but disturbing realization. I was walking on 9th Avenue, which in those days was nearly as far west as you could get in Manhattan. It was around eight or nine at night, and I got the feeling I might get mugged, as no one seemed to be around.

Where I was going and why, I've long since forgotten.

As I stepped off a curb, I came upon a wounded pidgeon. He was lying there with a broken shoulder.

What to do?

I felt powerless to help this poor creature and there was no where I could take it for treatment. I hadn't a clue if there was a vet nearby, and even if there was, no vet would be open now. I didn't feel right just passing him by to suffer for God knows how long before he died in agony, so reluctantly, I decided the best thing to do would be to put him out of his misery.

Nearby, were a number of empty crates. I picked one up and smashed the poor pidgeon repeatedly to kill it.

Intending to get this over with as soon as possible, I smashed down with murderous force. Shockingly, I enjoyed it. Something that felt like pure evil came over and out of me. I was like a sadistic nazi taking pleasure in inflicting pain. Normally, I loved making new and unexpected discoveries about realities that lived inside me, but not this time.

I was horrified this monster lurked inside me.

This realization left me more resolved than ever to learn how to use my shadow-self in service of the art form I was learning, lest it come out in real life in some catastrophic way.

COMING OUT OF MY BODY

It was now well into spring of 1979, and I was deep into my last year of training at Circle. I'd just completed a fourteen-mile run, followed by an hour and a half of yoga. In the best shape of my life, at the moment I was lying on the floor of my apartment, resting.

Suddenly, my back arched, AND I CAME OUT OF MY BODY!

My entire consciousness, every bit of awareness I could identify as *"me"* was now floating just above my prone, inert carcass. *"Whoa, I'm out of my body,"* I thought, astonished.

I felt incredibly free; completely liberated of the pull of gravity.

My first instinct was to explore this amazing, unexpected event.

Hovering in mid-air, I rotated my head left and right to identify the furniture in my room. Everything was grounded and in place but me. Then I thought, *"man, you better get back in your body or you won't want to."*

BANG! Instantly, I returned to normal.

Although I never explored or sought out this experience again, this single event, an unanticipated episode that took mere seconds, changed my entire conception of existence. After this, the thought of dying, at least as I now perceive it, became nothing more than moving from one breath to another. From this time forward, I identified myself as a conscious awareness that transcends my physical form. Likewise, from here on, I saw my body as a vehicle of experience and expression, but nothing more.

When my time comes to travel from this life to whatever's next, I'm not saying I won't be reluctant or afraid, but despite my final reservations, I know the universality of the cycles of life and death will sustain me. I don't require faith to live now; I have direct experience that I exist as pure spirit.

Living the Actor's Life: Embracing Temporary Insanity

The depth of my breakthroughs was thrilling but also scared the hell out of me. I wish I'd let my fear prompt me to go deeper but I didn't. I especially wish I'd done more sensory work. I didn't do that either. Pursuing both these pathways would probably have taken me to richer ground as a person and as an artist, but the price of admission was letting go in a way I didn't feel was safe.

One of the many things I learned about the emotional side of acting is that breakthroughs are always followed by contractions. I loved opening up and it was great to live larger than I'd ever lived before, but part of me looked at this and said, *"Hold on, what am I doing OUT HERE."*

I learned that the only antidote for a knee-jerk contraction is to anticipate it, feel it, express it, and then remind myself that growing in depth and dimension was worth all the effort I was making.

On the downside, by the time I was done with my first year of drama school, I was trying to catch up with all the preening, pretending, and bad habits most inexperienced, self-doubting young actors fall into.

In trying to erase any trace of regionalism in my speech, and along with it a whole chunk of what made me *me*, every time I spoke, I was dotting every **"i"** and crossing every **"t."** Maybe this was a necessary step, but I was turning into an insufferable, pompous and posturing asshole.

I went through a Grace Kelly phase where, like much of her film acting in the 1950's, I was over-enunciating my speech and my life. Workwise, I wanted to be the best actor I could possibly be but overemphasizing anything personal calls attention to yourself not to the character, and I hated that.

There was also a broader context to the struggles I was having as I learned my craft; the contrast between fantasy and reality.

This is the irony of the actor's life.

You work your ass off to become expressive, to get connected to something authentic and real; to exude a humanity through your work that's rooted in your soul, and then either through some combination of unresolved personal defenses, the pressure to succeed, the fear of exposure, the desire to be pampered, and/or the public treating you like a cross between Prince Charming, the Devil or a house pet, you wind up cloaking yourself in artifice except when you're playing a role.

In other words, once you get connected and real; once your groundedness centers and establishes you within your own being and in the so-called real world, that's the very thing you lose as you interact with regular folks, along with the catastrophic loss of your privacy.

Your work as a performer becomes your saving grace. If you work well; rooting your performance in your genuine humanity, it sustains you. But learning to navigate the world from the false and distorting vantage point of celebrity, at least in my day, was something no acting school in the world trained you to do.

The acting profession will challenge your sanity somewhere along the line. If you're not loco when you start, you're going to go nuts at some point. If you survive that ordeal, then you will probably have a useful perspective to bring to your work.

I was never successful in the commercial sense of having a career, fame, and fortune, but I had several encounters with renowned performers along the way that persuaded me being rich, admired, and envied was the last thing I wanted.

The truth is that I became an actor to become a human being; to excavate my buried humanity, and if I was lost when I started acting, by the time I quit I was very much on the way to being found. Instinctively, I always knew that giving myself fully to the process of becoming a fine thespian would liberate me and it did.

My most chilling experience of fame involved Eartha Kitt. Sometime in the mid-eighties, I was between acting gigs and working for money as a doorman at *Regine's*, a well-known Manhattan nightclub of the day named for its owner.

Today was Regine's birthday and loads of glitterati were there to be seen as Ms. Kitt, *Catwoman* before Michelle Phiffer and Halle Barry took the role, showed up in a limo and on her own. When she stepped out of her ride, Eartha looked terrified. I knew her manager, a twisted, charismatic, and Machiavellian character named Cecil. I dropped his name so she'd know I was for real, then asked her if I could help.

The moment she realized I had a connection to her inner circle, Catwoman clawed my arm and said, *"If you leave me, I'll kill you."*

My job was to guard the door, not watch over her, but the party was well under way so I figured it would be ok to take her to the main room. I gestured for her to lead the way, following her up the stairway to the club.

As she came to the top of the stairs, the paparazzi spotted her. Suddenly, a wall of flashbulbs exploded as Kitt went into a *Sunset Boulevard*, Norma Desmond-like pose as Catwoman. It made my blood run cold to see her body silhouetted by the flashing light. I was horrified by the contrast between the cold adoration of the press, her seeming confident pose, and her actual terror and vulnerability.

Just as the flashbulbs faded, she dug her nails back into my arm; *"If you leave me, I'll kill you."*

Ms. Kitty now dragged me into the party as the club manager's eyes caught mine with a, *What the hell are you doing up here*, look.

Spotting a photo-op, Regine herself came up for the obligatory peck-peck, cheek to cheek greeting. The moment they parted it was clear these women had zero connection.

Once more she sunk her claws into me.

Now, in the middle of the ongoing party, in deep shit with my boss, lamenting my good deed, and wondering how to extricate myself from Catwoman's death grip, salvation came in the form of Ebony Magazine.

"Oh, Eartha, said their reporter who rushed up her, *we've all loved you ever since you shat on the Johnson White House over Vietnam."* Seduced by more agenda driven adulation coming her way, Eartha released me. I flew back downstairs to the relative serenity of being

unknown, unsought, and uncelebrated and thanked my lucky stars I wasn't famous.

Of course, I took the seedy side of Show Business way too seriously. The other thing successful actors handle is all the bullshit and hoopla attendant to fame. At the end of the day, I was lucky as a performer to get reconnected to my core and to my natural self-expression.

For me, this was what I wanted from acting and it was more than enough.

Acting with a Board Up My Ass

Quasimodo was suddenly my roommate. That alone, should have given me pause. His real name was Derek Conte, and he was a mad, loveable, and dedicated disciple of the actor's craft. He also had a positive gift for judging, provoking, and pissing people off. We met at an audition for a tour of <u>The Hunchback of Notre Dame,</u> both of us got cast, we liked each other from the start, and decided to be roommates for the ten-week run of the show.

<u>Project: Educational Theater,</u> the producer of our show, was based just outside New Orleans and catered to middle and high school audiences in Louisiana and Georgia. Bill Crumb, PET's owner, employed writers to knock off adaptations of classic stories, then sent out bus and truck tours to community centers, auditoriums, and schools to perform them as plays.

Along with Derek as Quasi, I was cast as Phoebus, captain of the palace guard and a rake extraordinaire. The play was your classic beauty and the beast tale. Our young audiences adored Derek's character, loved our ingénue Esmerelda, and hated me. Esmerelda was in love with Phoebus, who's dark side she was blind to, and my character was so in love with himself that he had no room for anyone else. All Phoebus wanted from the Parisian urchin was to notch another conquest.

My physical appearance, the expectations it engendered, and my actual inhibitions collided in this role. I looked like the attractive, rakish, and arrogant captain, but I was too shy to strut my stuff. This reality, combined with the fact that my character was unsympathetic, made this a tough but valuable learning experience.

Derek suggested I play Phoebus as Ronald Coleman, a renowned actor of yesteryear, complete with that actor's nasal speech inflections, but I balked at reducing my role to imitating another performer. Quasi also suggested I tie a board to my ass than ran up the length of my back, to get a feel for my character's physical bearing and pomposity. After rehearsal one day, I tried the board bit at a party we had in our motel room, and it helped me get in touch with Phoebus' vanity and prissiness.

As we got into the run of the play, I struggled with being hated by our audience. We would usually perform at the end of the school day or during the first half of extended lunch breaks. Derek would hold court with the kids while our company ate together at lunchtime. Conte considered this part of his job, and he was great with the kids. Of course, the fact that they loved him/his character made this extra effort fun. Not one child, however, ever wanted to sit with me. I knew this was because I was one of the bad guys in the play, but it still hurt to be rejected.

Thinking back on it now, this was another instance of the split I felt between fantasy and reality. All performers must come to terms with this split, especially when you're playing the heavy.

What depressed me was fighting the feeling of being rejected. Worse still, the better I got at playing Phoebus, the more I was reviled. Whenever I could take a personal moment, I let myself storm and rail at being hated, and these "poor me" mini-breaks made things ease up. I learned not to identify too much with whatever character I played. I also learned that having my feelings in the moment kept me connected and present. Sometimes I even let myself enjoy being hated.

There were many more lessons I learned on the road.

Playing different houses day to day called for constant adaptations. When we played in huge civic auditoriums, the whole cast had to take giant strides to accommodate the size of the stage and to keep the timing of the show intact. In these big house settings, we would think in opera terms. Everything became grander and adopting this stylistic approach kept the timing of the show on track.

Conversely, when we played tiny houses, we had to play more intimately and slowly. There wasn't as much physical ground to cover so we had to stretch out the show a bit. The trick here was to go at a more relaxed pace but still keep our energy up so we wouldn't lose our audience.

One day, the lethal combination of a massive auditorium, a late start, and an ill-timed bell ruined the show. There were 1900 children in the audience, and the show was going well, but when a bell rang two-thirds of the kids rose as one to board their buses for home.

Everyone in the cast felt the air was sucked out of our lungs.

Bells had proved to be a problem throughout our run. Most of our actors pushed through when a bell rang, ignoring it, but I saw this didn't work. I decided to hold if a bell rang in the middle of a scene I was playing.

One Friday, we were performing on a small stage in a school cafeteria. There was so little room in the wings you could break your nose making an exit. We'd come to the love scene in the play where Esmerelda confessed her love to Phoebus in the moonlight to the tunes of a mandolin;

Esmerelda: *Oh, Phoebus, Phoebus I adore you so! Do you love me too?*

Phoebus: *What a question?*

Esmerelda: *Oh, tell me...tell me you do...*

Phoebus: *I have never loved anyone...*

(School bell goes off. I hold, anticipating a three count before I resume, but the ring continues for 4, 5, 6, 7, 8, 9, 10 counts, then FINALLY stops...)

...as I love you.

The time gap from the start to the finish of my line perfectly illustrated Phoebus' insincerity and the audience and actors exploded in laughter as Esmerelda stood onstage with proverbial egg on her face. It was an incident that upset the scene to a degree, yet perfectly illustrated Phoebus' insincerity, and it was also great fun!

Potter's Field and learning to play Shakespeare

I met actor Michael Moriarty in the spring of 1980, not long after he founded Potter's Field, a theatrical troupe he hoped would develop into a world-class Shakespeare Company. Moriarty was a uniquely gifted performer, probably best known for his work on TV's <u>Law and Order</u>. He was also a little nutty, as his odd exit from that show documents. His eccentricity was a blessing and a burden. It made his acting unpredictable, colorful, and alive, although I wouldn't have enjoyed navigating the perils of his personal life.

Michael was aware of all this, for he was nothing if not bright and perceptive. He had great range and originality, and I think he delighted in the vagaries of his personality, but an actor-manager he was not.

There are a few reasons that Potter's Field failed that went beyond Moriarty's capabilities and reveal an artistic climate that is unique to American cultural life.

Overall, Potter's Field didn't have the time and resources to develop at the level of, say, The Royal Shakespeare Company. Part of this had to do with a lack of demand for live drama in our country. Most folks outside the New York metropolitan area and the northeast corridor don't see many theatrical productions and those they do see are usually mainstream musicals.

There are exceptions to this, like the Guthrie in Minneapolis and Actors Theater of Louisville, both of which have established themselves over many years as strong regional theaters with dedicated subscribing audiences, or New York productions that travelled to Los Angeles, but for the most part, until you see a drama come alive and experience the intimacy and intensity of live theater at its best, you just don't know what you're missing.

There's also the reality of how one makes a living as a performer in the United States. An actor can make a very good living here and never be known to the public. Commercial and voice over actors find it hard to say no to these very lucrative jobs for the sake of developing the kind of core group and repertoire a national theater requires.

Because we lacked the theatrical tradition and expectations of a country like Great Britain, it was very difficult for Potter's Field to find sufficient backing to grow into an internationally renowned ensemble. The number of people necessary to support and sustain such a company, the time it takes to develop such a troupe, and the relatively small salaries available to company members, all mitigated against establishing a true National Theater of the United States. Moreover, the crucial corporate backing necessary to underwrite it didn't exist at that time, nor is it available to any nationally recognized theater company in America, today.

Primarily, this has to do with lack of demand. American audiences, as a whole, just don't see the need for a national theater because they've never experienced the tremendous value it can bring to their lives. Ironically, this is not the case in the world of ballet or opera, which both have a rich, worldwide tradition of community and corporate support in a many civilized countries.

New York City is renowned for several world-class ballet companies and for the Metropolitan Opera. But when it comes to theater, then as now, it's just not the same. Hollywood had something to do with siphoning off talent back in the day. Today, however, as Hollywood is no longer the epicenter of film production, Amazon, Netflix and other businesses are providing actors with multiple production options that dissuade them from making long term commitments to theatrical companies, too.

Our lack of a national theater also involves elitism.

Ballet and opera are cultivated tastes that are high-dollar pastimes for subscribers and lucrative for featured company members, especially guest artists. This combination of elitism and economy gives opera and ballet companies time to develop a strong repertoire and makes them immune to the drain on their supporting player pool.

Actors have much broader options, like commercials, voice-overs, and a vast array of guest starring parts. These often one-time, jobber markets can be too lucrative to turn down. This market reality tends to diffuse the exceptional artistic results that only come from long-term specialization and dedication to a body of work that has been nourished and developed over time.

But let me get back to Shakespeare and what I learned about performing his plays at Potter's Field.

What I warmed to in Moriarty's approach was that he removed all reverence from playing the Bard. He encouraged me to believe that everything history's greatest playwright wrote about lived fully inside of me. This freed me of intimidation. It was a wonderful way to approach Shakespeare.

I was not a member of the company but a student in classes taught by company members. My best experience in a Potter's Field production was playing Antonio in *Twelfth Night*. Just before my entrance where I confronted King Orsino for betraying me, my still, small voice, a voice I was beginning to heed said, *"start slowly and simply."* I did just that and my brief speech exploded in a passionate and very real tirade.

Suddenly, I wasn't acting, I was being, and being true to my personal reality in ways that merged with my characters truth.

In that moment, our passions dovetailed into a perfect blend of Antonio's outrage and my life experience of betrayal. The acting lesson here was that there is no character, there was and is only me; that my thoughts, feelings, and expression stood proxy for those of the character I played. This experience also affirmed that small parts, done well, could come alive, compelling an audience's attention. My work was to live the emotional and spiritual truth of the part, and if I did my work free of worry about the size of role, I would be noticed and progress.

This brings to mind a wonderful story about the great George C. Scott, an actor who both reminded me of my father and inspired me to become an actor. He was appearing on Broadway in Neil Simon's *Plaza Suite*. As his part was written, he was having an extramarital affair and in the scene he was playing he was supposed to abandon his wife, played by Maureen Stapelton.

Scott played this situation so close to the emotional reality that he couldn't exit the stage, *so he didn't*. He embraced Stapleton's character with a bear hug that said, *"I just can't leave you and I never will."* ONLY THEN, when he'd honored his authentic emotional impulse, was he able to find another compelling reason to leave the stage and continue the play as it was written.

Marion I

I knew she was a handful the moment I saw her. After a friendship of a quarter of a century, with many ups, downs, starts, and stops, a handful she remains. I met Marion D. S. Dreyfus in an acting class at Potter's Field in the spring of 1980. We agreed to work on a scene from *Antony and Cleopatra*.

Marion was curious about me. I was intrigued by her. She was a force of nature.

I'd never known anyone quite like Ms. Dreyfus. She reminded me of *Standing Woman* by Gaston Lachaise, which at that time was displayed in the Sculpture Garden at MOMA in midtown Manhattan. Like that iconic sculpture, she had the seeming constitution of an ox and could go all day and all night without sleep. She had an encyclopedic knowledge of a vast array of subjects from medical science and technology, to literature and the great outdoors. Marion was also incredibly well travelled.

My guess is that she thought of me as a barefoot mountain boy who had come to conquer or be overwhelmed by the Big Apple. I thought and still think she has the most amazing drive I've ever seen.

The first born of a raging Rabbi, if I thought I was supposed to have been a girl and that I disappointed my parents by being a boy, the same was true of Marion in reverse. I can't speak for her mother, but her father definitely wanted her to be a boy. The more I heard about him, the more my dad seemed placid by comparison.

Many things bonded us, first as friends and then as lovers. Our biggest similarity was that our personalities developed as reactions to what we perceived as our own deficiency. Both of us were Sagittarians. We both loved to laugh and argue. Both of us were curious, clever, and quick witted, although I found her curiosity almost compulsive, and I came see us as much like the Streisand and Redford characters in *The Way We Were*.

In many ways I still do.

Marion was sharp, suspicious, and assigned meanings to my behavior that I didn't always understand or agree with. We were two fiery personalities though her trigger point flashed quicker than mine. And like the protagonists in *The Way We Were*, we clashed over politics.

I was apolitical. Dreyfus was a passionate, pro-active, and vocal pro-Israelite. I suppose I was too focused on finding myself to get involved in what I saw as the indecipherable madness of the world. Marion, conversely, seemed to draw energy from politics, art, and from every other area of human endeavor. From my viewpoint, she had a terrible habit of watching CNN 24/7, angling her TV to reflect in a mirror so she could glance up to see it as she listened to whatever was being broadcast while simultaneously writing movie reviews or poetry at her computer.

"I'll be damned if I'll be controlled or dominated by you or any other fucking person," seemed to be the running inner monologue that played out within both of us. Our projections on this theme, led to our first parting of the ways. Marion's M.O. and mindset mirrored the vengefulness I was acting out in my relationship with my father, although I added to that a measure of withholding which she did not possess. Acknowledging all this would take me several years to see. Dealing with it would take even more years after that.

Forgiveness, self-acceptance, and grace applied in active service to the world, is what we both needed to do. Getting free of the need for retribution, as we would see in future iterations of our relationship, would take both of us the better part of a lifetime to get past.

Playing the Bard in the Company of Miserable Idiots

Just over a year after I met Marion, during the summer of 1981, I had my best experience playing Shakespeare in a professional company. Hopkinton Playhouse in Rhode Island was doing a season of *Macbeth, Auntie Mame, Cyrano de Bergerac, Cat on a Hot Tin Roof,* and *Frankenstein.*

The Artistic Director at Hopkinton was Angelo Malvasio, who preferred to go by Mal Angelo (Bad Angel) and his personality matched his name. He was a cross between the infamous Jed Harris and Darth Vader. Harris was a long dead Broadway producer so reviled Walt Disney based the Big Bad Wolf on him, and Laurence Olivier used as a human model for his *Richard III*. The Darth Vader in Mal came out via his raspy, self-amplified breathing. He had a bad hip, a gamey leg, heart trouble, he chain smoked, and used a cane to get around.

When he said something to eviscerate a young performer, which he had a real gift for doing, Mal was just trying to help. What's more, he was unaware of the negative impact of his comments or criticisms and seemingly surprised when he created constant meltdowns amongst our company. In the heightened, fragile, and savage world of the theater, he was a nightmare for many a young performer, but happily not for me.

Like at Circle with Nikos, Mal and I never crossed swords.

He was as tender as he was tough and notwithstanding his poor people skills, he had a powerful intuition. An ex-marine who loved the theater and gave many performers the opportunity to cut their teeth on great parts in great plays, Mal was a warrior/poet at heart. He just canted a little too much towards the destructive side of that tandem.

We had a quiet kinship with each other, and I liked Mal. I especially admired how he picked seasons top-heavy with great plays. He didn't pander to the lighter, more popular, and profitable summer fare most summer theaters opted for and relied on to survive.

When I think about it, I'm not sure how I dodged Nikos and Mal's criticisms, especially considering the chip on my shoulder I had with strong male authority figures. Perhaps the killers in them saw and respected the killer in me.

I was fortunate to be cast in the title part of the Scottish Play. I refer to Shakespeare's shortest tragedy this way because I experienced the curse legend has attached to the play. Macbeth was our season opener. No sooner than we begun rehearsal, than a member of our group stole the company station wagon, our Malcolm sprained an ankle, I nearly lost an eye stage fighting, and the production wound up having three directors.

The power of the Bard's poetry, of his monumental ideas and insights, and the feelings his thoughts and words engendered in me, was incomparable and unforgettable.

Playing Macbeth was like surfing a tidal wave; it was demanding, dangerous, and daunting, but it was beyond thrilling, too. I'd developed some acting chops by now and because I drilled and stayed sharp vocally and physically, riding this great wave was a peak experience.

I memorized the entire play; every single part, and I was so in love with this tragedy that I recited the whole play to myself every night before bed. This was a ritual I kept up from the start of rehearsals till we closed the show.

Shakespeare gives you everything as an actor. His sublime language takes you to realms that transcend everyday experience. Every night I played the "dagger speech," for example, became a brand-new seduction. For those unfamiliar with the play, the title character envisions a dagger in his ambition filled imagination and interacts with the blade, foreshadowing his murder of King Duncan and of many more courtiers in this parable of a soldier who betrays his code and thus himself.

Sometimes I would tempt and tease the dagger and then it would lure me in or bait me in reply. My connection to the speech was always fresh and my process went something like this;

> *I imagine the blade before me, floating in space. Look how it flirts and dances with me. See it coax and tease, see how it fades in and out of view, expressing it pleasure or disdain with my love play. See how it beckons me. I know full well the folly of my ambition yet go happily to my demise…*

Such was the evocative power of Shakespeare's poetry. In the process of exploring my imaginative dance with the dagger from rehearsal to opening night, and then from one performance to the next, I built up a trust fund of active images the made the speech come alive. I looked forward to playing this bit every night. I also kept track of how my moments worked and was able to accomplish everything I wanted to achieve in the part as a whole by the time we closed the play.

If heaven exists, I was in it that summer, but much of me was blind to this. I was playing Shakespeare in the company of miserable idiots and I, no less than they, was guilty of absurd complaints.

We paired up with our summer lovers, got food stamps to supplement our pay of $35 per week, and lived like well-fed Kings and Queens in our large, comfortable seven or eight bedroom house, complete with a barn, a 67' Pontiac station wagon, and a coterie of great plays.

Oh, so tortured, put upon, and ridiculous we were, like characters in a Chekhovian comedy. We were in paradise and didn't know it.

Darrell Hammond, who later would gain fame playing Bill Clinton on Saturday Night Live, joined our cast to replace the idiot who stole our Pontiac. I've long since forgotten the thief's name but remember he was enraged at not being cast as Macbeth. Hammond came to us as a forlorn, failed baseball player who drank too much, and he played Ross in our mounting of the Scottish Play.

Like me, Darrell was a southerner, and I laughed at his riffs on southern humor till tears rolled down my cheeks. Every night, as I did the dagger speech on stage, he'd match me word for word in the lobby of our theater, as he waited to make his entrance. While I played it straight on stage, Darrell played Macbeth as a southern Black mammy.; *"Is dis a pawk-chop I seez before mee, the handle towards muh hand?"* I was glad I couldn't see or hear him from the lobby because every time I heard him do this at rehearsal breaks, I laughed so hard the back of my head hurt.

The sweetness of my recollection now makes the "miserable idiots" we were an affectionate description. Our theater was an old church with a seating capacity of around eighty and the dressing room was an enclosed loft space directly above the stage.

Outside, there was a meadow on the north side of the playhouse. During the day we'd run lines, paint sets, or take breaks there. Joan and Helen's Café, a restaurant just on the other side of the highway that fronted our theater, was a lunch only establishment. Run by two retired friends, the cafe offered fantastic specials that were out of this world. You'd get homemade fare, like chicken pot pie with three freshly cooked veggies, apple cobbler for desert and all the lemon iced tea you could drink for $3.25! Absolute Heaven!

We worked hard doing the business of painting sets, and the day-to-day tasks involved in keeping up the theater. Our routine was to play the current show in the evening and rehearse the next production during the day. And so it was that we loved and hated each other and discovered how to work as actors and relate to each other as human beings.

Most of us were obsessed with learning the craft of acting and sought to become better and more expressive. Even on our one day off, Monday evening, we'd stay up late at our farmhouse debating the secrets of great acting. I argued that the audience didn't want to see some pre-packaged performance, asserting that what moved them was seeing us grapple from moment to moment with the given circumstances of our characters in each play. To me, live theater meant you had to be responsive to the moment and to your fellow players in each and every performance, so that each night you were subtly different and therefore fully present and alive.

I was passionately opposed to giving a "pre-formance." I felt rehearsal was to re-hear; to listen anew to what the play was saying; to explore the various possibilities of my part, and to develop an inner catalogue of options I could play in performance because I'd mined them as powerful trigger points in rehearsal.

My rivals countered that not to be crystal clear about all my choices and characteristics cheated the audience. They believed that being totally prepared, and to my mind, immune to the moment, freed them to become available for inspiration.

Acting at its best, combines elements of both these approaches.

Ten years after my season at Hopkinton, I was riding the M-86 crosstown bus in Manhattan. As we turned briefly up Madison Avenue, before continuing east on 86th street, a woman came up to me and said; *"I just want you to know that I saw your amazing Macbeth and I've never forgotten it. You were great."* Her kind comment puts the perfect tag on what was one of the great experiences of my life.

Susan Slavin's Actors and Singers Academy

One night in the fall of 1980, I was walking uptown on the west side of Broadway. As I passed by the Ansonia Hotel, I ran into Judy Knoop. She pronounced her last name KAH-NOPE and had been a classmate of mine at Circle. Judy was rail thin, smart, and sassy but beneath her up for anything exterior she was wound tight and very few people got close to her.

After we hugged each other with the warmth of former comrades, she told me she was taking an acting class with Susan Slavin and that I ought to check it out.

For the next decade before, during and long after my gigs at Hopkinton, touring the Hunchback, and other jobs, I took Susan's acting class in a variety of locations till she found a permanent home at Studio 912 in the Carnegie Hall Apartments on 56th and 7th Avenue.

In that decade, I fell in love for the first time with a girl I met in Slavin's class, was abandoned by her, began and ended talk therapy for the first but not the last time, met my future wife on the rebound, we married and divorced, wrote a play, happily ended my career as an actor and then briefly taught acting to singers.

In all that time, my core concern was becoming a more open, powerful, and successful, first as an actor and then as a teacher.

Or so I thought.

Firstly, I felt I needed to work on myself to resolve personal issues that blocked my fullest expression. Secondly, I continued to work on improving my craft.

Compared to these two pursuits, I didn't give a damn about money, either how much I made or spent. Making a living or being married or being in a committed relationship were subordinate to getting better and working as much as possible as an actor.

In retrospect this seems narrow minded, and it was, but that's where I was at the time. Perhaps if I'd been normal, I would have focused on building a family with my wife Paula, which is what she wanted, but I wouldn't be writing this book today if I had taken that path.

At the time I met her, Susan Slavin was at the end of her marriage to Larry Moss, whom I'd briefly studied with at Circle. They shared a seemingly identical approach to teaching with one fundamental difference. Larry knew how to let his students go. Susan did not. Whether her control issues contributed to the demise of their union I can't say, but I'd be surprised if they didn't.

Susan was a very private, canny, and guarded person. A Scorpio, she viewed herself as a work in progress and as an evolving, transformational self-creation. As time went by, I saw her morph into a slightly toned-down version of the divas on TV's popular *Dynasty*, the prime time soap opera of the day.

She surely dressed the part.

For all her prompting that we be authentic, there was an air of fantasy around Susan. She kept her students at a distance, and for the most part her private life was a mystery. Although she seemed straightforward in all her interactions, there was something about her polished image, the distance she kept, and her performance as teacher/entrepreneur that was unreal.

Sue asserted that I couldn't act what I couldn't live. At least not in any real, lasting way. She was right, which is why I studied with her. The more aware and empowered I became as a person, the more value I brought to my work. Susan's conception of acting was compelling but there was a hitch. In class, I could do top-notch work, but I couldn't bring that work or myself out into the real world and establish myself.

This was my problem, not Susan's, but my difficulty went deeper than my childhood withholding pattern. Although my issues dealing with becoming a working actor were largely self-inflicted, they were also exacerbated by Susan's teaching agenda.

From her viewpoint, there were a whole bevy of elements that needed to come together for us to find lasting success in a highly competitive, overcrowded marketplace.

Number one was self-awareness and the liberation that attends it. This required psycho-therapy so we could get clarity, mobility, and outgrow our personal blind spots, denials, and projections.

After therapy, in no particular order of importance was packaging ourselves, which meant knowing what type we were, (leading man, character actor, etc.), and polishing that image. Of equal importance was forming a marketing strategy, dressing the part, and applying the whole package with corporate uniformity and consistency.

Of course, it was essential, too, to continually sharpen our instrument, i.e. our voice, body, mind, and spirit. This not only included diction, dance and singing skills, but metaphysical elements. Here we used astrology with its past life perspectives to find our soul's intentions. There was image consultation, too, via her sanctioned practitioners. Among other things, this involved getting your colors done.

Last, but not least, there was cultivating a consciousness of abundance so we could pay for her class and all these essential services.

Susan counseled us to integrate and master all these elements with the goal of becoming successful, socially relevant performers. Social relevance was prized not for any genuine difference we would make in the community, but so we could be timely and on target with whatever was trending and in vogue at the moment.

The dark side of all this was the bane of all performers; *narcissism*.

Self-involvement is necessary to a point. You have to have a solid measure of introspection to be a fine actor, but what prevents toxic narcissism from overwhelming an actor's life is consistently contributing to society via your work and in other ways

This idea was and remains rooted in focusing on the art form of acting and comes from an artistic mind-set; not from a business-like, market-oriented perspective.

Inspiring an audience both balances a performer and fosters humility, connection, and a sense of community. It's important to recognize that there are things bigger, more significant, and larger than you, your needs, or your career as a performer.

Empowering others via my acting turned me on and inspired me, but I never found the social value of acting authentically supported at Studio 912.

In fairness, whatever Susan's influence, I withheld myself from the marketplace and my community and would have done so no matter what. To Susan's credit, she suggested I get into therapy, which I did. Nevertheless, with or without therapy, I still projected my childhood issues onto the world and would continue to do so until I was ready to let go of all that shit.

The crucial questions were; how long can you take to get your psyche together compared to the demands of building a career here and now? When and where did the demands of your career trump your need to heal? And how well could you function as a working artist when you had the kind of entrenched human frailties we all have?

Although I couldn't admit it yet, my inner commitment was the same as it had always been; deny my father any joy or satisfaction from my life, project my defiance of him onto the world at large, and deny myself any real satisfaction or success in the bargain.

Deeper still, I refused to acknowledge, much less face how **deficient** I felt. There was another layer beneath that, too.

Self-hate.

If I'd recognized my self-hatred and allowed my feelings of deficiency to wash into, over, and through me; if I'd simply, but not so easily, accepted the poisonous self-criticism I felt at the core of my being, I might have moved forward, but I didn't.

Denying my inmost feeling about myself shut me down.

In practice, I found talk therapy to be an over-rehearsed alibi for why I wasn't having the life I said I wanted. I saw this was true of most folks I knew who were *on the couch*. Head shrinking just seemed to take more time than I felt I had.

What I needed was a more expedient healing modality to get to and work through my deepest emotional blocks, but I didn't know how to go about that, so I stood pat with the advice of counselors and shrinks I trusted.

But let me focus more specifically on the work I did with Susan because it has relevance for anyone who wants to pursue a career as a performer.

Regardless of my personal pathology, there are elements of Slavin's approach that should serve as cautionaries for all performers.

While she was tacitly supportive of our being in action in the world, Susan put her primary focus on the performer and his or her personal needs. This quest for freedom and expression far outweighed any real commitment to serve others through our work.

In actual practice, Susan's Studio became an environment of eternal self-involvement. Nobody who worked with her, and I was there a decade, ever left the nest to become truly successful in an independent, self-sustaining way.

This was not because her students lacked talent or the ability to manage their careers.

We needed an approach to working that inspired us to get past our fears in service of something bigger and more important than our narrow-minded self-concerns. We needed to see ourselves as artists with a commitment to better our world through our acting, and we needed to understand that consistently working in the industry was the ongoing challenge we must consistently meet to justify society's support of our careers.

What was missing was clarity, perspective, and true commitment to something that inspired us to go beyond our fears and frailties.

Our personal quest for freedom, power, fame, and wealth was in many ways an insular pipe dream. As scary as working with our real feelings was, we knew we were in a very safe, *and as things turned out*, too safe, environment.

We did some fine and powerful work at Susan's Studio, but it was too cloistered. When all was said and done, I believe what most of us thought went something like this; *"Why go out and get beat up in the marketplace, when the most important work of my soul is being done right here in Susan's class."*

What was really going on was a fantasy pursuit of individuation and empowerment. On the face of things, Slavin supported us to become performers of prestige and significance. Underneath it all, her relentless drive to build and diversify her teaching business, *and other related services* like getting kick-backs from <u>her</u> astrologer who counseled <u>her</u> students, ruled the roost.

I don't know for a fact that kickbacks occurred but that would be perfectly acceptable if you had a marketplace mindset. And whether or not she got paid for our work with her sanctioned consultants, her involvement in the image side of her approach to being successful netted her a tidy profit above and beyond her teaching fees.

These related services were in conflict and suborned her primary duty to liberate our full expression and to bring the best of our artistry to the world.

The only way an actor or singer becomes strong and self-sustaining is by sorting themselves out personally, then mastering the rough and tumble of a performer's life in the world at large. That necessitates going out there and staying out there, while at the same time learning how to protect and nourish yourself as you deal with the war wounds you incur working in show business.

As I see it, teaching us how to survive and thrive, as well as how to master our craft, was Susan's primary obligation.

It's what we paid her for.

Consciously, or not, Slavin was about securing her own selfish interests by taking a cut of every new element "we absolutely needed" as we pursued the holy grail of self-liberation and career success.

It wasn't that she overtly declared that we should have our colors done (I was a spring) or dress for success (I looked like a pastel ice-cream cone when I went to her class). No, heaven forbid she distract us from what was most essential to the actor's work.

She was subtler than that.

She would always give us a choice about following her recommendations, but there was a conflict of interest, nonetheless. She had a financial stake that compromised her ability to guide us to find our own independent viewpoint and self-sustaining ways. Although from a business standpoint she was simply optimizing her profit opportunities, I feel Susan bred dependency in all her students.

Slavin was a fine and perceptive teacher who helped loads of performers become more authentically expressive, but she, like all of us, had her blind spots. By teaching us to mold ourselves as types in a marketplace vs. finding and speaking with our authentic artistic and spiritual voices, regardless of what was in vogue or how we were perceived from a market perspective, she compromised our individuality and whatever we had of genuine human value to contribute to the audience that paid our way.

When a performing artist doesn't focus on and cultivate his or her original voice, that person gets lost. Again, in fairness to Sue, finding the best blend of artistry, marketability, relevant service and making a living is a balancing act that all working artists must sort out for themselves.

The correct use of a conservatory, however, is to discover, nourish and solidify talent, not promote and profit from secondary concerns that may or may not enhance that fundamental aim. Mixing art and business is dangerous for someone who's primary function is, or should be, to enhance her students' artistry and the public good that comes from that artistry.

A teacher's first obligation is to do away with the students' need for teaching; to create performing artists who are sovereign, self-determined and self-sustaining.

In reality, Susan's first commitment was to herself and her business.

This is why, as I see it, her studio and her students never found the levels of success they might have. By comparison, the success of Larry Moss's students suggests he helped his pupils become autonomous. The fundamental difference that separated them as teachers, and probably as people, is that Larry could free his students and let them go. Susan helped liberate her pupils' expression, but she couldn't or wouldn't set them free to find and follow their own course.

My first year in New York, I had a brief encounter with a working actor who gave me some prescient advice. In essence, this is what he said; *"Beware getting involved with a teacher who makes the pursuit of personal freedom more important than practicing your craft for a demanding, paying audience. Your personal life is up to you, but your job and moreover your obligation is to perform. If your audience decides your work has merit, you'll survive and continue to work. If it doesn't, figure out how to make your work relevant or find another way to make a living."*

"Let he who is without sin cast the first stone."

My intention in sharing the basis of this phase of my training, and the perspective I have on it now, is to serve a higher truth, not to dismiss Susan as a teacher from some artistic higher ground.

I don't feel superior or inferior to her. Neither do I have a bone to pick. Moreover, I now believe I wasn't meant to be successful in the sense of having an acting career. The process of reclaiming my humanity via the acting process was what I was really after and I accomplished that in spades.

I hope that being open and honest about my mistakes and forthright in my current viewpoint helps other performers trust their inner guidance and to find their way.

It's been well over thirty years since I last worked with Susan. I hope in that time, because I expect she's still teaching, that Susan came to a method which empowers her students and sets them free. At the same time, and of equal importance, I hope the work her students do in the world serves society's greater self-awareness and well-being.

That's the real purpose of having and supporting the performing arts.

Living on the Periphery

Throughout my career as an actor, if you can call it that, I worked as a waiter or bartender in the New York City catering industry. The truth is I did much more serving than acting. This is the reality for many performers. The challenging part is telling yourself the truth about whether you're an actor, singer, dancer, or waiter.

When all was said and done, I became an actor to become a person. Although it took years for me to realize it, I never intended to make acting my profession. I was too insecure to handle the considerable challenges of an actor's life. But I was also seeking something much deeper and more substantial than fame and fortune. Riches and renown weren't important to me.

What I truly valued was following the path that was right for my soul and finding ways to connect to that.

I was an excellent actor, and I had a gift for the craft, but something more than personal insecurity wouldn't let me go at the business end as all out as I went at acting, itself. For years I puzzled over this. In time, I came to understand it.

To my mind, a famous actor is no more important than a parking attendant. Both have their paths and lessons, and one person's journey is no greater or more valuable than another's.

The only thing that's important is knowing and following the path that's right for you.

I've seen famous, celebrated and "the beautiful people" close up. Their lives can dazzle, but their actual existence is often as ugly as it seems to be sublime. Human existence is a mixed bag for all of us.

I remember when Dustin Hoffman won the Oscar for his role in *Kramer vs. Kramer*. He spoke of the community of actors and how deeply he respected actors who were driving cabs, scraping by, and continuing to work on their craft and careers, in hopes of getting a break.

He'd been there so his comments were heartfelt. They were also true.

Any waiter with aspirations to become a fine performer, or great writer, or a groundbreaking teacher, who has French served filet mignon to the crem de la crem of society knows or hopes that deep inside him or her there is a person capable of much more than being a hash-slinging vassal. Service of any type is a noble pursuit. I'm not putting down people in the service industries. I'm saying that we all are more than the roles we play or the circumstances of lives.

We're all more than the sum of our parts.

If you're lucky enough to have a place at the table of society's soirees, try to remember that the person serving you dinner may have the gift of genius raring to burst forth and judge not lest ye be judged.

One night, I was a waiter at a party for an organization that was the liberal counterpart to the conservative John Birch Society. This association was called The People of the American Way. Bill Moyers, the broadcast journalist, was being honored that night as their Man-of-the-Year. Gladys Knight and the Pips were performing, and they hooked into something spectacular. Those of us present who knew the difference between real artistry and phoning in a performance stopped what we were doing. Most who paused were waiters.

When the set was done, the applause was tepid. The Pips looked at Ms. Knight with an expression that said *"what the hell do we have to* do? Don't these folks know what we just did was great?"* The only ones in the room who got it were the wait staff, who as a body applauded the beauty of what they'd just seen.

It's time for me to step off my soap box but if you're still listening to my sermon, let me leave you with this; the next time you're at a catered party in a great city like New York, reflect for a moment on the humanity of the folks who are serving you. Consider they might prefer to be doing something else and ponder how you might feel if you were serving them.

The second coming of Quintin Tarantino or Daniel Day Lewis might just be busing your table or serving you *hor's d'oeuvres*. Take time to show these folks some real appreciation, then tip him or her a c-note and say to yourself, *"there but for the grace of God, go I."*

Paula

As I topped the gangway and came aboard the sightseeing ferry *Cabaret*, I saw her bent over, balanced on one leg. Her back was to me, as she draped a bar with a tablecloth. *"Excuse me,* I asked, *could you tell me where to sign in?"* The moment our eyes met I knew we would marry. Unfortunately, I was coming from a wounded and bitter place but in denial about it. I saw Paula DeNiro's neediness, vulnerability and heart, and knew I could play her.

When I first gazed at my bride to be, the idea I'd been mulling over for many months flashed into my head, *"I'm going to get this relationship thing down, then I'm gonna get married so I have a solid home base and launching pad for my career, and this is exactly who I'm gonna do it with."*

The fact that I didn't consider how she might feel about where I was coming from or value what she might feel, and that I didn't recognize what kind of bastard such a callous calculation made me, reveals how cold and monstrously selfish I'd become.

Yet I thought of myself as a good, kindhearted person, and in many ways I was. Using my bitterness to justify manipulating another person who had nothing to do with my pain was monstrous. Neither did I consider the harvest my attitude would reap.

It was now June of 1982. Paula and I were working as free-lance waiters in the booming Manhattan catering trade. This is how I covered all my living and acting expenses and how Paula paid her way as a modern dancer.

I traded on Paula's need for love to evade my own feelings of worthlessness. I lied to my future wife and to myself from the get-go. By the time I could admit this to her, I couldn't repair the damage I'd done.

But to fully understand my relationship with Paula, I have to go back to what happened before we met, to what I made a prior relationship mean, and how I justified my contemptable behavior.

I met Suzie Adams in Slavin's acting class a little over a year before meeting Paula. Suzie was a pure woman/child, an overgrown cheerleader with an infant's need for attention and an adolescent's urge for sex. A blind man would have steered clear of her by a mile, but not me. This is where I learned it wasn't a good idea to hook up with someone in your acting class, although it wasn't the last time I did just that.

The red flags were too numerous to count.

Suzie had married an Irishman so he could get his Green Card, and though they were living together, it was a non-sexual relationship of convenience. Or so she told me, and I believed her.

The two of us were attracted to each other, of course, and I remember the moment she decided to sleep with me.

We were in her tiny apartment at 1st Avenue in the upper 50's. I was sitting on the edge of her plywood covered bathtub that doubled as a kitchen table. I'd just told her I was attracted to her. I saw her review her sexual impulsiveness like it was a video game playing inside her head. I could sense her thinking, *"Should I sleep with Bob or should I be disciplined for once and not indulge my libido."* "Well," she said, after brief consideration, *OK!"* Whereupon she jumped on me, and we went at it like rabbits.

Where the Irishman was, I don't know and couldn't have cared less. If Suzie was good to get it on, so was I. I only wish I had credited the whimsy I saw in her face and been as cautious as my gut told me to be.

Relocating my brain below my belt has never worked for me.

The upshot of my relationship with Suzie was that I confused hot sex with love and fell for her in a way she initially dug but then felt threatened by. The fact that I blurted out in the throes of our passion, *"I want you to be the mother of my children,"* probably struck her as a little scary since she was essentially a child herself.

When she dumped me, I never found out why. She literally walked away, and I never saw or spoke with her again.

I carried the torch for Suzie like a fucking eighth grader. I just grinded and grinded on why she left me, and I held onto my angst in a way that was childish and just plain stupid. The worst of this was that I used the pain I felt at being rejected by Suzie to justify manipulating Paula.

To this day, what I did to Paula is the worst thing I've ever done to anyone, and I will regret it to the day I die. Nothing can justify the way I used her yet held her at bay, when Paula had all the heart, all the desire, and all the loyalty I could ever hope to receive.

Paula Marie DeNiro had a lithesome grace, a willowy, offbeat sexiness that reminded me of Ellen Barkin, a popular actress of the time. She also had a powerful intuition, though her neediness sometimes clouded her eagle eye. Underneath a cool detachment, Ms. DeNiro had a gushing desire for love and a childlike joy and playfulness. She was torn between her need to be cool and removed, and cutting loose with her fiery, all-consuming heart. She was practical, yet lyrical and impatient with my quibbling. Like all Italians I've known, she needed to be seen, loved, worshiped, and adored. She was also more than ready, willing and able to give what she needed back to me.

What I didn't see was how blind I was to my own faults and frailties, and what an exploitative asshole that made me.

"Give me time and space, I'll come around," I cried, so Paula let me move in with her. She always knew I was holding something back, but I couldn't *"come around"* till I faced how I felt at being abandoned by Suzie.

I kept my distance from Paula because I was afraid to confess I was using her to evade myself. I tried to build our relationship on the quicksand of my denial. At the time, I had no more capacity for intimacy than Suzie did.

At one point in our relationship, things came to a head in an all-night showdown. I fessed up to where I was coming from, but only partially. I challenged Paula with; *"Are you willing to jump through all the hoops I'll throw at you, just to test and prove your love?"* Paula said *"Yes,"* but she couldn't get past her own denial any more than I could mine. She too had a pain deep within her that she couldn't yet own up to or embrace.

The only way out of that pain, or any pain, is to go through it.

We were both playing hide and seek, reversing roles when one or both of us got too close. If I was a heartless manipulator, denying my pain and using Paula to cover it up, Paula had her own pathology.

The youngest of four children, my wife had a bratty side. She would make a commitment then go back on her word with no regard for how that affected others. Sometimes she just didn't give a shit about how anyone else felt. Paula made the effort with me because she wanted our marriage to work, but to a large degree, she wound up rejecting me for fear of seeing the taboo parts of herself.

If you crossed the line with her, or if you got closer than she allowed herself to be with herself, she'd cut you dead. I saw her do this with others but somehow thought she'd never do it with me.

I was wrong.

Although I haven't seen or spoken to Paula since our divorce in 1987, I'm sure her anger brought her low. While we were together, we tried some counselling. Just as we started to make headway, she pulled the plug. When I made a stand and said we had to do some serious work on our relationship, she showed me the door.

We probably never should have married. We both wanted to love and be loved but we were too self-involved, too selfish, and too defended to let love bloom. Before we tied the knot, we didn't even discuss if, when, or under what circumstances we wanted to have children.

Paula was at the end of her dance career, just as I was at the beginning of what I thought would be my lifelong profession as an actor. She couldn't wait to leave New York but there's no way I'd leave the Apple just at the start of my career. As a compromise, we bought a vacation home a year before we split, but she blew off our agreement less than a year after we made it and started up again about leaving Manhattan.

When this happened, I felt she'd quit on our marriage like I'd seen her quit many smaller things or other people when they didn't meet her expectations.

The vacation place we bought was structured on a ballon mortgage. We went 50/50 on the purchase price and when my end came due, I balked, leaving Paula holding the bag. This was the second worst thing I've ever done.

Near the end, there came a moment when we saw our marriage disintegrating before our eyes. We were standing in the living room of our tiny East Village apartment. We looked at each other in that moment with the dual realization that our partnership was coming apart. All we could do was embrace each other and cry.

I hope to God Paula forgave me, not for my sake, but for hers. I hope she had children and a happy, healthy life. Regrettably, I'll never know. When she was done with someone, she was DONE.

I wish we could have work things out, but once we separated, one of us would want to get back together and the other didn't. For a while we flipped back and forth between trying again, but it never happened.

I deserved no better than I got.

Don Quixote At the Crossroads

During my nearly thirty year run in the Big Apple, dad came to New York twice on his own, and twice more with mom. New York City was not his cup of tea. His second visit, this time solo and on business, came sometime in the spring of 85'. Now 64, pop was in town on a fraud case involving the accounting firm of Arthur Anderson and Company, and dad's client, the Hamilton Bank in Chattanooga.

My father was on the verge of a retirement he longed for and deserved, but clearly dreaded.

Paula and I arranged to meet him for breakfast at his hotel. He was staying at the Park Lane on Central Park South, and we were running late. I knew dad hated New York and he'd be anxious when we didn't show up on time.

As we entered the lobby of his hotel, I spotted him through its revolving doors an instant before he saw us. In that moment, he looked completely out of his element, like a frightened little boy. My heart went out to my father. As soon as he saw us, he stuffed down his anxiety and went into a Glad-to-see-yah routine.

During breakfast we ran through the predictable check-list; how's your weather been, how's mom doing, and a quick review of what all of us had been up to lately. Usually, dad could pull off the appearance of affability regardless of what he really felt, but there was a hollowness about him now that he couldn't disguise.

My father had always preached honor and self-sufficiency to me. He believed if you did right by folks, and you rigorously cared for yourself and your kin, good things would happen. This was his version of the biblical missive; *"The Lord takes care of those who take care of themselves,* combined with *"Get a good job."*

He also taught the concept of *nobles oblige*. His conviction here was that if you did good deeds and interacted nobly with others, they were more than likely to respond in kind.

At this stage of my father's life, however, he was exasperated by the level of greed and malice he saw in the world. I saw a futility in him that he'd never expressed and could no longer hide.

As a trial lawyer, dad was no stranger to the darker side of human nature. Nevertheless, the absence of honorable or even decent behavior in the world, an awareness no doubt prompted by the blatant fraud at the root of his current lawsuit, seemed to have shaken him to his core. I sensed he was questioning *nobles oblige* as a viable concept.

As he spoke with us about his current case, and laid out the evidence that Arthur Anderson and Company had clearly swindled his client, my father said, *"How could a company behave like that?"*

Although he had a point, I think what was really going on with dad was terror at letting go of his career and being out of harness. His expression and behavior seemed to say, *"What the hell am I going to do with myself when I retire?"*

Work had always been the central, defining reality of his life, even when he relaxed (for him) doing his weekend projects, he worked his ass off.

As our cab pulled away from the curb at the Park Lane, a stunning image came to me. I saw Don Quixote staring dumbfounded at the spinning vanes of the windmill he'd just charged. His life's purpose, as symbolized by the lance he used to stab a blade of the windmill had become a toothpick. As he looked skyward, he saw to his horror that little toothpick spinning round and round, and he was left facing the fact that his grand quest was a delusion.

The White Crow

In the late spring of 1985, I was cast to understudy the lead in an off-off Broadway, but well financed drama entitled *The White Crow*. Set in Boston at the turn of the twentieth century and based on a true story, it involved psychic investigator Richard Hodgson's efforts to expose the medium Elenora Piper as a fraud. Piper proved to be an authentic seer and, at least in the play, these two rivals fell in love.

The story essentially restated what Hamlet asserted to his friend and comrade; *"There are more things in heaven and earth, Horatio, than are dreamt of in your philosophy."*

The play was solid but overwritten and had a running time of nearly three hours. Our production had great atmosphere and effects and combined the best qualities of a thriller with a love story. I adored the period of the play and call me kooky, but I literally felt I'd happily lived at that time.

Hodgson was Australian. At the last minute, an actor named Peter Kent who *was* Australian beat me out for the lead. What burned my ass was I knew I was the better actor. The producers had gone for his authentic accent, but our director also suspected Kent's acting chops and he persuaded the producers to ask me to understudy with a guarantee of a few performances playing the leading role.

I accepted their offer.

The wonderful film *Shakespeare in Love* beautifully expresses the impossibilities of theater life. How everything works out, with all the interweaving of actors' working and private lives is, as the movie says, *a mystery*.

This was never truer than my experience with <u>The White Crow</u>.

It's an absolute of acting that you must be in touch with your moment-to-moment emotions to be fully present and alive. When our two leads did their first good work in rehearsal, I had to deal with how that made me feel or I would have shut down. I went home from the theater and wailed, pounding my bed with my hands and feet, till I went through all the shame, pain and inadequacy I felt.

As childish and horrifying as this may sound, my outburst was actually responsible and disciplined. What I was going through wasn't mere ego or jealousy, although some of it was. From a craft perspective, I was keeping my instrument, and the artist within me, open, attuned, alive and available.

As rehearsals progressed, I tried to beg, borrow and steal whatever time I could get from our principal actors when they were on a break. It wasn't enough. I worked hard to get ready on my own but to properly prepare I needed time to rehearse that didn't exist.

If the actor's nightmare is being naked, alone, and not knowing his lines, imagine how I felt as I took the stage playing the lead WITH NO

REHEARSAL in a three-hour play! My first performance was on a Friday night and thank God I'd arranged to use my acting class, which met earlier that afternoon, to prepare.

As I stood up in class, Susan asked me how I felt. *"I FEEL TERRIFIED,"* I said, and when she asked me speak about my fear, I described what I saw in my imagination; the floor I was standing on had holes to my left and right that ran all the way from New York City to China. *"What do you need to fill up those holes?"* she asked.

I reached up to the heavens and pulled down columns of light from what I guess was heaven, or God's divine mercy, or I don't know what, to fill up all the pitfalls around me.

Susan, God bless her, really helped me work through my dread and helped me to express my terror. I left class deeply relaxed and as fully prepared as I could be.

I felt open and ready until I got to the theater.

Then I flipped in the complete opposite direction. Suddenly, I couldn't get my breath below my Adam's Apple.

Talk about walking the high wire blind, with no net. When I made my entrance, my first bit of action was to silently investigate the study where most of the play took place. I was looking for tricks planted by the so-called clairvoyant so I could expose her, but none were to be found. *"Jesus Christ,* I said to myself, *I can't fucking breath, but I have the lead! I've just got to keep going, keep going, keep going."*

At no time in this entire performance did my breath get deeper than my throat.

I was clearly stressed but my preparation and training held. Although I usually relied on my imagination, I weaved some substitutions into my characterization to keep the work personal and alive. For example, I used the moment I met Paula, that instant of clarity and precognition that we would marry, to inform meeting Elenora Piper for the first time.

When I made my curtain call that night maybe the audience responded to my guts in pushing through my terror. Perhaps, on the other hand, I was better than I thought. Whatever mix of tension and talent came through in my performance, the reality is I received a standing ovation. I was shocked and puzzled by this incredible reaction because I was just trying to survive and do my job. I guess I did better than I thought and/or the audience admired my commitment.

To this day I don't know what really happened. I was bloodying my nose in the arena. I didn't have the luxury of a clear perspective, but the affirmation of my audience was one hell of a surprise.

Marion II and MacMillan

Not long after my divorce, I was having a drink after work with a new friend. Her name was Lynn. We both worked at MacMillan Publishing Co. on Third Avenue. Lynn was Executive Secretary to the company's President, and I was the part-time *Maître D'* in MacMillan's private dining room. The two of us were chatting in a restaurant near the Citi Corp building when Marion Dreyfus, of all people, appeared out of the blue.

Marion had a unique walk when she was excited. It was a combination of hop and skip a tip-toe with her shortish stride that looked like she was making tiny jumps on hot, burning coals. I saw her move this way as she approached our table, and I knew she was not only happy but thrilled to see me. We had lost touch over the past five years, and I was as happy to see Marion as Lynn was not.

We briefly caught up then Marion left. We promised to call each other and when we did, we quickly got back in bed together, too. This was a bright spot in a challenging time.

The cast of characters I worked with on MacMillan's dining staff was memorable.

George, the head Chef, was a paranoid, head-case, but as good with food as he was bad with people. The company was looking for a full-timer to take my spot. In less than a year, George burned through two men who quit, so management asked me to come in on a part-time basis, again.

Ramos was the headwaiter, and chief peacemaker between the floor staff and George's kitchen crew. Jerry was George's chief assistant in the kitchen, and as is often true of people who serve in the ranks, was an envious, venal little Iago. Charlotte, a waitress, was a childhood survivor of the Dresden bombings in World War II. She was only 55 but looked like she was 70.

Pettiness and power plays seemed to rule the day at MacMillan. I needed the income but not the full-time headache. I wasn't yet ready to give up my dream of being an actor for full benefits and a steady weekly paycheck.

Two episodes from my time at MacMillan bear relating.

One day a Jewish editor named Glickes came to lunch with a writer client. I sat them in Charlotte's section, gave them that day's specials and took their drink order. As I mixed their cocktails at the bar,

Charlotte came up behind me where she couldn't be heard and said something that chilled me to the bone.

Just before I turned to give her the drinks for Glickes and his guest, this odd and bitter woman said, *"Ah, this Jew Glickes, put him up against the wall and shoot him!"* "Jesus Christ, I thought, *this is the mind-set that created the Holocaust, I'm working with a Nazi!"* The poor editor must have said something to set Charlotte off.

This next episode was almost equally chilling but provided a deeper, sadder study in character.

Edward Evans was the CEO and Chairman of MacMillan's Board. My job was to serve him personally, to handle parties in his private dining room, as well as supervise the executive dining area.

One day, he ordered a turkey sandwich for lunch. No sooner than I'd served it than he buzzed the kitchen to take it back. Paranoid George went on tilt. Evan's complained that the turkey wasn't fresh. Technically he was correct. Like all executive kitchens we used a compressed and packaged variety of turkey. No one in Manhattan had real, fresh turkey available, so our CEO reluctantly settled for the sandwich he got.

Rumor had it that Evans father had invented the hostile corporate takeover. It was clear that while his father was pillaging the corporate world, he didn't give his son the time of day. Ned, the son's nickname, had wealth, privilege and status, but little more. In place of any real affection, all he had from his original family was pressure to uphold their vapid image. In lieu of genuine love, all he'd inherited were their expectations, demands, and money.

It was a bum deal.

As a human being, my heart went out to this Richard III-like character. As an observer of psychological gesture, however, the suppressed pain and rage that came sideways out of his body fascinated me.

C.G. Jung said, *"When an inner situation is not made conscious, it appears outside, as fate."* As it would with anyone, Evans inner life was revealed in his interactions with others. Ned's behavior was often desperate, sad, and sometimes beyond inappropriate.

One of his most revealing gestures was to reach down the front of his pants and readjust his balls for several minutes. Often, this would happen during a business luncheon in his private dining room. He seemed oblivious to the discomfort this created as his guests struggled with how to react and respond to such outrageous behavior.

I'd never seen such a cry for help expressed with such social contempt.

The Chairman would also crane his neck in such a display of discomfort, that it was clear with anyone with eyes to see that he was literally trying to get out of his body.

One weekend, I confirmed my deductions about Ned Evans and "poor little rich kids," in general. I was working for Abagail Kirsch, a Westchester County caterer, and we were in Connecticut at the semi-annual polo matches which were hosted there.

As luck would have it, when I took a break from bartending, the consultant Kirsch hired to supervise service was on her meal break, too. *"Excuse me,"* I said, *but I have a theory I'd like to run by you if I may?"* *"Sure,* she replied, *what's on your mind?"*

I shared with her how after a few years of doing this party I found myself going crazy every time I worked these matches.

"*What do you mean? she said, tell me more.*"

"*It's the funniest thing*, I replied, *I can start my day feeling great and once I get around these privileged folks, I get twisted up and angry.*"

"*How come?*" she probed.

I explained that there was something about being around these "beautiful people" that set me off and I was determined to figure out why.

"*These folks are like American Brahmins,*" I said, borrowing from the caste system in India. "*They represent everything we're told we should desire. They're well educated, well-spoken, well-traveled yet many of them are in agony. I mean, come on, they have every conceivable advantage; they have it all. So, what's up will all their angst?*"

Then she said, "*they don't have love.*"

Suddenly it all made sense to me. The consultant put her finger on the root cause of my observation. This was the basis of the pain I saw in Ned Evans. The fact that he had it all but didn't have a loving connection to his father, or apparently to anyone else in his family, made all his privilege a torture.

The consultant went on to tell me that this was the reason she'd moved to Florida. She came back once a year for the high fee she received to co-ordinate the polo matches, but she wanted no part of a world absent of real human connection and love.

After years of serving advantaged folk, I came to see that the extremes of being people of privilege but without love are most pronounced in the ruling class of our society. This is a cruel and challenging reality for many wealthy people. Confirmed now by one of their own, it was a reality no one in their right mind would ever envy and a reminder that appearances are often deeply deceiving.

Life without love isn't worth living, and although I can't say love is totally absent among society's *crem de la crem*, its absence lies at the root of the pain that so deeply troubles many folks who are beyond well-heeled.

Sherri

Marion was away in Israel and although we were going steady when she left, I went in a new and unexpected direction that split us up again. After my divorce, except for my reconnection with Ms. Dreyfus, which was a joy, a challenge, and a pleasure, I felt like a dump-truck had run over me. *"What is life trying to tell me? What is it that I most need to learn?"*

The truck was the wreckage of my marriage. This cosmic eighteen-wheeler paused for effect; pulled forward a smidge, then backed up on top of me again to make its point, before finally moving on. The pause was the truth doing its best to get through to me.

This truth-truck was hauling numerous realities such as; *what you give you receive; what you bring to a relationship, you take from the relationship; if you are true to yourself, you can be false to no one. If you lie or you exploit a lie, nothing good will come of it.*

All I knew for sure is that post-divorce I felt crushed, numb, and ashamed. I needed some serious R&R. What I most required besides some plain old fun, was a long, honest look at myself and my behavior. Luckily, I was able to channel all my feelings into my acting. Amidst my numbness, I had a thousand questions.

"Who, what and where am I? Why didn't my marriage work? What's wrong with Paula? What's wrong with me? What do I do with all this? What do I know that is reliable and real? What's it all about, Alfie?"

All this was going on inside me when a new woman came into Susan's acting class. You'd think that given my disastrous encounter with Suzie Adams, and how I allowed that to damage my life with Paula, that the mere idea of another liaison with a fellow student would send me running, but you'd be wrong.

Although I was single now, I was still as blind to reality as I was passionately attracted to Sherrill Wilkinson the minute she walked into Susan Slavin's Actors and Singers Academy.

If only I'd thought, *"Oh, Jesus, here I go again. Don't you dare get involved with anyone until you have a clue about who you are and can constructively relate to another fallible human being, who can also constructively relate to you,"* but instead it was *"WHOA, WHO IS SHE?!?"*

Who was it who said, *"Until learning occurs, punishments continue."* Whoever it was, I was the poster boy for Masochists Anonymous.

Now a whole new battery of questions came up for exploration and review.

What is love? What is lust? What boundaries must I maintain. Which ones can I shatter? How do I distinguish between the two, or is *that even possible? Just what is it with me and UNAVAILABLE WOMEN, anyway?*

No sooner did Sherri come into my world than I approached her about working up a scene for class. She agreed immediately and enthusiastically, and we arranged to meet at her apartment to go over some possibilities right away.

When I showed up at her place, I could feel how turned on she was. Sherri had a visceral appetite for sex. I could feel her desire, but I wasn't sure if her evident thrill wasn't just her excitement about making a transition from being a successful businesswoman to becoming a working actor. She kept herself in check, but she could barely keep her knickers on, and the conflict between her desire and restraint turned me on.

It would've been better if we could've been open and honest with all parties concerned. If Sherri and her husband, <u>*yes, her husband*</u> had been swingers or in an open marriage, that would've been OK. But even if she had his blessing to bed me, in time the toxic psychology beneath what I would learn was her history of extramarital affairs would have come to bear and she would have been off to a new man and a new way to be naughty.

The truth, at least in part, was that Sherri got off being bad. Had this element been absent perhaps our assignation would not have been as hot as it was.

Sherri was as pissed off about her childhood as I was about mine, but she wasn't conscious of this.

In her case, she was an only child who'd been raised by Christian Scientists. She was so angry at second guessing her impulses and at the imposed programming of her parent's religion, that she refused to harness the enormous power of her sexuality in a relationship sustaining way.

I had always prized myself on my discipline as an actor. The oldest and sleaziest con in Show Biz was to do a love scene with an actor and use the feelings it engendered to get her or him into bed.

More often than not, jumping into bed with your acting partner hurt you and your work. The worst part of this is that having sex broke loose tons of archaic crap in both parties that was incredibly difficult to navigate.

Still, when I found out Sherri was married it did nothing to lower my attraction to her. I simply didn't care. In fact, I thought, *"If he isn't strong enough to keep her, he doesn't deserve to have her."*

The reality that there's no fruit like forbidden fruit was about to hit me like a jack-hammer.

I did everything I could to be professional; everything I could think of to diffuse the bomb of pent-up passion and desire that was set to explode, and which very quickly fused us into a compulsive, addictive fuck fest that was destined to overwhelm me. But nothing I used to keep a safe distance, nothing that had worked in the past, worked now.

As we finally went to bed, yet again my poor, neglected still, small guiding voice said, *"If she betrays her husband, she'll betray you."*

Of course, I didn't listen.

The heat and fury of our chemistry blew me away. Our appetites seemed one and the same and so did our carnal enthusiasms. The only problem is we were out of integrity with ourselves and with the people to whom we were supposed to be devoted. I with myself because I went against what I knew to be right. She with her husband because they were not in an open marriage. For my part, I was once more, attempting to build a relationship on quicksand.

There seemed to be tons of *"Here's mommy"* coming out of me and *"Here's daddy"* coming out of her. The real problem when you get to that deep level of intimacy and need, is that your pathologies about mommy and daddy rise up, too.

Suffice it to say that although we tried several times to work together, our acting was compromised by our hidden affair. Sexually, when she needed a hot, passionate fuck, I was only too happy to oblige, so she'd come to my place to get her fix. We'd be close and joyful in our stolen moments, then she'd go her own way till she needed another dose.

After an agonizing back and forth of months like this, I drew the line and told her I was done being a yo-yo. I loved our passion, but I'd become a sex addict; no longer a person but a thing. When I found the strength to say no more, she walked.

Again, I'd confused sex with love. Sherri was blind to what I wanted to create with her, which was a long-term committed relationship that worked. But I was blind, too. Given what went on inside each of us, we'd never be capable of having something real.

Sherri was spoiled and narcissistic; seemingly incapable of loyalty or creating an enduring intimacy with a true-life partner. Until she dealt with her unconscious rage, she'd destroy any relationship with her selfishness.

And I guess, at least in part, the very same was true of me.

I told myself I wanted to do whatever was necessary to form a bond that would last, but did I?

I was biased, of course, but the truth is I tried to make more of our relationship than it ever really was. On her end, I'm not sure Sherri knew what she was missing. She was at her sexual peak, she was hot, and she knew she could get pretty much any man she wanted. Her sexuality gave her power and as long as she could trade on that she could do as she damn well pleased.

At the end of the day, my lover wasn't the marrying kind. Our affair broke up her second and final marriage.

Once my need for integrity and personal dignity caught up with and overtook my desire for Sherri, I grieved the loss of my passion with this poem;

"Oh Eden lighted angel
Whose every depth and breadth I glimpsed
Essence of my own but lost to soon; soon;
Whose fiery damsel-ness I championed day and night on lightening steeds of love, love,
A timelessness we shared; wordless, unspoken;
language and law unheeded, no longer needed.
Whose windvanes of finest lace I sought, Quixote-like and lost.
Your gift to me as mine to you was past our understanding,
my insistent insecurity exposed this life not withstanding
For in the anguish of your loss and my never-ending plight, as I wallowed, lost in a never, ever, ending wrenching day and night...
Salvation came by way of seeming slight;
And by your unloving loving; unknowing knowing, was I restored to self and soul.

Was ever there a greater fool for love; nor one blinder to female wounding, vanity, self-indulgence, and fickleness, than me. The truth as I perceive it is that Sherri felt the pain of her childhood exempted her from the rules of maintaining a lasting intimate relationship, open or not. But again, so did I as evidenced by my manipulation of Paula.

As the more conscious and self-aware one between us, I should have known better than to engage in this sordid, sweet, and sour affair, but like with Suzie, my brains had wandered south of my belt again. Looking back on my failed relationships, I reminded myself of the old missive, *"If wishes were horses, beggars would ride."*

Perhaps it was a coincidence when she ran into me at the Museum of Modern Art. I was bartending an opening there and she had come to that opening with her new beau.

"Oh, Bob I can't believe you're here. HOW ARE YOU? Sherri said, as I withered into an infinitesimal smudge of misery. I mindlessly muttered *"Nice to meet you,"* as she introduced me to the man who was fucking her in my place. Inside, I died a thousand deaths.

Surely, she knew how painful it was for me to see her there with him.

"Goddamn, I thought bitterly to myself in the middle of this terrible encounter, *a merciful, even semi-sensitive person would have turned away in compassion to spare me from seeing them together."*

She was getting back at me for drawing the line. I knew and she knew there was no way the man she was seeing now could match the heat we generated together.

Perhaps the only thing Sherri valued more than hot sex was avenging her lost childhood.

I kept my dignity, but knowing what I'd lost, however untenable it was, launched me into a new round of moping and crying when I got on my own.

Nevertheless, our sex life together was so elemental, that even now, nearly forty years after we parted, I'm glad of our liaison. I had to swallow a bitter pill to awaken from this delightful delusion. Nonetheless, I'm grateful to have been passions fool though I never got involved with a married woman again.

When all was said and done, what happened served me right. No matter how attractive Sherri was to me, I should've known better than to involve myself with someone who's dishonesty with herself, I now fully understand, mirrored my own.

Twenty-nine years after I lost touch with Sherri, I tracked her down and invited her to come to South Africa with me. We had a nice reunion on the phone, but she declined. I kept in touch with her for seven more years, texting her on her birthday. Not once in all that time did she reach out to me on mine.

I'm sure she didn't and doesn't remember my birthday. Of course, I would have gladly reminded her, but she made no effort to find out.

That's when I finally let go of her.

A New Start and The Invitation

When my divorce came through in 1987, a ton of psychic energy broke free within me. Sometime during my separation from Paula, I used this emerging energy to begin a project that would prove to be the next step in my journey. This new chapter involved grappling more directly with an idea I'd pondered for years; exploring the feeling of being alive and dead at the same time.

I began my inquiry with this multi-layered question;

What if I was 500 or even 1000 years old; if I could do, be, or have anything or anyone I wanted, anytime I pleased, and I could live forever, too, what would give my existence meaning and value?

This question drove my exploration of the vampire myth as I began to conceive a new play based on Bram Stoker's classic tale. I loved the period and setting of *Dracula*, and I planned to stay true to it, but I set out to investigate the Count's dilemma and character in a whole new way.

The existential implications of Dracula's situation and how it might drive him to become more fully conscious, intrigued me.

Stoker's novel became the jumping off point for dealing with the dilemma of a creature who has it all yet suffers never-ending loss and unique isolation. In a sense, Dracula the individual embodied both the fulfillment and the dissolution of the American Dream. Moral considerations aside, his immortality and ability to have or take whatever he wanted expressed the longings and dreams of many people I observed, some of whom I knew.

What lies beneath and beyond one's narcissistic fantasies; what is it that gives enduring meaning and purpose to existence? It was delving into the up and downs of this immortal's reality that grabbed me.

From the beginning, I envisioned a scene at the core of my play between what I saw as the animus and anima energies of the shadowy

Dracula and the more consciously aware, presumably moral, but deeply disenfranchised and conflicted Van Helsing.

Contrary to Stoker's conception, I felt it was vital that Van Helsing be not only an iconic character but also an almost a super-woman.

My Count was seeking a higher way of being he could not possess; liberation from a kind of addictive reality and to live in spiritual light. Conversely, my Van Helsing was a wise figure who knew the ways of light and truth but was in denial of her own anger and darkness; someone who used her intelligence and hostility to unsuccessfully mask her rage at being dismissed, ignored, and marginalized as a mere woman in the Progressive Era that followed the Gilded Age.

I saw these two titanic figures exchanging energies, roles, and understandings. Their intimate, private, almost clandestine meeting was the crux of the play. This was the hardest scene for me to write and here's the core of that scene;

DRACULA

Teach me to live and you live, evolve as you have evolved, transcend as you have transcended.

VAN HELSING

Walk into the light.

DRACULA

But why must I die?

VAN HELSING

Because you fear it.

DRACULA

Would you not fear oblivion?

VAN HELSING

Death is no oblivion. It is the passageway to all that is, that was, and will ever be.

DRACULA

What if for me there is no higher realm?

VAN HELSING

It is a soldier's death to fall upon your sword; to walk into the Sun would be no less.

DRACULA

To die selfishly; without purpose, loveless and without honor?

VAN HELSING

Your battles for fortune and glory have long since passed. Pride, alone, defeats you. Your vanity dishonors you, even as you endure.

DRACULA

And if I die, what then?

VAN HELSING

You will be reborn as I was; renewed again and again in the endless cycle of time.

DRACULA

But I live now and forever.

VAN HELSING

And thereby are barred from eternity by your addiction to physical life, forever lost to the life beyond. My death is my evolution; it is the gift of my mortality.

DRACULA

Then pledge to me in equal measure that which you ask of me.

VAN HELSING

Why?

DRACULA

That I may know wherein lies your trust, your faith, your heart.

VAN HELSING

So be it. Make me yours and together we will kiss the glorious morning Sun...

By the time I finished writing this scene and the play, which I entitled *The Invitation*, I came to the conclusion that only growth, evolution, and integration make life livable. That, of course, and most important of all, the ability to love and be loved.

Ironically, it all started in Slavin's acting class. Susan suggested we work on characters and material that spoke to us, and if we couldn't find such material, that we write our own. As I went about searching for interesting material on vampires, most of what I came up with was mere fluff.

Anne Rice was the only writer I found who truly took on the dilemma of the *Nosferatu*. Rice thoroughly addressed the undead's need for meaning. She concluded that in order to go on they must abandon their remaining humanity. Her vampire mission statement was this; *reinvent yourself as something new and unique; leave the past behind.*

Rice nourished my take on the myth but I went in a completely different direction. For me, the vampire was only compelling if he or she struggled to resolve the humanity that survived their life as humans. As I saw it, they could not cast it aside. As much as blood sustained them now, it was the meaning humans seek that impelled them to find purpose and direction beyond their survival needs.

My personal struggle with the myth involved integrating my own shadow. The understanding I came to is that I must embrace my dark side. I must own, experience, and express it, not literally but symbolically.

For me and the Dracula I wrote; only by embracing my shadow could I transcend it.

Writing *The Invitation* was the most intense experience I had up to this point in my life. As a first time playwright, I loved being in absolute control of and yet free to explore my creative destiny. Once the first draft was done, the next step was to secure a workshop production, then cast, rehearse, and perform the play to see how it did on its feet.

That process began when I met Robert Baker, a remote but spiritually gifted man who "just happened" to live in my apartment building in the Washington Heights neighborhood of upper Manhattan.

We first encountered each other riding the elevator in our building. Casual hellos led to brief conversations until I mentioned one day I'd just written a play and asked Robert if he'd like to read it. When he said yes, I gave him a copy of the manuscript.

Two weeks later, during which time I secured a production of the piece with a new works festival called T.W.E.E.D., Robert got back to me and said he loved the play and invited me to discuss it over dinner at his apartment. The upshot was he would like to direct this new age Dracula and when I told him I now had a venue, a producing partner, and date to open the play, we agreed he would direct, and I would co-produce and play the Count.

Robert never wanted me to play Dracula. If the truth be known, he would have loved to direct and play the Count, too. We butted heads about this, but eventually he conceded that it was my choice as playwright and co-producer to cast the lead as I saw fit, and that no one knew my Dracula's intentions better than me.

There was some competition for the director's role, and though I considered my friend John Jubak for that position, I stuck with Robert. *I had a strong sense that my association with him had a future dimension that was far more significant than my play and who would direct it.*

Creatively, Baker and I were incompatible. He was controlling, rigid and his conception of the Count was far too old-school, Bela Lugosi for me.

CLOCKING the GOOSE

My desire to explore the character in rehearsal also ran counter to his approach. He didn't really get what I was going for with the Count, but Robert had great style, an excellent sense of pacing, and access to a treasure trove of period costumes, so I stuck with him.

Again, this was mostly because of my sense that something after the play was produced would come of our relationship. It was also true at this stage of development that *The Invitation* was more an outline than a finished piece of writing. When we video-taped the last festival performance I saw a play with wonderful tempo and production values but no real life. It was essentially stillborn and certainly fell short of the existential exploration I'd intended.

Ironically, this too turned out to be a blessing in disguise. In the aftermath of our production, I dug deeper to write a much stronger piece. My intuition about Baker also panned out. Not only did I work with him in life changing ways later on, but his mentors, June and Jim Spencer saw what I was going for and helped me to round out the play.

As an actor, I learned from watching my performance on video tape that I must always hold something in reserve. If I exceeded my limits, if I hit my top, I'd lose my audience. Hereto, I learned that pacing must always be grounded in something human and real. Most of all I came to realize that my experience of the emotional reality of my part must always be subordinate to the audiences' experience of the play.

From a writer's standpoint, I learned that writing for the stage was about pairing dialogue down to the bone; that one must capture and keep the audience with discourse that advanced action, built tension and conflict, and that forced the audience to go with you or be left behind.

Career-wise *The Invitation* marked the end of my acting days. This was fine by me because I left the stage writing and producing something I was proud of and that expressed my values and concerns as a human being. I didn't see myself topping this experience and although I loved the process of building a role, I detested show business and could not reconcile the two. I was glad to be free of the horrors of the actor's life, and I've never missed performing or second guessed my decision to stop.

By now, I'd learned that it was far more important to follow my truest inner voice than conform to someone else's expectations of me. I needed to follow my sense of what was right and true for me. My purpose in life was to experience and explore the themes that moved me, and to seek whatever was next in my journey, regardless of whether my choices made sense to anyone else.

In a way I'll expand on shortly, I'd come to understand that acting was familiar to me in a past life sense, and that I had been highly successful acting in prior incarnations, but now I was meant to go beyond what life would have been for me had I remained an actor.

What I was seeking went beyond self-expression or celebrity; and way beyond what performing alone could now offer me. I'd been falsely instructed that to be successful I must package myself like a human tube of toothpaste, and I'd have none of it. What I needed now, which I'll also expand on soon, was to empower other people free of the pressures of the spotlight.

I refused to be trapped by anyone else's preconceptions. I also feared I would sell out if I limited myself to acting, alone. At the time I quit acting in 1990, I didn't have the clarity I have here and now, I only had the sense that it was time for me to move on.

CLOCKING the GOOSE

It would take a few more years to put all this together and to understand my true calling.

Mom's wedding engagement-1945   1953 - Early troubles with Dad

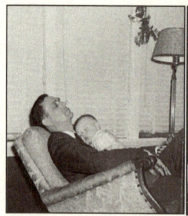 

Pop and me - two warriors in repose   1955 – Rick watching over me

A stranger in a strange land or Why am I sitting on this guy's lap? 1956

The two Bobbys – Angelic and Naughty Bob – Who will win the day?

Robert Moseley

A photographic metaphor for how I was raised – 1964

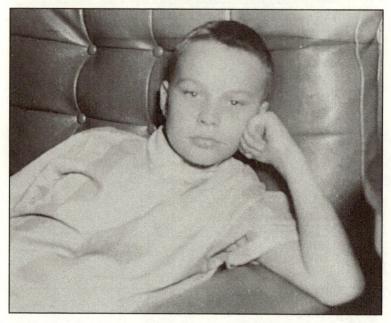

The young writer within the fighter pilot

CLOCKING the GOOSE

The Moseley kids 1960

Two photographs of our happy family 1964 and 1968

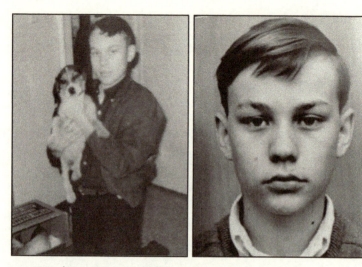

My 11th birthday December 12 1963 with Sir George Beagle and my first passport photo 1966

June 1966 - The Great Pyramid at Giza and the Sphinx

Local transportation in Santorini 1966   Acne 1969

After my final performance as MacBeth - June 1981

Pop and me on my wedding day May 19, 1984

Family vacation in Penscola. Notice Rick's "tell" – 1996

Mom in her dotage, around 2010

Dad at retirement - 1987

Machu Picchu – May 1997

Indiana Jones at the railhead Machu Picchu – May 1997

Chillin in Dunfermline, Scotland, June 2023

North Berwick at Twilight-rear view of the course from the 17th green, Scotland, June 2023

Bob sinks a birdie putt at Kinross, Scotland, June 2023

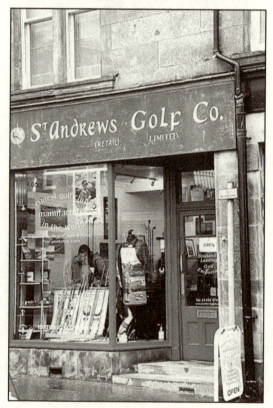

A Classic Scots Golf Emporium

The Wrecking Crew gets TOASTED, Edinburgh, Scotland, June 2023. From the left Mat, Jimbo, Me, Michael and Travis.

Robert Moseley

Bob at home - August 2024

CHAPTER VI:
Life gets Metaphysical

Loose Ends and Angelic Interventions

These next several stories relate to my experience as a spiritual seeker and my start/stop career as a teacher in a variety of fields. It was during this period I returned to my roots and broke new emotional, philosophical, and professional ground. As I now entered an entirely new phase of my journey, at times I found myself at loose ends. I taught acting, which was a joy, then left teaching for a while, only to return to it as a golf instructor, and then as an astrologer.

Despite the fact that I was going from one type of work to another every few years, I see now how beautifully one job led to the other and how, when taken as a whole, each of these steps directed me back to a fuller connection with my heart.

I'd always wanted my career to be an expression of something that I loved and in ways I didn't fully understand yet, a process of reduction was occurring. It began as a quest to reclaim myself, moved into a reunion with the golf I first loved as a boy, and progressed into a metaphysical career as an astrologer, and today as a writer.

During this period I would learn the essence of being an effective teacher, encounter mystical and extraterrestrial energies in Peru, learn from a difficult new woman in my life how to love myself by accepting my self-hatred, and apply all this to writing this book.

In this time, I also began to realize that life was not a destination one arrived at but an ongoing series of experiences, experiments, and explorations. My life was made up of periods that had their individual rhythm and meaning but were also connected to my existence as a whole. By allowing these different episodes to flow from one to another, by going with the process of change, these experiences also helped me identify my working values as a person and connect to a truer sense of purpose.

Taken all together, going with these many changes empowered me to be of service to others by reconnecting to myself.

<u>Gabriel</u>

When I met Robert Baker, I connected to something powerful I couldn't quite put my finger on. It wasn't so much a personal vibe as a transpersonal energy. This vibrancy, and what it led to, took me to a place deeper than I'd ever been; the experience of feeling truly alive.

When Robert began to channel the archangel Gabriel in November of 1990, I knew this was the real purpose of our meeting. The transpersonal aura I felt when we first met was Gabriel's energy.

What I learned from Gabby, our nickname for him because he had so much to say and spoke at a rapid clip, made all my conflicts working with Robert on *The Invitation* seem as trivial as they were.

I can understand how many folks might take exception to the phenomenon of channeling. My original thought, however, was, *"it only seems fair to me. With all the shit we go through in life, its only right that God would give us an angelic heads up from time to time, provided we're open to applying the guidance."*

The challenge came with doing whatever was necessary to shift my beliefs and behavior so I could apply what I learned. I didn't see much difference between channeling and doing affirmations or praying. The more I thought about angelic guidance and spiritual work, the more confident I was that taking part in these gatherings would be a major part of my continuing evolution.

A group of us began to meet at Robert's apartment in my building late every Sunday afternoon. At each of these sessions, I imagined myself in the core of a spiritual/nuclear reactor. Somehow, I knew I would get the benefits of this divine energy just by showing up. I was right about this and for the next dozen years working with angelic and spiritual information would be my primary focus.

Gabriel's fundamental message, and that of every religion and wisdom tradition world-wide is *"the kingdom of God is within us."* To me, this means I have everything I need inside me to do whatever I intend, especially if that creation is truly aligned with my heart, mind, and spirit. The key to tapping this power is to stay open to ALL my emotions, regardless of how I feel about having them.

It was a simple formula. Applying it was and remains the challenging part.

Understanding how attachment works was a big piece of growing spiritually. All my life I'd pushed away my "bad" feelings about things that happened to me. In truth, this resistance and denial just made me hold on to those experiences and to the negativity that came with them. The story I made up about my life felt real, but it was just a story.

My victim viewpoint skewered my view of reality, and I stayed in a negative behavior loop because of it. Again, as I've acknowledged in earlier stories, I was terrified of feeling deficient; of feeling what Gabby called *"not good enough."*

Worse still, I'd developed the habit of *thinking about* myself vs. *allowing myself to be*. The default belief I held as a child had been *"what's wrong with me."* Now it had devolved to the point that I viewed my entire being as a negative object; a flawed thing. I was no longer *living life*; I was reacting to *a concept of me* that alienated me from my true self and blocked me from being the person I was meant to become.

Seeing myself as a broken object that needed fixing, as opposed to a fluid and evolving creation that could always adapt, froze me, and kept me at odds with myself.

Once I fully grasped that I was not a broken object but a living, breathing, adaptable work in progress, I began to transform.

The real work of liberation came in learning how to have my feelings, not to let my fear and hatred of my emotions shut me down. The key here was to allow and experience the feelings I hated most, because denying them healing expression denied me life!

By blocking my killer, or my brat, or my rage, I cut off my power source. Once I cleared out the cobwebs of my distorted and denied emotional memories, once I'd reclaimed and released those threatening old feelings by finally letting myself fully experience and express them free of judgment or condemnation, the next step was to commit myself fully to my goals without attachment to results or how the outcomes of my actions showed up.

In liberating myself, I gained awareness, too, that all the darker shades of my inner life; anger, hate, bitterness, resentment, and all the rest, were actually my allies. Properly understood and integrated they restored my boundaries and my inner equilibrium. Letting these once repressed and despised feelings out but keeping safe boundaries doing so, was like letting an internal thunderstorm clear imbalances in the personal ecosystem that was me.

My emotions had two purposes; one, to energize and sustain my life force, and two, to restore my stability when I got off kilter.

Overall, I discovered that my state of consciousness was determined by my deepest emotional commitments. It was the depth of these commitments, regardless of whether they were positive or negative, conscious or denied, that was at the crux of my personal reality.

If I shut down any part of me, I shut down all of me.

This was true in spite of my age or level of awareness. So, if I cut off an emotion or a person when I was two years old, as I had in Tyson Park, it was necessary for me to revisit and reframe that experience. Doing this brought me into the present moment and gave me the energy to create the life that was right for me.

Finally, I learned from Gabby that there's a light and shadow element in all things, at all times. All the parts of me I'd shamed, dismissed, or denied lived in my shadow-self in a sort of spiritual layaway. Until I reclaimed these disowned parts, I would never be happy or wholly human and alive.

To say all this was exactly what I'd been looking for would be a colossal understatement. It was the perspective I needed and had searched for my entire life.

Appropriate to the size and significance of this insight, the power of my willfulness and my desire to say NO to all these liberating perspectives came up in spades.

This was confirmation that I'd hit upon something real.

So, I had a choice to make, and it was mine alone. What was refreshing about all of this is that I now realized my old commitment to negative action mirrored my positive potential. My desire to punish and deny joy to others by hurting myself was the shadowy reflection of my force of will.

Now I could move forward. My darkness and rage could be turned to the good, if only I would make way for it by finally and fully dealing with my shit.

Inevitably, the group sessions with Gabriel evolved into private sessions with Robert, but I resisted this. I suppose I judged Robert. He had many destructive traits that made me mistrust his ability to help me help myself. Baker smoked, drank, and drugged himself to medicate his inner demons. Despite this, working privately with him became trendy and fashionable, too, and I wasn't comfortable with that either.

To my thinking, Gabby's message and guidance transcended his channel's personal limitations and addictions.

At that time, Ron Baker was Robert's partner in life and in the healing business they created. Although I felt more *simpatico* with Ronnie, I also felt he was the driving force behind the expansion of their healing business in ways that made it feel like the related services I'd took exception to when I was in Slavin's acting class.

For all these reasons, I decided to stand pat with the Sunday group lectures and work on myself by myself.

The shadow side of our Gabriel group, also similar to what had happened in my acting class, took the form of narcissism rooted in too much self-involvement.

Nevertheless, to some degree, I used my viewpoint to avoid working on myself as deeply as was necessary.

When Ron and Robert opened <u>Children of Light,</u> a healing center on the upper west side of Manhattan, it appeared they were bringing the information that emerged from years of Sunday group sessions out to the world.

In my observation, although there may be facts I was unaware of, COL seemed to be about Ron and Robert and their vision of themselves as successful healers. What was missing for me at COL was a true sense of giving back to the community, of providing guidance free of charge for folks in need of spiritual grounding and direction but without the resources to pay for mentoring and guidance.

Who to subsidize vs. who to charge might have been problematic, but I felt that could be worked out in some sort of exchange of services arrangement. Sadly, at least from what I could see, no real community outreach element happened at the Baker's healing center.

What is more, the training that people paid for who aspired to build a clientele of their own seemed to exclude partnership with the center to help them grow their own businesses as healers. They were left to their own devices in this, at least as I perceived it, and I felt there should be some part of their training that helped them find and cultivate their own clients.

Spiritual pilgrimages to sacred sites around the world, also became a big part of the healing agenda at COL. This involved group trips to Egypt, Tibet, Peru, and other spiritual centers across the globe. Preparations for these journeys were elaborate and the trips cost several thousand dollars each. If the kingdom of God is within me, I didn't see the value of these pilgrimages relative to their cost.

At COL it wasn't the message that I found lacking, but Ron and Robert's agenda. Both of them worked hard, they truly helped people, and they deserved to be well paid for their efforts. Nevertheless, the personal transformations they promised would take place if you made these trips didn't happen.

People had their personal shit, and that shit remained for them to deal with whether they went to Egypt and Tibet, or not. Everything I needed to work on was right in front of me, here and now.

I did make one trip with our Gabby group to Peru, and it was a wonderful experience, but it wasn't life-changing, so I didn't feel drawn to make the many other pilgrimages that followed.

Over time, I found myself wanting to do more in the world with what I'd learned from Gabriel. I wanted to work with regular folks; to see what might be possible, not just be surrounded by spiritual acolytes.

As I began to separate from COL and even the Sunday sessions, I got involved with a men's organization called MDI. It was there we conceived a Fathering Forum program where dad's mentored dad's to be better at raising their kids.

Along with the spiritual excavation I accomplished by learning the craft of acting, I count my experience with Gabby one of the most significant and constructive pursuits of my entire life. I wouldn't hesitate recommending any true seeker work with Ron Baker, although I didn't do so myself.

Sadly, Robert died suddenly of cancer in 2013. He made a great contribution to the quality of my life and the record of Gabriel's lectures available via Children of Light's website is a treasure trove of solid, life-enhancing information and guidance.

Although I feel Robert's bad habits exacerbated his declining health and death, I'm glad I trusted my gut and stayed in relationship with him long after we worked on *The Invitation*. Knowing him made a powerful, positive difference in how I live, and I'll always be grateful for the contribution his work made to my life.

No where Man in a No Man's Land: Finding and filling my Own 0Void

The spiritual perspective I developed with Gabriel opened my frame of mind. I was becoming more accepting of myself and others The years from 1992 to 95 were pretty much an in-between time for me. I mostly served at catered parties, played some golf, and attended to my work with Gabriel.

Though no clear theme or activity marked this period, I was doing serious and consistent work on myself. Looking back, it feels like I was in an extended period of incubation.

I was still unconscious and resistant to seeing the reality of my emotional conflicts and commitments, but now I was becoming more intentional, and less habit driven. At the same time, although I had implicit trust in Gabriel's information and guidance, I didn't really trust Robert as a spiritual practitioner.

Fundamentally, this was an evasion on my part. It didn't make a damn bit of difference what Robert did or didn't do. The work I needed to do <u>was the work I needed to do</u>. Still, from a human perspective I looked to Robert for leadership.

Something similar had happened when Paula and I were in marriage counseling. Roland Reed, our therapist, was wrapped up in some personal shit and this kept him from being fully present in our sessions. I wasn't quite sure how to call him out on this so one day I just said, *"hey, man. if your gonna lead us through the valley of the shadow of death, I want to make damn sure you have a firm grip on the flashlight."*

Reed got my point and became more focused. Perhaps I should have said as much to Robert, but I didn't.

I had no intention of following his lead just because he had a connection to "dispense" higher guidance. Until I saw him get his personal shit together, and in my view he never did, I would only rely on him as a conduit of spiritual information and insight.

Just as I began my journey with Gabriel, I was ending my studies with Susan Slavin. I guess this was a case of one door closes and another opens. As I was headed out Susan's door, which was the death knell of my affair with Sherri, I started dating yet another woman I met in Slavin's class, (surprise, surprise).

Sharron Crocker was from rural Maine, but she had a style and sophistication that belied her humble origins. She was blissfully available, without major prior wounds or baggage, and was joyfully self-sufficient.

Best of all, we were good to each other and good for each other.

We began seeing each other after Sherri and I were done, and while I was still in Susan's class. Getting to know each other at a very relaxed pace, we agreed it was best to keep our burgeoning relationship on the QT. Part of this was because Susan had figured out that it wasn't such a great idea for her students to get involved with each other. So, Ms. Slavin asked us to keep things professional, although go figure, she herself married one of her pupils.

Talented, sensitive, and beautiful, Sharron was genuinely compatible with my mad, passionate but also tender, demonstrative, and loving self. We didn't have the heat of my affair with Sherri, but we communicated well, and we built a very solid, happy sex-life. I loved that Sharron and I had good rapport and our union worked.

I'd long since let go of cloning my father as a way of being and now I was moving past Slavin's market driven image system, too.

I guess I'd finally grown up enough to be comfortable finding my own way.

The one thing missing in my relationship with Sharron was agreement on the Gabriel work. She was never open to it or comfortable exploring it. We were happy but never really considered marriage. Sharron was content with our companionship, but I wanted more.

After nearly three years together, we broke up. From my perspective, we stopped growing together. She didn't protest because she knew I needed more, and for the first time in my life, I ended an intimate partnership without an ounce of angst and just moved on.

Sometimes I think this was a mistake, but long term I believe moving on was the correct choice.

Alone again but free now of my lover's doubts and resistance to my spiritual perspective, I felt able to explore my possibilities with a free hand.

Still, I could never have anticipated what would come next.

On Teaching and Being Taught

When I began to consider what I'd do after acting, I was still in Slavin's class. Susan had done all she could to help me become conventionally successful. After a decade of working with her I had grown as an actor, learned how to work effectively, developed confidence in my skills and done some fine work.

Neither Susan nor I had been able to figure out why I held myself back. Near the end, knowing I'd made the decision to stop acting, she took me through an exercise to explore what might be next for me. When I said I might like to teach acting, something I'd never considered before, Susan tried to hide it, but she squirmed in her chair like I'd put a hot poker up her.

It was crystal clear she thought I'd steal her secrets. Suddenly, I was the competition and the enemy. Well, I'd paid nearly twenty grand for her tricks of the trade, many which I dismissed, and I'd use them as I damn well pleased.

Her reaction made me angry and sad, but I wasn't entirely surprised. In terms of becoming an independent, empowered, self-directed and working professional actor, I'd been studying with the wrong person for years.

In a way, Susan and I were very much alike. We were both enormously willful. For all her skills as a teacher, she was unprepared or incapable of seeing beyond her viewpoint and agenda. For all my skills as an actor, I refused to realistically pursue a career. It was good that I didn't, too, but learning why would only become clear to me as I got further down the road.

After the "hot poker" exchange I left Susan's class and didn't think further about teaching acting. Jean Hammons, however, a peer who also studied with me at Slavin's studio, taught a musical performance class of her own. She made note of my interest in teaching.

Shortly after I left Studio 912, Jean contacted me about taking over her class. She was leaving the Big Apple and wanted me to do a teaching audition so her pupils and I could feel each other out. If this went well, Jean would offer me the opportunity to buy her established class.

Hammons had several people audition to teach her class so her students could evaluate a broad range of instructors and teaching styles. I'd never taught anything but decided to give it a shot. After several people vied for the assignment, her pupils picked me.

We agreed that for a specified time, Jean would get a cut from the set monthly fee of each one of her established students, and I would keep that entire amount for individuals I brought in on my own.

Suddenly, I was in a position to give of myself in the one area of Show Biz I loved; the craft. I was my own boss, and free to teach as I saw fit. I made it clear to my new charges that my background was in acting so acting a song would be the central focus of our class. I shit canned finding your color palate and all the image stuff and focused on what was unique about each one of my students. I shared my belief that they needed an artistic focus, though it wouldn't hurt to have a business plan, and that they needed to devote themselves to serving the public.

I developed a catch phrase that summed up my philosophy. *"The only thing more important than success is deserving to be successful."*

The implication here was that each of my students must bring real value and social commitment to their paying audience. Devote yourself to the work, not to your image or ego. Offer your audience characterizations and productions that stur the pot of conformity. Make them think. Become athletes of the human heart and spirit. Let your acting and singing mirror your audience's complex and contradictory humanity.

This is what it means to be performing artists.

Soon I came face to face again with my *"No success allowed self-sabotage."* I found this same mechanism existed in most of my students, too. Moreover, I quickly discovered that the majority of my pupils were committed *to looking for <u>but not having</u>* success.

I'd bought a group of *wanna-bees*.

Despite these limitations, I did my best to educate, expand and inspire my singers. I taught them how to break their songs down from a craft perspective and left it to them to prepare vocally.

Several elements are needed for a class to produce disciplined, working performers. All these qualities must be present in the teacher and the student and are of equal importance.

1.**Talent**. One must begin with talent and the desire to fulfill it. Talent is an intangible. You have it or you don't. It is made up of your voice, body, mind, and imagination. All these elements must flow into a singular ability to create the given circumstances of a character in relatable, intriguing yet believable ways.

Performance Therapy for 9 to 5 working folks is a profitable cottage industry, but if you don't have talent, you've got no business being in a class with people who do and who are committed to becoming professional performers.

2. Self-Mastery. The desire for self-mastery. It's up to the actor or singer to gain access to their deepest parts and then get command of them. Containment is the key function of self-mastery. Most people develop personality traits that mask their inmost reality. An expert performer can and must be in touch with their molten core, then craft characteristics that comply with or deny that core energy. The heart of a character and the traits that disguise that nucleus are often very different.

3. Discipline. It takes hard and consistently challenging work to become a craftsperson. Once mastered, your voice, body, imagination, and movement skills need to be utilized, nourished and drilled to stay sharp.

4. Context. To sustain a career and the hazards a performer faces, he or she must have a compelling *"why"* to contextualize their *"how."* Why am I performing? For whose benefit? What is my social commitment and how can I be loyal to that larger purpose in ways that inspire me to endure all the hardships that attend the performer's journey.

Ironically, even with my real passion for acting and the deep and detailed perspective I had on it after years of study and practice, I still couldn't make of my teaching what I knew it should be. As I taught, I felt I was showing my pupils how to recycle their old wounds to get their character effects, instead of moving through and going beyond those wounds.

At this point, getting past my wounds was what I really wanted to do. I wanted to go beyond all the goddamn drama, and get centered in something authentic, lasting, and real.

Just as therapy had become an over rehearsed alibi for why I didn't have the life I SAID I wanted, performing kept me an infant. This is a big piece of WHY it wasn't good for me to have a successful career in show biz.

For me and where I was in my soul's journey, acting was about recycling old wounds to produce real effects, but I wanted and needed to go deeper than that. I needed to do more than dramatize other people's stories.

Once I realized this, my heart went out of my teaching, and I let it go.

Machu Picchu & an unexpected turn in a familiar direction

"You simply must go on this trip. It will change your life in the best way possible forever," was the implied message regarding all the Gabriel pilgrimages. Each and every trip was certain to transform me.

Oddly, I didn't see this happen for any of the folks who regularly made these journeys.

When I finally decided to go with the Gabriel group to Machu Picchu in 97', I thought I'd use the trip to renew and recommit to my teaching business. But the truth is I was done with show biz in all its forms.

Although our trip was only ten days long, the rituals we did in Peru were so intense it felt like we were there a month. My friend Peter Frame, who had been a principal dancer with New York City Ballet, and was now a much beloved instructor there, roomed with me. The reduced oxygen in Cusco, which was 12,000 feet in altitude, was a major problem for Peter and some others in our group.

Aware of this hazard, the Peruvians at the airport gave us coca leaves to chew when we our plane from Lima arrived. This revved-up our internal organs and helped us acclimate to the thin air.

We were also instructed to rest. As I laid on the bed in my hotel room, I remember my entire circulatory system was stressed to the point that I could feel all my arteries and veins carrying blood throughout my body. It was an odd but fascinating sensation.

What I liked most about Peru were the heart-centered people. They were simple and kind and they created a vibe of serenity and grace. Geographically, I'd never seen earth toned colors like those I saw on our day trips. I also loved how the water in a flushed toilet spun opposite its normal direction because we were south of the equator.

The night before we got to Machu Picchu, which highlighted the trip, we travelled to Ollantaytambo. While there we did a ritual on the mountain top, and I brought and buried my wedding ring there as a sacrifice to make peace with the bad juju I still carried from my marriage to Paula.

Tim Chambers, another healer in our party, stayed with me when we decided to sleep on the mountain top at Ollantaytambo. Neither one of us got a wink of sleep but when we saw an amazing spaceship appear our lack of sleep no longer seemed to matter. *"Do you see what I see?,"* Tim said. *"Oh, yeah,"* I replied. The UFO we were watching was the size of the mothership in *Close Encounters of the Third Kind*, and it instantly shifted position several times, covering several miles in a flash.

By the time we got to Mach Picchu I was exhausted and the cabana-like hotel we stayed at in the valley below the ruins there provided us with much needed respite after the mostly spartan accommodations we'd had up to that point.

Not long before we arrived at Machu there'd been a jungle fire that burned out of control for several days. The natives were concerned their famous ruins would be overrun. Miraculously, a monsoon appeared out of nowhere and doused the flames which came right up to the edge of the site.

The entire perimeter of Machu Picchu was black for months and the border area had barbed wire with skull and crossbones signs every few feet.

The worst part of our journey was when we came back to the states via Miami. At the airport there I felt bombarded by wave after wave of commercials, and a glut of other media blitzes that all seemed to scream the same message; *"you're not enough, you're not enough, you're not enough."*

From my viewpoint now, America is a great place relative to the corruption and troubles that exist elsewhere in the world, but we're corrupt and troubled, too. Peru had a lot to teach everyone everywhere about living from a heart centered place.

Roberto Borgatti and following my Bliss

By now I'd completely and happily let go of performing. Probably because I'd given my heart and soul to acting, I didn't miss it. Now I was free to move on. The space this created inside me opened up my gift for coaching, but I'd neglected if not sabotaged my teaching business much as I had my acting career.

Deep down inside I knew I'd reclaimed massive chunks of my humanity via my training and performing, and I finally realized this goal had been my real reason for acting all along. Although I enjoyed teaching acting, and it was free of most of the bullshit that managing a performer's career required, it was also a way of holding on to a life way of life I no longer needed to pursue.

Drama, both making it and teaching it, was over for me now, or so I hoped. At any rate, it was past time for me to walk away from show business. Happily, I got what I needed from acting and was able to steer clear of being chewed up by the destructive elements of what show biz wanted from me.

Joseph Campbell, the famous mythologist, said *"follow your bliss."* I tried now to do just that. To keep my sanity during this transition, I played golf because it was the only thing that brought me joy while I resumed cater-waiting to make a living. Almost as an aside and to save money, I volunteered as a marshal at Vanny so I could golf for free while I sorted my life out.

One afternoon at Vanny, as I took a few practice swings to loosen up before driving off the first tee, I was blindsided by a warm, booming voice that proclaimed to everyone in earshot, *"with a backswing like that, you must be a Pro."* "Who the hell is this," I thought as I turned to see who was analyzing my swing.

Roberto Borgatti grinned at me with an engaging smile that could defang an angry cobra on its worst day. He combined the best of Enrico Caruso, with whom he could compete as a singer, and the best of Walter Hagan, who was America's first touring golf pro, and with whom he could have competed as a player.

I quickly discovered Roberto had a fantastic personality.

A former All-America golfer at the University of North Carolina, he'd been a teammate of the successful tour pro, Davis Love III. Currently, Roberto was an independent instructor with a following of students at World of Golf in Manhattan. He also had a group of players he taught at City Athletic Club. On this day, he was giving a playing lesson to a student on my home course at Van Cortlandt Park.

Originally from Massachusetts and a generation younger than me, Roberto was a renaissance man of enormous energy, grace, and ability. It was a measure of his confidence that he made an excellent living without being affiliated with the PGA of America, and therefore was free of their rigid regulations.

In other words, he was his own man living on this own terms.

A born teacher with a great ability to play the game at a very high level, Robo also had a seemingly flakey side, though he was anything but a flake. No one who played golf at his level lacked the ability to concentrate. Roberto's uniqueness was due to the unusual cant and scope of his mind.

Amidst the clutter inside his Nissan SUV there were always several books of wide-ranging subjects. Next to a tome on *The Philosophy of Mathematics*, there might be a book on operatic vocal technique, or one entitled *Communism in Modern Dance and Geopolitical Art*.

Borgatti would stay up all night reading in between love making bouts with his current flame. He had a thing for sopranos, and seemingly had a string of girls he was seeing or planning to take up with. Amidst the frenzy of his joyfully active life, for when he rested I don't know, he'd get up at dawn to pick up two students for 18 hole playing lessons at a rate of $500 per pupil, grab me too, giving me a massively discounted lesson rate, and shoot 68. After all this, he'd treat our entire party to lunch, drop us at our homes and move into the night combining a new book to read, a vocal recital to give, and a new girl to take out on the town.

To this day I have never met a bigger-hearted, more energetic, or infectiously joyful soul.

From the very beginning Roberto saw my love of golf. Moreover, he saw I had an excellent eye for swing technique and a gift for teaching the game. Since he knew I was in a transition phase, one day he said, *"hey, why don't you teach golf for a living?"*

The Royal and Ancient game had been my first love but my talent and ability to play it at the level necessary to become a pro was missing.

At least, that's how I saw it then.

But golf wasn't all about playing the game. There were many ways to make a living in the industry. What was missing in my ball-striking was counter-balanced by my analytical eye. Moreover, I was good with people, articulate, and I had the ability to feel what was going on in someone's body as they swung and fix their flaws.

"Maybe Roberto is right, why not teach golf?" I began to think. And so, what began as a fantasy, moved to a possibility, and finally became a viable goal. My new friend quickly became my mentor and greatest advocate. The tenor-pro went out of his way to teach me his conception of the golf swing, a subject whose study had been a life-long passion for both of us, and then he got me work teaching golf.

Roberto was an indispensable inspiration. He helped open my heart to go for something I'd always loved, to start pursuing a career in golf from where I was now and instilled in me the belief I could eventually become the head professional at a fine golf club.

Whether it was in golf or life, the lesson I learned from my newfound guardian angel was that my dreams could come true when my talents, commitments, and my heart aligned. My bliss was and always had been golf.

The ease of my transition into the game both amazed me and left me feeling it was the right thing for me to do now. I didn't question this, and I didn't allow my modest playing ability (I usually shot in the low 80's) dissuade me from believing in my ability to teach the game.

In no time, Roberto turned me onto Max Galloway, the head pro at the Bronx Family Golf Center. Max needed a teacher and was an intriguing figure in his own right. A Class "A" PGA pro, Galloway was as skilled and resourceful as he was remote. On the surface he could be friendly and was always professional, but at heart he was an introvert and a loner.

Family Golf had expanded rapidly, too rapidly it would turn out, and our facility on Gun Hill Road in the Bronx was the last of several sites the undercapitalized and over-extended company built.

The best thing about the company was its unbeatable program of lesson packages at low rates. This approach gave participants access to practice under the supervision of pros. I'd never seen a more constructive training program. Roberto arranged for me to audition my swing and knowledge of the game with Max. We discussed the spot he had open, I got the job, and soon became very successful selling lesson packages, in addition to giving lessons.

After only one season, Family Golf went bankrupt, but I didn't skip a beat. Billy Castner, another PGA pro of long standing in the area, offered me a place teaching at another driving range close by at Turtle Cove. I was able to set my own rates there, and he also hired me to work at Mansion Ridge Golf Club in Monroe, New York.

Mansion Ridge was a signature design of the great Jack Nicklaus. It was a fantastic track and a fairly easy commute by train. I worked there during the week and taught at Turtle Cove in the Bronx on weekends.

The beauty of a great golf course at dawn or twilight is like heaven on earth, at least it is for me. That's how I viewed Mansion Ridge as I played the course for the first time. It was an early spring morning, dew was on the fragrant, freshly mown turf, and the fact that I was working now at a course designed by my hero Nicklaus, made the combination of playing challenges and serenity there all the more special to me. I was 48 going on 49 and beginning a new chapter in a life that had been anything but doctrinaire or predictable.

The layout at Mansion was first rate. The fairways were generously wide and depending on which tees you played, the track was as friendly or as challenging as you wanted to make it. After a gentle start, the holes became progressively harder till it was all you could handle at the end. From the tips, Mansion played nearly 7400 yards, and when the wind came up it could be brutal. If a breeze was blowing against me, I could hit my best drive from the blue tee box and not make the front of the fairway on many Par 4's.

My favorite holes were the 5th, 9th and 10th and the finish from 14 through 18. Set in the rolling and hilly parklands of southeastern New York, you could walk the course with or without a caddie if you had a death wish, but it really called for a riding cart.

The Ridge provided a variety of risk/reward scenarios that always tempted and tested my abilities but pleased my eye and enhanced my senses. The challenge of golf was to tack like a sailor through nature in all sorts of weather, using my mind, body, and spirit, the use of which varied with my moods and physical condition. Being honest about my capabilities day to day was crucial to scoring but so was luck.

This was never truer than when I took my PAT (Player Ability Test) at Mansion Ridge.

The test required me to play thirty-six holes in one day in 156 strokes, or less, which translated to two rounds of 78 or better. This would put me on track to get my own class A PGA professional card.

Two pars, the second from a long putt on the par 3 second hole had me off to a good start. On the third, I slightly pushed my drive which settled on a gentle upslope, leaving me 175 yards to the center of the green. Using my 6-iron, I struck this approach shot beautifully, but the uphill lie shortened my normal carry, and my ball landed in the deepest bunker just right of the front of the green.

Two shots to exit the bunker and two more to get down and I'd doubled bogeyed number 3. SHIT!

When it comes down to it, golf is a game of the mind. Your game always reflects your belief in yourself, your resiliency and focus, and most of all your self-esteem. Golf can expose you to the bone and that's what happened in my PAT.

All this came to bear on the fourth hole. The confluence of my negative self-concept, the lack of entitlement I felt, and the anxiety I had about moving through all that crap to build a life I truly wanted, appeared as a foozled approach shot that I semi-shanked out of bounds to my right. The shot was an anomaly, pure nerves. I then went on a bogey run that seriously damaged my chance to make the grade.

The *coup de grâce* of my hopes came on the ninth. A par-5 and the signature hole at Mansion, it required a good drive to the right side of the fairway, a lay-up shot, then a short wedge to its elevated green.

I hit a solid drive and had 164 yards to a waste area that cut across the entire fairway and was death to many a golfer's score. My ball was four inches above my feet, requiring me to grip down on the 8-iron I picked for my second shot on this uphill gem. From a level lie, I normally hit an 8-iron 160. There's no way I could reach the trouble from this distance with that same, but now much shortened club.

Perhaps my total confidence made my swing flow with a heaven-sent ease, for the pass I made at the ball was sheer perfection. The contact of clubhead to ball felt effortless and my Pro VI launched precisely on the line I intended. I'd just made one of the best swings of my life, but my ball flew like a rocket dead in the middle of the waste area, putting a dagger in whatever hopes I had left of shooting a qualifying score.

"You've got to be fucking kidding! I can't believe that just happened to me!?!"

I couldn't recover from the shock. My body said, *"You just made a phenomenal swing,"* and my scorecard said, *"and that once in a lifetime swing just killed your last chance to succeed."* The extreme dichotomy between what I felt in my body and how badly my mind knew I screwed up put me on *TILT*. I'd never felt so good and done so bad. I was toast.

THIS WAS THE GAME; finding a way to master myself in any situation and being ready, willing, and able to do so regardless of any circumstances. This is what I loved and now hated about golf.

I staggered through the rest of the day in a fog.

Billy Castner was there when I finished and he couldn't have been kinder. When I saw him, I said, *"you can fire me, but I won't quit."* He smiled wryly and replied, *"why would I fire you when you're just getting your feet wet. Don't worry about it, we'll get 'em next time."* A couple of days later he treated me to lunch, and we went through my two rounds shot for shot, to identify my weaknesses, analyzing my play in detail. My putting was solid, the best part of my game, but I was swinging over-the-top, and my sand game needed major improvement.

No sooner did I set out to fix my swing and improve my short game than I found out I had Lyme disease.

During the week when I was in Monroe, I stayed and a B & B just across the street from the club. When I woke up one morning shortly after my PAT, half the face I saw in the bathroom mirror had dropped towards the floor like it was made of melted candle wax.

At first, I thought I'd had a stroke. I'd noticed some fatigue lately and I'd been irritable, but I thought this was an emotional reaction to blowing my playing test. Once I checked around the club to see if anyone else was sick, I discovered one of our greenskeepers had Lyme and that this area was known as a hotbed for the disease.

Luckily, as soon as I got back to the city, I went to my local hospital and had them test me for Lyme. When they confirmed I had it, they put me on doxycycline and after a day and a night in the hospital my face zipped back up in place and I was fine.

I was very, very fortunate to have caught and diagnosed the disease so quickly. My ex, Sharron, got it while hiking but didn't find out she had Lyme for years. Periodically and without warning it wreaked havoc on her body and mood, sapping her energy.

Deer ticks carry Lyme Disease. They are tiny little creatures, the size of a pinhead, and I figured one had jumped me as I crossed a fescue area between the club and the B & B.

Not so luckily, it turned out I wasn't the only one having a rough time that season. Although my woes were with my game and my health, dealing with American Golf, the low-ball management company that ran Mansion Ridge, and enduring the commute from Staten Island, where Billy Castner lived, nearly killed my head pro.

It was all too much. In short order, both of us would discover other worlds and other possibilities. The coming golf season would have surprises for both of us, and both of us would wind up going in new, unexpected directions.

Dead, Buried and Born Again; Again!

Bill Castner left Mansion Ridge when American Golf cut his salary in half. He took me with him, and our new home for the next season was Colt's Neck Golf Club in the New Jersey town of that name.

The mostly open links at Colt's Neck was a good track but predictably far below the quality of the Nicklaus design at Mansion. This season I would again work in the Pro Shop, managing and merchandising. I would also give golf lessons there, which was a new responsibility I looked forward to.

On the plus side, the practice area at Colt's Neck was much better than at the Ridge, and I could workout in my free time using the club's gym. I also got to practice free of charge.

A dentist named DeGennaro owned the club. Oddly, he didn't play golf. He viewed the facility as an investment and his indifference to the game would prove to be a problem down the road.

When Bill first asked me to join him at Colt's Neck, it didn't seem possible. I didn't have a car, didn't have the money or credit to buy one, didn't want to go into debt getting or maintaining wheels, and had no intention of taking on a commute similar to the one that nearly killed Billy when he was at Mansion.

Then I remembered that my friend, Brian Brennan, lived near Billy's new club in Red Bank, New Jersey. If Brian could put me up during the week, I could work my same schedule as last year. I would simply replace Mansion Ridge with Colt's Neck during the week and teach at Turtle Cove on weekends.

I knew Brian well from our time together in the Sunday Gabriel group. When I asked if he could help, he agreed to put me up on his couch at no charge. Once again, guardian angels in human and celestial form seemed to be watching over my new career.

As I began my new duties, I was struck by the many joys of the game. I loved the solitude of golf. Once my work in the shop was complete, I could play anytime I wanted without the need to organize a game with others.

There's also something about the game that leaves you renewed and refreshed when your round is over and it's time to go back to real life. Playing golf was so demanding of my attention that when I finished my round, I felt better able to deal with my life's challenges after taking a break from them.

Things were going along fine. I enjoyed managing the Pro Shop now that I had a season under my belt, and I found time to work on and improve my game. This time, I felt my chances were good to pass my PAT.

Perhaps most importantly, I had time to think about my game and refine my approach to swinging the club and to my playing procedure.

The idea of a golf shot was to make the simplest, highest percentage play possible in any given situation. Developing a routine approach to any shot was a big part of building consistency in my game. I used Nicklaus as my player/model.

Here is a present tense breakdown of how I play golf;

First, comes visualization. Picture a mini-movie of the shot I intend to play in detail. Factoring in the current weather conditions, both outside and within me, see and feel the flight of the ball to its target on the line and with the shape and trajectory the shot calls for. See and feel it land and observe the ball's behavior. Now backtrack the shot from finish to the start of the swing. Assuming you're right handed, if a pin is cut on the left side of the green, you play a right to left draw shot. The deeper the pin is cut, the flatter trajectory my ball should take. Conversely, if the pin is front right, see and feel a fade flying from left to right at the highest possible trajectory.

Once I visualize the ball's behavior upon landing and then its flight to the target, I focus on the sensation in my body that will produce the flight pattern I intend.

Here I have a catalogue of swing keys/feels/sensations I call on that I know will produce the shot shape I want.

In all this simplicity and specificity are the crucial overall principles.

So, ideally, I may have one physical feel for my backswing and one for my downswing. The fewer *"feels"* I need, the better I'll play.

Likewise, I must factor in my confidence, my mood, and how my body feels. Here, what I go for is comfort. The idea is to make the easiest, simplest motion possible in a way that's connected to my entire state of being.

A golf swing takes roughly two seconds.

Inside the player, the time it takes to make a swing can feel much longer, but the trick to keeping your concentration is to establish a playing rhythm that allows you to relax between shots, and to coach yourself as you walk to your next shot, so you maintain an optimal focus and equilibrium, and then have a pre-shot routine along the lines I've just described, that takes no more than twenty or thirty seconds to conceive, program, and execute.

The pre-shot routine must be identical on every swing, although the specifics of each shot differ, and any interruptions necessitate starting all over again till your visualization and swing are complete, and the ball lands on the target you establish in your mind.

Self-reliance and self-trust are essential to mastering one's playing procedure and concentration.

Bearing all this in mind, my practice and play were improving, and I was well on my way to becoming successful.

Then something unexpected happened.

I got fired.

No one was more surprised than me when Billy had to let me go. Monday of that week, I missed an earlier bus from Manhattan down to Colt's Neck. This was in the pre-cell phone era. I called the Pro Shop at the club before I left Manhattan to alert them I'd be late and then again when I arrived. It was bad luck that only one person was at the Pro Shop when I called, and from the club owner's viewpoint, the damning error was closing the shop to come pick me up.

Once I arrived at the club, I took over a kids clinic that was in progress and thought no more about what had happened.

Just a few days later, Billy called me into his office at the end of the day and told me the club's owner fired me. I was shocked. Apparently, DeGennaro, who I'd been warned was notorious about terminating people for no good reason, had heard about my lateness, and told Castner I had to go.

Billy felt terrible and he agreed that it was an overreaction to something that could happen to anyone, but it was out of his hands. Later that same season, Bill wound up leaving the club too because the owner cut his salary by a third, breaking their contract.

"Now, what?" I worried.

Deep down inside, in ways I'd never been fully conscious of, I always wanted to be of spiritual service. For some time, too, I had been told by friends who knew of my fascination with the stars that I ought to become an astrologer.

So that's exactly what I did.

Bill did what he could to help me get another golf job, but it was too late in the season. I was not by then a top-notch golfer and may never be. However, I know and love the game and although I was essentially out of the golf business from now on, I've continued to love playing and teaching golf whenever I can.

I will be forever grateful to Roberto, Billy and all the many people who helped me get to this new and unexpected place by nourishing my love of the greatest game of all. The real gift of my time as a golf professional was that I reconnected to my heart. By spending time in the game that was my first love as a boy, I became inspired to take another leap of faith to be of service in a new and profound way.

Becoming A Starman

For me the fun in life, the real juice, is to connect to people who value soulful growth. When I do something that serves them that way, I love the look in their faces and the gratitude I feel in their hearts. Helping like-minded folks become more self-aware, more internally connected, and to live more intentionally, gives me much more joy and satisfaction than I ever got from acting, playing golf, or teaching both those disciplines combined.

My primary vehicle for serving others now became Astrology.

When I realized I could make a truly soulful contribution to people via their stars, which I first began to investigate in high school but didn't fully appreciate till I stopped acting and seeking a career in golf, I began to spend more and more time on astrology.

My heart and desire for self-possession now found full expression in this ancient art/science. At every level, astrology deepened my understanding of myself and everyone around me. Studying the stars became a way for me to take a deeper cut at life in a wide variety of ways. It also empowered me to assist other likeminded folks to do the same.

Looking back now, everything I experienced prior to my deep dive into the cosmos prepared me for this new journey.

From a practical perspective, the end of my golf career was the beginning of my professional life in astrology. I opened my star practice in 2005 and continued to study the craft. In 2012 I became certified as an evolutionary astrologer via Steven Forrest's training program.

Evolutionary astrology is the examination of any birth chart from the perspective of karma and past lives.

For those of you unaware of astrology as whole or who have doubts about its value, let me briefly explain how this great wisdom tradition works and how to use it.

If considering this information is hard for you or it runs contrary to your ideas about reality or religion, suspend your disbelief like when you watch a movie. Let the story of astrology speak to you and just imagine the following information is valid and true.

Feel how it feels. See if it makes sense to you.

Let's begin with a description.

It's helpful to think of astrology like the weather. Nature's ebb and flow; the tides of the ocean, the cycles of the moon, and the movement of the stars and planets in their orbits, affect us deeply.

The outer manifestation of the weather and of the seasons also reflect an inner process, a sort of internal weather, that takes place inside you and cycles through all of us.

This is what is meant by the phrase; *as within, so without.*

Whether you think it or not and whether you believe it or not, the tides of the universe that we see in the orbits of the planets have a direct and explicit impact on you.

If you think about it, this is not such a far-fetched notion.

There are tons of invisible forces that impact us all the time. When you go outdoors, the invisible rays of the Sun burn your skin if you don't use protection. If you work at your computer for an extended period, your eyes become unfocused, or you feel drained because of the unseen rays it emits. These simple examples have more complex, internal effects when it comes to how the movement of the planets affect our internal vibrations and possibilities.

We measure all this through the template of the natal (birth) chart and other charts, also known as horoscopes. Once a person learns to read their chart, and then compares it to a chart of current planetary transits, the timing and intensity of our interface with whichever planets we study become clear, predictable, and most of all, useful.

I recommend two reference books, both non-technical, to help you understand the historic and cultural influence the planets and stars have on us;

The Passion of the Western Mind and Cosmos and Psyche both by Richard Tarnas.

There are many charts that help us understand our inner nature, to define areas and activities that serve us best, and to time our actions in the world. But for simplicities sake, let's focus primarily on the birth chart.

Drawn from your date, place and time of birth, your natal chart is like a blueprint of your entire character, warts and all. Learning to "read" the chart, or hiring a professional astrologer to interpret it, helps you become conscious and intentional in every area of your life.

Astrology is a wisdom tradition, not a religion. Belief or faith have nothing to do with it. It's effects are specific and measurable, but only if you're conscious, open, intentional, and self-aware. Denial shuts down our ability to make use of astrology, just as it shuts us down as human beings.

I have no interest in *converting* you to astrology because, as I've said, it's not a religion. If you're reasonably conscious, self-aware, and curious, investigating your stars on your own will be convincing.

Pick up a copy of <u>Astrology for the Soul</u> by Jan Spiller. It deals with one vital aspect of the birth chart known as the nodes of the moon, that isn't technical. All you need to know is your birthday. Read her book and apply what Spiller says. If this is your only foray into the stars, you'll find this one book will enrich your life significantly.

OK, now what does astrology provide?

If you're clear about what I written up to now this can be summarized as self-knowledge, a sense of life direction, and timing. I've never found another wisdom tradition that comes close to how astrology explains human character in all its nuances, contradictions, and detail.

If you read a book on your rising sign or ascendant (they're the same thing) it will explain how you see things and illuminate your blind spots. This part of the chart is determined by your time of birth. A book on your Moon will clarify your feelings and how your emotional life works. Examine a book on the sign and placement of the planet Saturn in your chart and you'll understand the areas of life that are most difficult for you. You'll also discover how mastering these areas can transform them into becoming your greatest strengths.

I could go on, but following your intuition will lead you to the information that most benefits you. You'll also find that one or several facets of your character contradict other parts of your personality. These contradictions fall into the category of the first idea I cited in the introduction to this book; *that all of us, everywhere, are obliged to grapple with the light and darker angels of our conflicted human nature.*

Here, I would only add that if you're looking for a religion or philosophy that eliminates inner conflict or frees you of all pain; if you're seeking a belief system that allows you to live on a sort of automatic pilot, you're cheating yourself of the full dimensions of what it means a conscious, responsible, and intentional adult.

Real life isn't about security, and never will be. It's about coming fully alive and free to live the life that's best for you. The universe doesn't give a damn about your comfort or your idea of fairness or injustice. It cares about your growth, your total self-acceptance, and your shared humanity.

This brings us to consider the second idea I cited in the introduction; that *to fully realize our creed as Americans, (and moreover our potential as people) we must develop a healthy relationship with our pain.*

I believe pain is meant to instruct and purify us, not to be avoided at all costs. In its highest incarnation, our existential pain calls on us to deepen and grow.

This is a human reality of worldwide dimension.

Lastly, for the purposes of examination, let's look at how your stars can help you identify and become your best self?

Once more, for simplicities sake, let me cite one or two elements of astrology that I think are most valuable.

Understanding the function of the Nodes of the Moon is crucial.

For example, your overused, dried up, but familiar life patterns are summarized by the sign, degree, and house placement of your South Node/SN.

I like to envision this from the perspective of past lives. The South Node shows us where we were most successful in the majority of our prior incarnations, but it also shows where we got trapped in ways that compromised our soul's needs.

Invariably, you'll find that you want to hang out in the area of your life that is denoted by the placement of the South Node. This is usually the case for most folks up to around thirty years of age, but it's also an area they need to move away from now.

Conversely, the North Node of the Moon/NN shows the new area of life and/or way of being that you must now cultivate in order to come into balance and true happiness. If you don't believe in reincarnation, I would simply say the NN reveals the direction you need to go in here and now. Risking new behavior in these new arenas helps you find real joy and fulfillment.

My South Node is in Leo and my North Node is in Aquarius. This alone tells me that I've had many experiences, too many in fact, in a starring role. Being the center of attention, which is a Leo preoccupation, can be seductive, but it undermines what you really want to do because you fear rejection. This is why acting from a career perspective never worked for me. It helped me develop emotional discipline and reclaim my full humanity, but the hazards of public life were something I didn't want or need to experience AGAIN.

All this is reflected in my Leo South Node.

Conversely, my North Node in Aquarius tells me that I'm most happy serving and empowering other people in a consulting, behind-the-scenes fashion. That's what this book is about. I don't get compromised by the seductions and the traps of the spotlight, and since I'm free of social scrutiny and worry about my popularity, (I don't currently participate in social media) I can give of myself fully.

My life experience bears out the presence of the South and North Nodes in my birth chart in ways that have helped me become the person I most want to be.

The second important astrological element I would emphasize has to do with where you live. Astro-cartography is a subdivision of astrological wisdom that can overlay your birth chart onto a geographical grid of any location on earth and identify the best place for you to live according to your primary values.

I live on my Chiron line. That's a line of longitude that aligns with Chirotic/healing energy. Living on this line supports my desire to have a healing influence in the world, starting with my local relationships, and then expanding to people I work with who live all over the world.

Essentially, the myth of Chiron has to do with developing *a healing orientation towards living* whether we heal our most deeply personal wounds, or not. If you want to explore what Chiron is all about, read one of several books on this centaur of Greek mythology by Barbara Hand Clow.

In summary, astrology is one of humanity's oldest wisdom traditions. It appeared simultaneously in multiple cultures worldwide around five-thousand years ago. The only reason its survived countless efforts to purge it from civilized society is because it works.

This doesn't mean you don't get out of bed and go to work if you have rough planetary aspects, it means you learn to function more consciously and intentionally with the challenges you face, and in ways that help you live with more depth and dimension.

Enough said. I hope you'll educate yourself about this fantastic wisdom tradition in whatever ways feel right to you and that your explorations enrich your life as much as my study of the stars has enriched mine.

Virginia

I hope my *never say die* relationship to true romance is a sign of resilience not delusion, but it's probably a bit of both. When I met Virginia Sanchez Navarro, whose first name I only recently learned is Monica, it had been nearly five years since I'd been with a lover.

We met at one of Robert Baker's Sunday Gabriel gatherings in the spring or summer of 2002, not long before I left that group.

I will call Monica Virginia because that's the name I knew her by. Why she didn't tell me her Christian name I don't know, but in retrospect, it doesn't surprise me. She had many secrets, and although she was a gifted, perceptive woman, Virginia had massive blind spots, too.

Once more, there were red flags that should have warned me, but they had no real effect on my attraction to her or my desire to be with her.

If she didn't have a bad relationship with her father, it was certainly problematic. A famous Mexican actor named Manolo Fabregas; all Virginia told me about him other than his fame was that he had a double standard when it came to performing. It was fine for a man to become an actor but, according to Virginia, he felt a woman with that desire wasn't much better than a prostitute.

I wasn't quite sure if this was her father's view alone and/or a cultural double standard. Whatever the reality, it infuriated her. Virginia had also lived a lesbian lifestyle for ten years, or so she told me, which changed it seems somewhere around the time we met.

Ms. Sanchez Navarro was alluring and beautiful but dangerous. Standing about five feet and five inches tall with gorgeous chestnut brown hair, she had a scorpion-like sexuality I found compelling. I loved the lilt of her resonant voice which had a slightly smoky quality as if it had been aged in an ancient oak cask. Virginia had a regal, smoldering libido and a penetrating look that transmitted deep passion and ferocity. She saw herself as a queen and certainly gave that impression, but she was tormented by demons of regal dimensions, too, and her anger easily matched my own.

Among other things, we shared a passion for astrology. Virginia was a Pisces and therefore squared my Sagittarius Sun. In plain language, this meant we tended to clash. For the most part, we didn't see anything eye to eye.

From my viewpoint Virginia was hypercritical. She self-righteously projected her shit in a painfully judgmental, dismissive, and distancing way, and frankly, I found her to be a controlling bitch. *Still, just as I sensed there was something significant that would come of my relationship with Robert Baker, I felt the same about my involvement with this beautiful, volatile, and perplexing Mexican.*

Virginia had a behavior that was particularly upsetting to me. When I hugged her, because I was taller than she, I would drop my head so I could place my cheek next to hers. For some reason, this infuriated her. She would berate me as if doing this emasculated me somehow and I never understood her problem with how I hugged her.

V was the sort of person who would place a protruding crystal in the floorboards of her apartment for a spiritual reason, then become angry and resentful when someone stepped on it by accident, who didn't even know it was there.

Once, we were driving somewhere in an intense rainstorm, I attempted to parallel park, but I couldn't see to back up. I asked her to crack open her passenger side window a bit and help me see the curb. You would have thought I asked the Queen of Sheba to demean her highness with such a pedestrian request.

The worst example of her cruelty came when I created a party for Virginia and her students from Landmark Education Inc. Landmark was at that time the latest iteration of what was formerly known as EST.

Virginia had led a course there and at the conclusion of their time together, the group she instructed gathered at her apartment on the upper west side of Manhattan. Completely on the spur of the moment, I created a party for them so they could celebrate. I ran to the grocery, bought the food, plattered and placed it, and then kept everything functioning smoothly while Virginia held court.

Of course, she told me in no uncertain terms that my efforts were wanting. If I wasn't convinced that something special was to come of our relationship, in no uncertain terms I would have told her what a thankless bitch she was and to fuck off.

Still, I'll held my tongue.

My ardor for Ms. Mexico was not completely masochistic. Something sacred transpired in our difficult relationship. The upshot of our liaison is that Virginia gave me perhaps the greatest gift I ever received from a lover or anyone else. She confronted me with and then helped me to embrace my self-hate.

Although this sounds insane, it was a crucial life lesson delivered in the nick of time.

Had Virginia not taken me to this place, a place I would never have gone to on my own, I don't think I would ever have become fully myself. For only when I embraced the depth of my self-hatred; only when I fully owned it, could I realign and reclaim my full energy, get past my refusal to fully engage with life, and begin to love and accept all of me.

Everything came to a head one Sunday evening at a Gabriel group lecture. Virginia wasn't even there, but the accumulation of her criticisms and the inadequacy of all my efforts to please her, came pouring out of me in a torrent of self-loathing.

Over time, we both recognized that our fire and water partnership would never work. Nevertheless, I loved Virginia deeply. Time and again I'd been there for her, and despite our clashing energies, I knew she cared deeply for me, too.

Inevitably, the time came for us to say goodbye.

Our moment of parting came as we were walking together on a sidewalk somewhere in Manhattan. Nearby, I saw a small stoop with three tiny stairs and realized that if I placed Virginia atop that stairway we would be the same height. I guided her to the topmost step, then hugged her deeply and fully with all the love in my heart.

Free for once of her violent reaction to my embrace, I'll never forget how good it felt to love her without being pushed away. She hugged me back with a love I'd never experienced from her before.

It was too bad we hadn't had such a moment together till we parted, but it was a wonderful way to say goodbye. When we separated, she went wordlessly on her way, as did I, and we never saw or spoke to each other again.

As I think of Virginia and how it was to be with her, I'm prompted to recall a poem I once wrote.

If it is choice by which we love, then why did I love you?
When mind was clear and saw our truth,
why did heart ignore the proof?
And why when knowing our star-crossed fate,
did love ignore our broken dates,
and give my battered heart the essence of your own.
To me the ways of love are strange, that I should choose a broken end,
and yet by love, our fate transcend...

Saying Goodbye to Gabriel and Grounding His Message in the Real World

"The kingdom of God is within you." This was the central message of Gabriel over the past dozen years I'd attended Robert's Sunday evening lectures.

I finally got it.

When I did, it was time for me to move on and do something in the world with what I'd learned from Gabby.

Essentially, what I'd learned is this;

Real life shows up when I take on all my feelings in the moment. This means having my emotions fully *as they occur* and letting them flow through me without editing them or attaching judgements to them, one way or another.

What I took with me out into the world was the awareness that everything around me mirrored my commitments. What I see in you reflects back to me my own acceptance or rejection of whatever issue is at hand.

The game, then, is to embrace all my experience, whether I like it, or not; to have it, to let it have me, and then let be and let it go. When I have no resistance to what is, I'm at liberty to play the game of life full out.

That's it and that's all.

It's a simple notion, as Gabby would say, *it's just not always easy to apply*.

Well, easy or not, now it was time for me to make that effort.

MDI

Men's Divisions International was and remains an organization within the Men's Movement. As it turned out, it would play a significant part in my efforts to bring Gabby's teachings out to the "real" world.

David Turk, a caterer I worked for on a jobbing basis in the early 2000's, was a member of MDI. My relationship to the organization began when he invited me to come to one of their meetings. In the beginning, I didn't like Turk. I thought he was a covertly self-righteous boy scout, who tried but failed to hide his sense of superiority. David played things close to the vest, keeping his real feelings to himself, but I usually saw through such people. Over time, however, I learned he genuinely cared for me and for people in general.

Turk was always professional, but he lacked the human touch and warmth of a natural people person. Still, he expressed real empathy through his actions, and I liked that. The more I got to know David, the more I came to love the man he was striving to be.

We both had a deep desire to become the best possible version of our potential. For David, as it was for the majority of the members of MDI, I think this was an idealized vision of his highest self; moral, ethical, compassionate, and a person who left everyone and everything in a better place than they found them.

For my part, I didn't care what combination of good and bad was inside me, I wanted to become fully human and alive, regardless of how that looked.

I'd rather be whole than good or bad had become my inner *zeitgeist*. In this context, wholeness wasn't about being perfect or perfectible; it was about owning my whole humanity and everything that comes with being completely alive.

After a few low-key invitations from Turk, I attended an MDI meeting in August of 2002 and liked it. I felt this was a group of men I could work with to bring Gabby's insights into the "real" world.

MDI had roots in the Sterling Men's Weekend. Created by Arthur Kardashian, who changed his name to Justin Sterling for reasons I could only guess. His operation had begun as a reaction to the "feminization" of men who reacted negatively to the Feminist Movement.

I wasn't sure what feminization meant from Sterling's viewpoint, but he seemed to assert that men were losing their masculine essence in modern day America. I also wasn't sure when this so-called feminization began. The Sterling Movement seemed to a throwback to a sort of fundamentalism asserting the belief that men are from Mars, women are from Venus, and a desire to keep gender boundaries clear and concrete.

What I liked about MDI, which was more egalitarian and less rigidly doctrinaire than the Sterling group, was the potential I saw for conscious, intentional action to make the world a better place.

MDI was a new iteration of the Sterling Men's Weekend and each of the organizations had a core event. The older group had the Men's and Women's Weekend. MDI had their Legacy Discovery event. I did Legacy Discovery in October of 2002 and the Men's Weekend the following spring.

I found the Sterling Men's Weekend predictable and simplistic. Our group was manipulated by Sterling, who was posturing and controlling, and reminded me of Gen. Jack D. Ripper from Stanley

Kubrick's movie, "Dr. Strangelove…" I had no interest in his outdated, ostensibly Alpha-male approach to what was termed "mature masculinity."

On the face of it, "mature masculinity" appeared to be a phrase emphasizing honest, direct, no-bullshit interactions between men who always addressed each other by their last name. Such straight-forward interactions were meant to be free of unspoken, codependent relationships that were rooted in the idea that *"I won't call you on your bottom-line shit IF you don't call me on mine."*

In my experience, authentic mature masculinity was and still is very, very rare. This was especially so with non-introspective folks locked into their everyday habits, patterns, and denials, which was my reading of most of the membership of both organizations.

My Legacy Discovery moved me deeply, however. The first night I was at my LD, I was asked what I intended to get from the event. When I said, *"I came here to get straight with the vendetta I've had with my father my whole life,"* I was shocked at my frankness.

Since I promised to keep what happened at this event confidential, I can only share my own experience and what I learned there but suffice it to say that the various components of my LD put me in touch with myself at a profound level.

When it came right down to it, I think what drew me to MDI was the age-old idea of a community taking care of its own.

Once a man's entry event was completed, he was assigned to a Point Team, supervised by MDI members with leadership experience, so he could learn how to function on a men's team. That point team was split up after several weeks training and each newbie was installed on an established team.

This was always a tricky situation because the new men had become very attached to each other. One of the biggest reasons to break them up was to avoid closely bonded cliques from challenging the established hierarchy.

The dysfunctional side of MDI, at least as I saw it, was its adherence to a heroic ideal that failed to get fully into and then go beyond men's defenses and wounds. Many of us had a genuine desire to make a positive difference in the world, but so long as we operated on the surface of our wounds and defenses, I saw we'd never become the positive social force we aspired to be.

As I thought about it, a phrase that was popular in our circle seemed to encapsulate both our aspirations and how we blocked them. Stated in the form of a question we constantly asked ourselves, *"Are you being the man I always wanted to be?"*

Considering this impelled us all to assess who we were now and who we wanted to become. It also required clarification; *was the man I always wanted to be a superman, or was he fully human and conflicted but alive to all his positive and negative potentialities?*

For the vast majority of us, he was a superman both inside and out.

And that was my problem with MDI.

If you're gonna become the man you always wanted to be, whether he is super-man or super-human, you damn well better deal with the man you're terrified you are right now.

First as a team captain and then as my Division's Coordinator, I tried and failed to bring this distinction to my boys.

For me, the question was; *Am I going to embody an idealized fantasy or become a fully authentic human being regardless of how I come across to others?*

I started trying to breakdown the idealized "Man you always wanted to Be" zeitgeist by introducing shadow work. The new and younger men in our circle got what I was going for and were open to exploring the underbelly of their masculine hopes and ideals, but the older guys who'd been around for years were uniformly against such self-examination.

Eventually, when I realized this was just the way things were and would continue to be, I "completed" my membership, which meant I moved on from MDI. To their credit, the men in my division supported my decision, because by the time I made it, I'd started the process of writing this book.

My boys saw my memoir had become a consuming passion for me, and we both knew that I'd done what I could to lead them in a new direction they just weren't willing to go. So, we parted ways by mutual consent.

My proudest accomplishment with MDI was beginning The Fathering Forum. This idea was rooted in the belief that the most important job a man has, if he's a father, is to raise his children to become the best versions of whatever potential they possess. This was a mentorship program where older fathers mentored younger, less experienced dads, using what they had learned along the way about what did and didn't work in parenting.

I left MDI nearly twenty years ago, but The Fathering Forum we started is still alive and well.

As regards MDI, I came to the conclusion that most of the men there wanted to feel masculine and strong in their identity, but not if they had to examine themselves too closely. They were committed to the image of mature masculinity, not the reality of their contradictory nature as human beings.

Most of all, at least from my perspective, no one there seemed interested in finding the gold that was contained in their shadow selves…

<u>Confessions of a Prodigal Son</u>

"What did your father give you that you're grateful for? What did you NOT get from your dad that you wish you had?" Answering these two questions helped me to begin making peace with my father.

These queries were part of an MDI exercise I did that prompted me to write dad.

Along this same time, I became aware that several people I knew who were working on themselves in a sister organization, Landmark Inc., the newest version of Werner Ehrhard's EST, were also working on their memoirs.

For the first time in my life, the idea of writing my story came to me. The thought of doing this was intriguing.

But, once more, I'm getting ahead of myself.

With regard to the letters we wrote to each other and the two questions that began our correspondence, what I got from dad that I most grateful for was a passion for excellence. What I didn't get from him was the freedom to go for what I wanted in life. Dad had the capacity to go for his dreams and for his everyday goals. I seemed always and forever to get in my own way.

In his reply to me, Pop said that what he got from me that was valuable, *as distinguished from what he was grateful for*, was my commitment to my goals and the courage to go after them. He also took pride in my growth as a person and the expansion of my perspective as a human being.

What he didn't get from me that he wished he had was peace of mind about the solidity and security of my future.

What I really hoped for in our exchange of letters was a real heart to heart, give and take conversation about our relationship. Given my father's blind spots, that was probably unrealistic. By shifting his response to valuable from grateful for, dad also stayed in his lane/role as teacher/mentor.

Still, the cat was finally out of the bag. I'd cracked the ice between us and spoken frankly about my pain and shame with my father. Our letters didn't settle any outstanding issues between us, but they were a start.

AUTHOR'S NOTE: *These next few stories overlap. Timelines in each interweaved with the other recollections written here, and in some of the following stories, events occurred almost simultaneously.*

Fayetteville I-Making a new start with Chiron

By now, the end of 2005, my memoir had become a compelling passion and I felt I must give priority to writing my story.

The next step was to return to my roots. I had to reconnect to vibes of my family and my old stomping grounds. Infusing my stories with this energy was essential if I was to write with feeling and depth about my origins and getting over my childhood wounds.

My plan was to stay with each of my siblings and with mom and dad for a total of six months, then evaluate my progress.

At the same time, I had the impression my brothers and sister were committed to write their own memoirs, after which we'd work together on a joint venture that compared and contrasted growing up in the same family from four points of view.

Once I arrived back home, we had a sibling-only retreat to discuss the individual and group aspects of this grand project, but whenever someone got close to opening up, Rick sabotaged our conversations. Steve had a hunger for our endeavor, but he didn't have the time to partner his spouse, parent his kids, sustain his struggling law practice, and give his own memoir the attention it needed. Diane was similarly engaged with her family and busy freelance career. As far as I could tell, she wasn't emotionally ready to dive deep into her story or ours.

Sis was a lot like me. IF she was going to write about anything, it would have to be authentically and deeply felt or else why bother.

After our abortive retreat, it was clear I was on my own.

I'd been living in Tennessee and then in North Carolina for a year and a half by the summer of 2007. My writing was going well, but beyond the book, it was high time I decide what work to pursue and to choose the right place for me to live.

It was also time to give my family a break. Except for dad, they were uncomfortable with my project but they'd all been more than there for me putting a roof over my head and making a place for me at their table.

I was aware of astro-cartography and knew it was very useful in finding a home that would suit me. When I did a web search, I found Julian Lee, an astrologer who specialized in location, and he coordinated my birth chart with ACG maps which showed the angular positions of the planets at the time of my birth. These maps also indicated where each planet was rising and setting when I was born. The planets' positions created *'areas of influence'* that would uphold, support and resonate with the dominant vibe of the place I chose to live.

Once I decided on the energies I wanted my new home to embody, Julian promised to find locations that would support my preferences. If no such places existed, he also said he wouldn't charge me.

I wanted to be as physically close to my family as possible but gave priority to living in the best energy I could find to support my process oriented approach to astrology. That approach was evolving but it basically involved regular explorations of my client's birth charts using voice and body improvisations.

Two weeks after I hired him, Julian completed his analysis and made five recommendations. The two places that I responded to were Fayetteville, Arkansas, a college town in the northwestern part of the state and Albuquerque, New Mexico, which was Julian's recommendation.

Just five minutes into his review of Fayetteville, I knew instinctively it was the place I was looking for. According to his findings, I would be moving there to live near my Chiron line.

The wounded healer of Greek mythology, Chiron was about cultivating a healing orientation towards life and living. Living in this kind of ambiance and aligning with this energy to support my practice, was exactly what I was after. I wanted to have a healing effect on my clients and the people in their lives.

I was by this time living with my oldest brother Rick and his family in High Point, NC. I'd saved money for relocation, but my funds were tight. Rick, as he always did, helped me anyway he could. Once I decided to make the leap, he rented a truck for me to move my belongings to Arkansas. In the meantime, I borrowed his spare pick-up for a quick drive to New York to close my apartment there.

Once I returned from New York, I headed for Arkansas. I didn't have a job waiting for me and didn't know a soul in Fayetteville. I'll never forget clearing Memphis westbound on I-40. *"What the hell are you doing?"* I thought to myself as I crossed the Big Muddy westbound to an unknown future. All I could think in self-reply was, *"Trusting my gut!"*

Just over two hours west of Little Rock, I turned north onto I-49 and headed towards my final destination. About ten miles up this last leg of my journey, I felt a shift in energy that felt really, REALLY GOOD!

Now I got excited.

Of course, as revved up as I was becoming, I was also flying blind and terrified. I didn't like this split within me, but I figured that was the price of admission to what I hoped would be a soulfully connected new life.

Once I arrived, I decided to rest and start fresh the next morning.

After a good night's sleep, I got up early and started exploring Fayetteville. First, I worked my way through the University of Arkansas campus. Fayetteville was situated on a plateau just north of the Boston Mountains and was fourteen hundred feet in elevation. The south part of town was mostly flat, but the campus was hilly, then the ground levelled out again just north of the university.

At the northern end of campus, I saw a rental office for Pierce Properties and stopped by and see what apartments were available. School had started so most of their units were rented, but they had a one-bedroom on North Garland Ave, so I drove there to check it out.

When I got back to their office, the Pierce folks asked me if I liked the place and offered me a year's lease. After living in New York, where this kind of quick access to housing was impossible, I said YES, wrote them a check, and began moving in right then and there.

I took the weekend off to nest and explore more of my new hometown. Although I don't really remember what my expectations were, once I settled in and got a feel for it, Fayetteville was SO MUCH better than I hoped it would be.

ANYTIME I COULD SEE THE SKY, DAY, OR NIGHT, I FELT PLUGGED IN AND AT HOME IN WAYS I'D NEVER FELT BEFORE.

Then I had an odd reaction; I froze.

I had a bit of nest egg left but needed a job and for far too long I refused to even look for one. Perhaps my inner thought was *"This is too good to last."* Maybe, too, I needed to make things more problematic than necessary because I was used to living that way.

Eventually, after a couple of my buddies sent me money to tide me over, I got a job at Ozark Natural Foods as a first shift stocker. I was now in my mid-fifties, making just over $7 bucks an hour, but I was there on my own terms and embarked on a new adventure.

I was happy living in my new hometown and excited about what would happen next.

Slowly, I got to know my new hometown and began to explore various groups to see if they felt like a good match. One group I connected with was a writer's workshop that met weekly at the excellent local library on West Mountain Street. Writers would read their work and then fellow scribes would try to improve each other's material. Bob Ford, a local playwright who happened to attend Circle in the Square just after I graduated, led this group and I enjoyed being part of it.

The only other assembly I found interesting was at St. Paul's Episcopal church. The church had a reputation for welcoming people of all persuasions. Their website declared *"Whoever you are, and wherever you are on your pilgrimage of faith, you are welcome in this place."* When I found this was true, I got involved in four ministries there.

The first was called Caring Friends. It was a respite ministry that provided relief for families who were dealing with ALZ. We would meet on Thursday mornings from 11 am to 2 pm and spend time with early onset patients to give their families a break.

The Sageing Group I joined at St. Paul's discussed concerns that confront people in their third act. Here, questions of a spiritual nature occupied our bimonthly discussions.

There was a Rosen-movement class that meet right before Caring Friends, so I started attending it regularly, too.

The last group I joined was The Friends of Jung. These folks had been meeting bi-monthly for over thirty years and were devoted to exploring the work the great Swiss psychoanalyst.

I felt welcomed in all these groups but with the exception of the movement class and the Jung group, I never feel fully accepted, probably because I made it clear I wasn't a Christian.

Until the Covid epidemic hit in 2020, my religious status didn't seem to be an issue, and maybe it never was, but not one person from any of the groups I was involved with reached out to me with any fellowship during the pandemic, so I let go of all of them but the Jungians.

Just before Covid hit, Rev. Evan Garner took over from Noel Grisham and this changed the vibe at St. Paul's. Garner was a highly intelligent, manipulative, and political animal. His *modus operandi* with everything was *"How is this going to look, how much will it cost, and how will I be seen."* No sooner had he arrived than he applied for the bishop's position in our region. That told me everything I needed to know about who and what he was devoted to.

Noel Grisham's *M.O.* had always been *"how can we include everyone who wants to be in fellowship with us."* As far as I was concerned, this egalitarian openness went missing with Garner's arrival.

I also withdrew substantially from my involvement with St. Paul's because I started a part-time job working at the Fayetteville Senior Center in mid-September of 2019.

This was one of the best decisions I ever made.

As of this writing, in late summer of 2024, the only group at St. Paul's I still meet with is the Friends of Jung. We continue to explore existential questions and to examine things from a Jungian viewpoint. I've always been a deeply spiritual person but was never religious. I found the formality of services at St. Paul's alienating. With the

Jungians I don't feel the burden of dogma or any concerns with looking good or being pious; just the freedom to explore.

By now, you probably know how important that kind of freedom is to me.

CHAPTER VII:
Great Loss Opens Me to Deeper Ground

Losing Dad

At the end of January 2008, dad phoned me at my place in Fayetteville. I was happy to hear from him and we spoke for around an hour. He was having a heart procedure done the next day. He mentioned this so casually that given everything else we spoke about; I didn't realize he'd just reached out to me in case he didn't survive.

When this hit me, my back went out for a month.

Now 86, my father survived his surgery, but that night went into an unexpected and surprising coma.

A considerable part of his recouperation was spent at a place called National Health Center/NHC. Based in Franklin, TN, where mom and dad had recently moved to be close to my sister's family. These jokers were Christian based, which was fine as far as it went, but this facility was dysfunctional as hell on a number of fronts. The staff there was so programmed with a corporate mind-set that they didn't listen, and they didn't hear. Our observations and requests were filtered and denuded through NHC's Stepford-like, pseudo-Christian, care and concern.

When a tech was feeding dad breakfast one morning, pop threw-up and developed pneumonia. He then fell out of bed, injuring his hand. They gave him a shot of morphine that nearly killed him, and he landed back in the hospital again. After this rinse and repeat pattern continued all summer, dad's doctors told us they'd done all they could for him.

It was not long after this, in July or August, that the decision was made to send my father home to die. In the meantime, I'd returned to Fayetteville and when mom called me with this news, she asked me to come home and help care for papa. I'd been in Arkansas for just under a year. My employer was aware of my situation and gave me their blessing, so I quit my job and flew to Nashville right away.

Mom hired a battery of caregivers to tend to pop 24/7 and eventually I joined their ranks, making him as comfortable as possible.

I thought I'd prepared for the eventuality of my father's death, but I was wrong. Way wrong.

The fact that dad was dying freaked me out. Of all my siblings, I was the worst at dealing with this reality. The irony was that of all my siblings, I'd probably done the most to directly address the unresolved issues I had with dad from growing up, via the letters we wrote to each other.

Writing letters was a good start, but it wasn't enough.

Actually confronting things man to man was what we both needed to do. Unfortunately, I didn't see how I could bring up ancient history now that dad was confined to his bed and dying, so I shut down. This is one of my greatest regrets. All papa wanted was someone to be WITH him. I watched over him as a caregiver, but our human interaction was almost non-existent.

Life is always full of surprises, and from time to time there was unexpected comic relief in this otherwise untenable situation.

As he was about to receive a bath in bed, dad declared, *"I never could stand a woman's naked bottom sitting on my back."* There were several people in the room. For some his comment was funny. For others it was TMI. All humor aside, however, a pall descended over my parents' house as the extended family gathered to keep vigil or say their goodbyes.

Pop got a good job on dying. What I mean, again in his parlance, *is that he got with it*. At one point near the end, he even said with some impatience *"Let's get this show on the road."*

One day dad asked me to go to the kitchen and see where the golden staircase led. This was something new in my experience. The kitchen in my parents' home was down a long corridor from their master bedroom and dad could see me as I combed every nook and cranny of it. Convinced I'd given it my best shot, dad accepted my report that although I'd looked all over, I just couldn't find the staircase or see where it led.

One afternoon, after my shift watching dad was over, I'd arranged to help my sister do something. Dad was always pleased when we did things for each other. He looked at me with so much love and affection that I knew I should reschedule with Diane and just sit and talk with him.

This was the moment we could speak frankly about all the things I'd complained about in my letters to him. He was open and ready to hear me.

I chickened out. I told him I'd promised to help sis and had to go. I regretted this the moment I said it and will for the rest of my days.

Inevitably, the show got on the road just past midnight on October 12, 2008. As his lungs filled with fluid, most of us were gathered around dad's bed singing hymns to him,. Diane sat with her head on his chest, and I was at the foot of the bed gently rubbing his feet. The rest of us surrounded him touching his arms, hands, and thighs, doing our best to comfort him.

I could see panic in his face as his lungs continued to fill but all we could do was be with him. At ten past midnight he stopped breathing. The family scattered to various parts of the house to grieve in their own ways. I stayed at dad's bedside. I felt his lifeforce leave about thirty minutes after he passed. The caring presence he exuded and that I'd always felt from him even when I lived in New York, vanished as his spirit moved on, never to return.

Surreal is the only way I can describe this event. None of my immediate family had lost a parent till dad passed and it was just impossible to process.

My father's attentiveness to every nuance of his family's need for safety, love and protection had been one of his foremost features. Dad was always on duty and standing watch, and this gave all of us enormous comfort and confidence that whatever happened we'd come out OK.

Now the King was dead. He was gone forever and there was no one to replace him. This realization gashed a giant hole in all our souls; a void so deep and wide that, at least for me, it took years to reassemble my psyche.

Some things in life you never get over, you simply move on as best you can, moving forward with a kind of spiritual limp.

For the next several years, life was like that for me.

From Hamlet, this line spoken by the Dane of his father, came to me;

He was a man, take him for all in all, I shall not look upon his like again.

Taking a deeper dive into WHAT'S WHAT

It took me a long time to come back to life after my father died. Losing papa was a psychic and emotional body blow. For several years I was angry about losing him. Grief affected me in odd, unusual ways. During that time, for example, I'd want to jump out of my skin whenever I used the turn indicator on my car, so I stopped using it.

Everything changed for me.

I launched into a deep dive, reviewing my astrology and how I delivered it. The lecture format of reviewing a client's birth chart and then recommending they make life-changes, the standard counseling methodology, didn't work and never had. That information went in one ear and out the other. For the most part, depending on your true intentions and level of consciousness, listening to a summary of your chart was never going to change your habits, patterns, or perspective.

It became clear that several of my client's couldn't really hear my coaching. I had to confront the truth that many who sought my counsel weren't committed to growing in spirit or self-awareness, they just pretended they were because they liked the way it made them look.

I confronted this tendency in myself in several areas of my own life.

These were hard realizations.

From my viewpoint, there was no point bothering with astrology if it didn't help you live a measurably better, happier, and more useful life. This involved becoming self-aware and then changing your beliefs and behaviors. I was determined to find a way to make what most folks thought of mere fortune-telling useful in a pragmatic, day-to-day way.

What good would it do for me to tell you that you'd meet Prince or Princess Charming on Wednesday at 10 am if you didn't have the capacity to be your own best friend. Best friends tell you what you most need to hear when you least want to hear it. Useful astrology was about growing in self-knowledge and self-acceptance so you could live a life that worked for you, regardless of your passing circumstances or current limitations.

Having Princess or Prince Charming in your life would do you no good if you didn't have the capacity to relate to yourself constructively.

I had to find a way to make it my client's charts *experiential*, so they could connect to and actually feel their inner dynamics emotionally and physically. I became driven to sell them on the fact that working on their charts, especially the painful bits, was vital to their freedom and independence.

I cut my fees by two-thirds to encourage folks to work on the dynamics in their charts on a regular basis.

I starting having them do voice and body dance-like improvisations to explore and imaginatively act out associations they had to facets of their charts that I knew were crucial to their growth and integration.

I let them make sounds but wouldn't let them speak or use word descriptions during these explorations. This approach opened them up and connected them to their creativity, as well as to their conflicts.

Only after they'd completed what I called a structure would we actually speak about and attempt to solidify what they'd just experienced.

The result of all this was that more of my clients got directly in touch with their personal issues. They grappled with these issues using their bodies, intuition, and imagination in sound and movement. This helped them integrate their various conflicts in ways that made them feel much more self-accepting. It also freed them up.

This approach to astro-counseling didn't free them of their blocks, but it reframed their relationship to those blocks in liberating ways. The goal was to become more fully human, not to be perfect or to look good.

As a consequence of losing dad, I also re-examined my life both internally and from the viewpoint of what I saw happening in America. I was searching for the essence of what it was to be or become my truest self. As a populace, I felt we needed to reconnect with our creed and heritage by becoming more connected to ourselves and each other in authentic ways.

All this broadened the scope of my memoir into something that would speak to all Americans about the genuine pursuit of happiness.

In dad's parlance, I was striving to *get a good job* as a useful astrologer. In a very real way, losing pop and how I responded to that crisis made me a better man and a more effective counselor.

Nancy: The Feeling of Being Home, At Last

This was a day I'll never forget; Friday, April 20, 2005. My friend Michael Beneat and I left the Edvard Munch exhibit at MOMA at around 4:30. It had been 26 years since the last Munch exhibition at MOMA. That showing coincided with my class's presentation of "*A Dream Play*" by August Strindberg, which was our 1979 graduation project at Circle in the Square.

Our director, Ed Berkeley, told us that Munch and Strindberg were contemporaries. He suggested we see the show at MOMA to connect with the milieu of the play.

And so it was that in the spring of 1979 I witnessed this Norwegian artist's paintings for the first time. The instant I walked into the Munch exhibit, I fell into a black hole. His art was breathtaking. I'd never seen human subjects in such visceral pain. His characters seemed to swoon off the canvas with a profound and haunting power. Although I didn't know it at the time, the artist and I shared a birthday. As kindred spirits, this intimate personal connection helped me grasp Munch's inner life. The impact his work had on me was unforgettable.

For those unfamiliar with Munch, (December 12, 1863-January 23, 1944) here's a summary of his artistic motifs and influence taken from MOMA's press release in 1979;

...Munch expressed through his art the intricate and often despairing life of the emotions. In his artistic interpretation of the psychological and physical hardships of the human experience, he foretold during the last decades of the 19th century the complexity and alienation of the 20th-century mind. Considered one of Europe's foremost Expressionist artists, Munch translated the themes of love, obsession, sexuality, melancholy, and death into compelling visual images...

The artist's themes and my life experience were deeply aligned. Looking back, I wonder if the 2005 show both foreshadowed and triggered the most powerful, passionate, and painful relationship of my life.

When we left MOMA that afternoon, Beneat and I went to his appointment at Dr. Jay Liss' office near Columbus Circle. Both men were fellow MDI'ers, and Liss had a central treatment room where he worked on up to four different clients on separate tables at the same time. His unusual approach to chiropractic delivered adjustments like improvised jazz riffs. Michael was up next. I was waiting for him in a tiny office next to the treatment room when she walked in.

The instant I saw Nancy Lynne Edington time stopped. My jaw dropped and I felt a vivid, multiple past life connection to her that took my breath away. I WAS TOTALLY AND COMPLETELY IN LOVE WITH HER AT FIRST SITE!

My Jungian friends would say I was caught in the grip of an archetypal moment; that I was projecting my subconscious fantasies. No doubt this was true. But reality is rarely singular or reductive; seldom "either/or." Reality is nearly always both/and, with several elements converging, merging, and often clashing at a single moment in time.

This was precisely the distinction I tried to make for my brothers in the men's movement but most of them didn't get it or refused to acknowledge the complexity of their human nature.

Seeing the 2005 Munch show connected me, if only subconsciously, to the karma of my intimate relationships. When I took in *The Scream* or *The Vampire*, I connected to the bleak emotional fabric of my multiple incarnations. This was deeply painful but *participating* with Munch's art, and beyond that, coming to terms with the karma of all my past and present relations had the potential to heal and transform me.

Hereto, by the time Nancy came into my life, I fully trusted my intuition. The karmic connections I felt with her were, are, and always will be undeniably real.

When you're in the grip of an archetype, you have no choice. Suddenly, this was my only reality. I'd gone off the deep end with women before, but this was my deepest, most unprecedented leap of faith. I couldn't imagine taking a deeper dive then, or now.

There was something in my connection to Nancy akin to the relationships I'd had with Robert Baker and Virginia. Something soulful and compelling that touched me in ways that transcended even Gabriel's guidance and the liberating power of embracing my self-hate.

By the time we met, we were both in our fifties. I recognized Nancy instantly as my one and only; my choice of life partner for the rest of my days.

Of course, she didn't feel the same.

Nancy wasn't smitten by me, but she was interested and curious about who I was. For my part, I wasn't going to walk away from this fated moment without making a maximum effort to win her heart.

So, I took on a simple tactic to convince her I was trustworthy and deserving of her love. I decided to be there for her, **no matter what**. This approach wasn't so much a conscious strategy as it was my intuitive sense of how to go forward with her.

Nancy tested me.

She took full advantage of how crazy I was about her. Knowing I wanted to spend as much time with her as possible, when she wanted to do yoga in Inwood Park, she asked me along because she knew I'd protect her. I did exactly that.

If she wanted to swim a mini marathon in Long Island Sound, she'd ask me to come along for the same reason. Again, I was there for her.

Once she got what she wanted, especially if I was getting too close, she'd abandon me by shutting down and refusing to communicate in any way.

This became our pattern and through it all and **no matter what**, I was there for Nancy time and time and time again.

Ms. Edington had a tendency towards emotional attachment that left her feeling stuck and made it hard for her to let go. She categorically denied this, but she was reluctant to get too close to anyone because when she did, she lost herself. She was also deeply intuitive and went into a shell of self-protectiveness whenever she felt uncomfortable or too exposed. In addition to all this, Nancy had a deep-seated resistance to allowing anyone to have too much influence on her. Most of all, she refused to let anyone have authority over her.

I made my position clear to her. I wanted her and I would wait till she was ready. If that didn't happen, it didn't happen. I wasn't going to rush her or demand anything from her. Moreover, I was ever ready to heed her call; available for any reason at any time.

Eventually, my tactic worked. When she was ready, she revealed more of herself to me, then we slept together. It had been so long since I'd been with anyone that I couldn't match what I felt with my lovemaking. But I was certain of my feeling for Nancy, so I trusted that our sex life would reflect that. Gradually it moved in a positive direction.

When we were intimate, however, there was something odd that happened I couldn't sort out. Nancy went to a very deep, very private place when we made love that did not include me; I wasn't invited there, nor would I be welcomed in this, her most private place.

When I first experienced this, it felt like the sex we had was somehow professional, not personal. No one could ever feel let down or cheated if she bedded you, but intimacy with Nancy somehow included her competency and skill, but also a lack of genuine connection.

This did not disturb me, as perhaps it should have. It made me see I had more work to do to reach the amazing person I knew was deep inside her.

My one and only lived in a large, beautiful two-bedroom apartment of the art-deco style in Washington Heights. An entire bedroom of her home was filled with art she had made over a quarter century. Nancy decided she wanted to do an exhibition at her place showcasing her work in multiple mediums.

This was quite an undertaking, so I wound up staying with her 24/7 for two or three weeks to prepare. Along the way it became clear that Nancy was afraid of exposure on multiple fronts, so I did my best to comfort and support her.

She ordered an elaborate lighting system to display her artwork to maximum effect, but it wouldn't work. I saw this as a symbol of her conflict between being seen and staying safe. Clearly, Nancy wanted to be known yet had major resistance to being fully seen.

We continued to work on the lighting problem as we went about clearing her place of furniture to create a gallery effect. I used my catering experience to assemble food and drink that would complement and accentuate her show.

There was lots of hard work involved in putting everything together. Sometimes it was a pain in the ass but since it was for my baby, I loved it. It was going to be a first-class, stylish event, and I contented myself knowing that Nancy had direct experience of my commitment to her happiness by doing everything in my power to make it so.

Her show came and went and was a great success. My love got tons of recognition, and the event was very well attended. Even the wonky lighting system worked, enhancing her work just as Nancy intended. I handled all the service aspects of the show. This left her free to interact with everyone who attended from both our women's and men's communities, as well as many of our other friends and work associates.

On my end, I'd begun my first preparations to write this book and told Nancy I planned to leave New York for Tennessee in January of 2006. I needed to reconnect to where I grew up. I planned to be away for six months. As soon as possible, I promised to send her a plane ticket to visit me and told her in no uncertain terms that I wanted her to meet my family.

She agreed to this plan.

I wish I'd stayed in New York longer, now, because we needed more time to solidify our bond. Looking back, however, I'm not sure there would ever have been enough time for Nancy to drop her defenses. She didn't object to my leaving, however, because she knew

I was as committed to writing my memoir as she wanted to be to making her art. I hoped and intended to make further plans to be together when she came south.

Eventually she did come, but much, much later than we first planned. When I sent her a plane ticket as promised, which was around six weeks after I left New York, she no-showed, without a word of explanation.

I was disappointed but firm in my resolve to keep pursuing her.

Nancy was a beautiful, intelligent, and gifted person. She was tall, she was elegant, and she was hot, but she was also a wounded, angry soul who had a barely suppressed, rage-ridden relationship with her father.

This fundamental rift dominated her life from top to bottom, blinded her to my love and to letting it nourish her, and constrained all her possibilities.

At heart, Nancy was a deeply intuitive and gifted artist. Her father was a corporate type. From her childhood on, he indoctrinated her in that way of thinking. Nancy's particular adaptation to his influence manifested as her determination to prove she was better at anything than any man.

I understood this reaction emotionally because I had a similar history with my dad. But I also understood, as Nancy did not, that this knee-jerk reaction to her father's coercion would never come to good.

The more I got to know the woman of my dreams, the more I learned about her painful past.

CLOCKING the GOOSE

Sometime along the way to getting her degree at the Rhode Island School of Art, I assume when she was in her early twenties, she had an affair with a Black professor and got pregnant. She decided to have the child, which I'm sure thrilled her narcissistic, controlling father no end, but then suffered an ectopic pregnancy. Nancy not only lost her baby but any possibility of having children.

After all this, my beloved completely changed direction and got into the dog-eat-dog world of Wall Street. She never explained to me this polar leap into a world so radically opposite her artistic sensibility, but I'm confident it had something to do with impressing and defying her father at the same time.

The middle child of five siblings, my girl was extremely capable at whatever she took on and she had a laudable work ethic, but nothing ever seemed to pan out for Nance in the way her abilities and dedication should have assured. I could see this unspoken frustration in her, and I knew why it was there.

Nancy had a vendetta with her father just as I had with mine, and vendettas never lead to fulfillment of any kind.

Ours was the sort of extreme, consuming passion the Shakespeare referenced in his sonnet 129, at least it was for me;

> *The expense of spirit in a waste of shame*
> *Is lust in action: and till action, lust*
> *Is perjured, murderous, bloody, full of blame,*
> *Savage, extreme, rude, cruel, not to trust;*
> *Enjoyed no sooner but despised straight;*
> *Past reason hunted; and no sooner had,*
> *Past reason hated, as a swallowed bait,*
> *On purpose laid to make the taker mad.*

Mad in pursuit and in possession so;
Had, having, and in quest to have extreme;
A bliss in proof, and proved, a very woe;
Before, a joy proposed; behind a dream.
All this the world well knows; yet none knows well
To shun the heaven that leads men to this hell.

Perhaps the best I could hope for in this relationship was to be purified by the depth and fire of my passion, but here and now, I was focused on doing everything I could to win my lover's heart and soul.

Nancy Lynne exuded a quality of purity and self-containment. This belied the extreme differences between making art and doing business that framed her past. She was also remarkably open and frank with me about that past. The most intense aspect of her story was somewhere along the way she became the madam of a house of joy.

This shared tidbit would have scared off Jesus Christ, but by the time she revealed it, I was too far gone to run. It also made me understand the distance she kept when we made love. It was a survival tactic she developed from consorting with strangers.

For my part, I wondered how she could exploit women to rent their bodies for money, as Nancy did herself with some frequency. In retrospect, however, I see this was a twisted but perfect way for her to express her contempt for her father, for herself, and yet assert her power as a beautiful, self-sufficient, and passionate person.

Not long after I returned to Tennessee, Nancy decided to become a chiropractor and this time things worked out. She applied to and was accepted at Life University in Marietta, GA. By this time, more than a year after we'd initially planned to rendezvous, my father had died. I was living in Franklin, TN now and mom and I were taking care of each other.

Completely unaware of this, Nance reached out to me via email, and I responded at once. I wanted her as much as ever. Maybe this time she'd come out of her shell long enough for us to gel.

Sometime before we did her art show, I asked Nancy to marry me and she said yes, but then she wanted to think about it. We decided to revisit matrimony after her exhibition. I looked forward to this, but she'd planned to get away to see her family before I popped the question, so again we put it off.

When she got back, we didn't deal with my proposal before I left for Tennessee. Now, with so much that had happened to both of us, my marriage request was still pending.

Once we reconnected, I wound up driving to Marietta to help her move to a new apartment. The last time I'd seen her was nearly two and a half years ago, in early January of 2006. Back then, we'd been happily making out in the street and walking around her apartment naked.

Sadly, I learned upon arriving at her place that she wouldn't sleep with me. This pissed me off. She knew damn well what I wanted, and it was manipulative of her to ignore or avoid my obvious desire without addressing it BEFORE I drove all the way from Nashville to help her.

Nevertheless, I held my tongue and slept alone in her living room. She was surprised I didn't try to jump her during the night, but there was no way I was going to force myself on the woman I loved and wanted to marry.

Once we'd moved her into her new digs, I drove us to Tim's Ford state park about an hour's drive west of my hometown in Chattanooga. I rented a cabin for us overlooking the Tennessee River, so she could have a pleasant break from school, we could relax together and get reacquainted. This time we tried sleeping together, but she still didn't want sex and that drove me nuts. I told her I was only flesh and blood and I IMPLIED how much I resented being played and used all this time while my own needs were ignored.

When it became clear to Nancy that she would have to deal with our relationship while she was also finishing school, two realities she'd hoped she could handle at the same time, she balked, shut down and abandoned me again.

Enough was enough.

From the moment we first met, she'd always been my priority. I was never more than an option for her. I was fed up. I didn't have a stencil on my forehead that said, "*Piece of Shit*", and I was done being used. I drove her back to Marietta and this time when she ignored my calls, I stopped reaching out.

Predictably, several months after she graduated, Nancy called me with a bullshit apology. It was the same old game; a booty call with no booty, but my frustration with her went far beyond sex, and this time I wasn't going to be played. It was gonna take a helluva lot more than a phone call for her to get back into my good graces.

It had finally become clear to me that she would probably never face herself, and failing that, she could never partner anyone. She told me that she'd shown me her worst parts and it was high time she shared her best sides with me, but Nancy didn't want to love or be loved. She wanted to control and dominate.

I simply told her time would tell if her apology was real.

For once, I needed her to go out of her way for me. I needed her to be the one to stretch, as I always had, to bring us together.

By my response to her apology, she knew I was calling her out. Her rage was palpable, and I thought to myself, *"so this is the best of her?"*

I no longer gave a shit.

That was fourteen years ago, now, and in all that time I've never heard a word from her.

After Nancy, there was never gonna be another woman for me. Spiritually, and despite our difficulties, I felt with her that I was at home at last, but we never got to the crux of what kept us apart.

I tried dating other women, but nothing came of it. I tracked her down in 2023. She'd closed her chiropractic practice in 2019, then married the year after that. I wrote to her, but predictably, she didn't respond.

Orthodox wisdom says there are two great tragedies in life; one when you get exactly what you always wanted; and the other when you don't.

In this relationship I got a combination of both these outcomes.

Perhaps if we had worked out, I would have been disappointed by Nancy in time. Probably so, because her rigid defenses were so firmly entrenched. Perhaps I taught her to disrespect me by allowing her to get away with using me. But when it comes right down to it, I still trust my gut that she was and always will be the girl for me.

If I could speak to her now, I don't know what I would say but it might go something like this;

"Who the hell do you think you are!?! What kind of human being are you? I never loved anyone as I love you and no one could ever love you more. A catatonic robot could see the truth of this in a second, but you pushed me away and pushed me away and pushed me away till you pushed me away.

The only way you could mistake my devotion to you was because you were so filled with pain and shame and rage that they blinded you to all the love anyone could ever want. Maybe you are better than me or any man at whatever you do; that's bullshit, and we both know it but even if it's true, what's the value of being superior; what's the point of existence itself; if you turn your back on the kind of love that makes life worth living..."

I still haven't fully come to terms with Nancy and everything she meant to me, but I'm getting there and time heals all wounds, or so they say. I still hold on to her, or rather to the realization of who she was for me.

So-called realists would say I was delusional; that she clearly never loved me but was perfectly willing to use me. At some level that's clear. But for all my efforts, I don't think I ever reached her heart.

If I had, things would have been different, but no one could fault the efforts I made. And beyond that, Nancy never faced herself. She stayed a safe distance from me because she had to stay a safe distance from who she was being. A part of her always couldn't wait to run away. When I called her out, that's exactly what she did.

It's been said of the malignant narcissist that what he or she cannot love they seek to control and what they cannot control they destroy.

This was the legacy Nancy probably inherited from her father. Just as probably, I showed this same toxic narcissism in many of our shared past lives.

Odds makers would bet on the fact that I'll never see or hear from Nancy Lynne Edington again. But if not in this life, then in a life to come, I'm certain I will.

Maybe next time we'll get it right.

Here and now, she wasn't good to me or for me, so I put a stop to her abuse. She taught me how close the line between love and hate really is. But I do and always will love and want Nancy with all my heart and soul.

For me, that's just the way it is.

Losing Mom

Much like my oldest brother, Rick, mom was always low key. She was always curious about what other people were up to and how they were getting along, and this interest in others extended to her curiosity about the world.

Although I wasn't conscious of this at the time, I felt mom ought to get a chance to nourish that curiosity after dad passed, and she felt free to take better care of herself. I decided that the right thing to do now was to live with her for an indefinite period and do my best to care for her as she'd always cared for me.

The truth is mom took care of me every bit as much as I watched over her. We both needed love, care and protection.

It's been said adults should never live with their parents. I suppose from the parent's perspective that's because they always somehow view their adult children as their little boy or girl. Mom behaved like this, but only slightly.

It helped that I was her favorite child, but that didn't exempt me from her lifelong lack of sensitivity. Mother was a much simpler person than I was, and she was more cut and dried about almost everything. Her lack of sensitivity was sometimes grating.

This issue came into focus when Nancy came up from Marietta on a break from LIFE University to visit. Mom made it clear to me that she didn't want us having sex during her stay. I made it clear that wouldn't happen at home.

If Nancy and I wanted to be intimate, I'd take her to a nice hotel where we could enjoy our privacy.

I considered this subject fully addressed but mom felt compelled to bring it up with Nancy, which put my girl off, and which was none of my mother's goddamn business. The last thing I needed was my mom getting involved in my sex life. This really, REALLY pissed me off. I told my mother she had my word on this issue, and all she'd done now was introduce an extra, unnecessary element of tension in my relationship with Nancy, who locked her bedroom door the entire time of her visit.

SHIT, PISS, FUCK, GODDAMIT!

By the time pop passed, mom and dad had been married for 63 years. Although I was never gonna fill dad's place in her life, all in all, we got on well together. It helped that amidst our considerable differences we both adored each other.

What surprised me, as I took on all the shopping and meal making duties, was that I could never drag mom away from her newspaper in time to give her a hot meal.

In our family, *"come and get it"* always meant *"come and get it NOW!"* Frankly, it pissed me off to work as hard as I did to make meals mom would enjoy and then have her fail to come to the table till everything went cold. It was as if she was in a new phase of life now, and she no longer considered how she would have felt had our places been reversed on this score.

Alive Hospice in Nashville had helped with dad's care while he was sick, and they had grief counseling available for survivors of people who'd been under their care. They offered group grieving sessions and individual counseling. Mom and Diane decided to join a group and I opted for both group and individual counseling.

I didn't feel comfortable sharing some of the things that troubled me with my mom and sister in a group setting.

Our group had other limitations, like blanket statements made by some that all was in God's hands, and similar religious presumptions. It was good to be able to talk in my individual sessions about everything that had gone down with me and my family over the years, but talk therapy always felt limited and way too slow for me.

For therapy to work you must arrive at the point where you were traumatized, reexperience that event, reframe it from a place of raw, emotional integrity, and only then can you move on.

I think you get to the crux of what sidelines you from your own life by doing play therapy and body work, and that these approaches to healing liberate you much faster than talking yourself into returning to the scene of the crime, so to speak.

Time heals all, they say, or maybe you just move on because if you're going to remain alive and engaged with life that's all you can do after a great loss.

Mom moved on by moving in with Diane. I moved on by moving to Albuquerque. That's where I was when sis called one day in the early spring of 2015 with news that mom had been diagnosed with stage 4 pancreatic cancer.

This was tantamount to a death sentence and sis and I both knew it. Mother took the news with remarkable poise. She even did her best to comfort the young doctor who had to deliver this devastating news. The medical industrial complex offered my mother a new chemo protocol that would have extended her life a month at best, but her quality of life would be abysmal, so mom declined.

Mother decided to let the cancer take its course.

She had by now moved from Diane's home to a retirement facility called The Heritage that was state of the art. It was expensive but just within her living budget and living there was a joy in her last year of life. It also enabled her to leave an estate for her children because the apartment she bought was sold when she passed, and the entire new purchase amount went to her estate.

When sis called, we decided I'd come home to care for mom as I had with papa. Near the end I would sleep with mom with my head at the foot of the bed so we could comfortably hold hands.

Mother had the softest hands ever.

If I'd fallen asleep, she'd give me a squeeze if she needed me. Mostly, I think she wanted me with her for to feel less alone. Mama was remarkably determined to be self-sufficient right up to the time we had to transfer her from her new home to hospice.

I remember one morning she got herself up to brush her teeth. I'll never forget her strength of character and determination to do for herself. Her courage made me cry.

Early one morning at the beginning of July, mom refused to take her pain meds. For the first time she was irrational. Mother believed I was trying to poison her. I called Diane, then Stephen, then Rick, to see if they could persuade her, but none of us were successful.

That's when we knew she could no longer manage her pain and it was hospice time.

On July 7, 2015, just past 10 am mom passed away at Alive Hospice in Nashville. As with papa, the entire family was gathered around her. When death came, mother was kinda of out of it, not fully present but not delusional, either. As dad had, she simply stopped breathing.

Now I knew the meaning of Hamlet's final words when he said, *"The rest is silence."* Death comes and the finality of it robs you of the capacity to express what you feel. Words seem beyond inadequate. There's a void with death that seems to suck out all the oxygen inside you and leaves you deaf, dumb and numb.

Mama was a good and caring woman who had issues being intimate with the people she loved most. Sometimes she didn't protect us from dad as much as she could and should have. Still, I know she loved us with her whole heart and it's a tribute to the quality of her love that despite her limitations we loved and adored her, too.

"The rest is silence."

Coming Home again; at least part way

When mom got sick, I realized that living 1200 miles away in New Mexico didn't work for me. I'd moved to Albuquerque a few years after dad passed because I associated Fayetteville with his death. That was understandable, but I found there was nothing close to the good vibrations in Albuquerque that I'd connected to in Arkansas.

Once I had been back in Tennessee caring for mom, I decided to move back to Fayetteville. The last thing I wanted was to go all the way out to New Mexico to close my apartment there, so I hired my friend, Devin Sherwood, to pack up my belongings and meet me in the Ozarks.

This time, I chose to live at a facility called the Links at Springdale, which had a nine-hole golf course onsite. It was the best nine-hole track I could find in the area and playing it was included in my rent.

I leased a two-bedroom apartment on the west side of the complex and it was a four-minute walk from my door to the 7th tee. Lindsey Management ran the facility, and they did an excellent job keeping the entire complex in good shape. My little golf course had bent grass greens that were fun to putt, Bermuda rough that was a pain in the ass, and a short game practice area at the clubhouse where I could work on that crucial part of my game.

I loved my little nine-holer and played it often. The only things I didn't like about it were that the prevailing wind always came from the southwest. I had to fight that wind most of the time I played my one par 5. The bunkers had no base which required a sand wedge with almost no bounce, and the first hole was too narrow for me to ever feel comfortable playing it.

For the most part, however, at least till the end of my time there, I enjoyed playing the links as much as possible because playing the game kept me happy and healthy.

Losing Stephen

Losing someone you've known and loved your entire life is awful and as trite as that sounds, because of course it's dreadful, what no one tells you is that the loss of a sibling is very different from losing a parent. So, it's terrible in its own unique way.

Worse still when we lost Steve, it was unexpected.

Before I knew his health had become an issue, we arranged to spend the day before I moved to New Mexico golfing at the Bear Trace in Crossville, TN. Steve hadn't played golf in years and opted out of teeing it up with me, but we shared a cart and I played with a work buddy of mine and his dad who had come on their own, as I had, from Nashville.

After the round, Steve and I sat alone in our golf cart for quite a while and talked.

Although we weren't close growing up, we became so as adults, and Steve always felt he could confide in me. So, when he told me that afternoon that he'd been having weird symptoms like a racing pulse that would pop up for no reason, or periods of deep fatigue that had no clear connection to what he was doing and that spooked him, I said he must get some tests done ASAP.

I drove to Albuquerque the next day but made a point of checking in with Stephen as often as possible to get updates. Not long after I moved west, his test results came through.

He'd contracted two blood cancers; multiple myeloma, and a rare secondary condition called amyloidosis, which caused protein deposits in his heart.

We were all in shock.

Steve started coming monthly to Vanderbilt Hospital in Nashville which had a strong reputation for effective cancer treatments. Whenever I was visiting Nashville from New Mexico, if he was there and scheduled for an appointment, I'd drive him to the hospital and hang out with him as much as I could. His chemo treatments were done closer to home in Knoxville, where he lived.

We never talked about it, but there was a terrible loneliness about going through all the steps one felt obliged to take dealing with cancer. Maybe this is why being together in this situation came to mean so much to both of us.

Somewhere along the line, his doctors decided the best course of action was to do a bone marrow transplant to harvest my brother's stem cells, then literally kill his infected blood, and re-introduce "clean" blood infused with those cells.

I was in New Mexico when this stratagem was settled on, but we were in constant touch with each other, and it was then that my brother and I began to have long phone calls twice or more a month.

Steve and I never said it explicitly, but the context of all our conversations was that he was living on borrowed time. Consequently, we talked about things that seldom enter everyday conversation. The trivialities of Tennessee Vol football, or bitching about taxes, and complaining about the government, which were such passionate concerns for him at one time, quickly vanished from my brother's priorities.

Now we got into the meaning of life. We talked about our legacies and what we feared but also hoped we'd leave behind. We spoke about creation and existence. He talked about Brenda, his wife, about his kids, and he shared his deep faith in Christianity. I told him why I wasn't a Christian; about how and why Astrology was such an anchor for me.

I'd grappled with life's meaning since I was a boy. Steve had always been more conventionally inclined, so he came to these queries later, but he was catching up fast. He told me that he felt he could talk with me about things that he couldn't address with anyone else, so we got exceptionally close.

Of course, going through all this was tougher on Steve than it was on me. For example, he'd always been quite a physical specimen. His hands and forearms were massive, the result of spending so many years on crutches, when he was recovering from several procedures he endured to treat the polio he had as a boy.

His arms now became more like toothpicks.

My big brother had a beautiful, thick, full head of hair that virtually disappeared when his chemo treatments kicked in. To counter this, I sent him an Elvis wig and some rock and roll sunglasses that befit "The King." Someone took a picture of Steve in his Elvis get-up, and we all had a good laugh.

With time, by trial and error, it seemed he'd found a blend of medications and chemo that seemed to work so he could maintain his struggling legal practice.

The day before he died was a good one. He'd spent it at his office and made good progress helping a client with a tax problem.

Brenda said they had a wonderful time that night, although in retrospect some of his comments seemed odd to her. Mostly, he reassured her that she'd be OK after he passed because, he said and/or she thought, his affairs were in order.

Sometime after midnight on July 26, 2017, Stephen passed away in his sleep.

In some ways, losing Steve hit me harder than mom or dad's deaths. My parents were mythical figures to me. Stephen was just three and a half years my senior. Losing mom and dad rocked my world, especially losing dad, but my brother's passing put me much more in touch with my own mortality.

At Stephen's memorial service I said what I felt and believed to be true; that matter cannot be destroyed; it can only be reformed. Steve was with us and just because we couldn't see or feel him didn't mean his passing was the end of him or of our relationship.

I'm sure most folks attending this gathering thought I was off the wall, but I didn't care. Whether he was with us or not, however, we all had to deal with the fact that Stephen *as we had known him* was forever gone.

The irony of Steve's life, for me, was the split between his many accomplishments when he was young and how lost I think he felt in his professional life. He was a man with considerable capabilities and a rock-solid work ethic, but he found little satisfaction or fulfillment practicing law. This is why his life as a Christian was so important to him, although its anchoring effect didn't absolve him from dealing with unspoken resentments and upsets I had no idea tormented him.

One of the traits I share with most of my siblings, living and dead, and for that matter with most of my extended family, is a propensity for resentment. Holding grudges seems to afflict us all.

This family trait was a challenge for Stephen despite his faith. So, at the end of the day, I wish he'd been more open about his anger and who it was directed towards, so it didn't come out sideways in his relationships with others who weren't the real source of his pain.

Ultimately, I've learned that the buck stops with me when I'm upset; that I must own my feelings and look to myself to get past whatever troubles me. No amount of faith or spirituality, religious or otherwise, can exempt you from dealing with your upsets and the feelings that go with them. Our deepest emotions always find expression one way or another, whether we acknowledge or deny them.

I had no unresolved business with Steve, so I don't suffer from any lingering resentments with him. I wish I could say this is true of other family members. But at this point, it's on whoever has outstanding problems with Steve to take on his or her feelings and work things out.

The only regret I have now is that I'm not as close to his surviving family as I once felt I was. Perhaps the closeness I felt with Brenda and their kids was an illusion because as adults Stephen and I were always so tight.

If there are unspoken resentments Steve's surviving family has with me, I hope one day they'll come to me, so we have the chance to work things out. I suspect they don't have all the information they need to get a clear picture of how things were with us, though this may apply more to how Steve's family views his relationship with other family members.

I miss Brenda and her kids. We've lost touch despite my efforts to reach out to them, and I'd like to be much more in touch with their lives.

The Saving Grace of a Part Time Job

I began to wind down my astrological practice when I found that most everyone who came to me was resistant to working on themselves, via the template of their birth chart and other relevant charts.

For me, the whole point of astrology was and remains to actively connect to and integrate all the energies that make up being fully human. This kind of work necessitates getting the dynamics of whatever chart you were working with into your body. Wordless voice and body improvisations based on the dynamic aspects of the chart are essential if the person involved hopes to experience him or herself in full. It's also crucial to becoming consciously connected to your inmost reality.

Most of my clients just wanted to be fixed. What was missing was ownership of all their human parts. More and more, I seemed to encounter passivity in my new clientele and even with folks I'd worked with for years.

Although the type of client I attracted may have mirrored passivity in me, I had no interest in talking folks into my way of thinking, so I found myself doing less and less astrological counseling and more charity work in my community.

This community service work brought me to St. Paul's Episcopal church in Fayetteville. With less money coming in from my astrology practice, most of my income was now from investments I'd made and my retirement benefits. In the summer of 2019, I decided to get a part time job in service of some sort. This would be a good use of my time and give me more of a financial cushion beyond the monthly distributions I already received.

Christopher Hallett, a buddy of mine who also volunteered at St. Paul's, had taken s social service job several months before and I asked him if he knew of any part-time jobs that were available where he worked. He told me that his employer, The Fayetteville Senior Wellness and Activity Center, was going to need a taxi driver and had me apply for that job online.

The first thing I said to Chase Gipson, the director of the center, was *"you have a good spirit."* He probably thought I was shining him on. My gut observation about him proved, however, to be more than true. My relationship with Chase has been a boon and a blessing in my life.

The Senior Center was the only place I applied to, and they hired me right away.

The new job didn't pay much, but it was only a twenty-five-hour weekly commitment, and I hadn't taken it for the money, anyway. I took the job to help folks in need. As I saw it, the difference between what I made working there and what I was worth would be my charitable contribution.

For me, Chase was the perfect boss. Pragmatic, low key, and full of uncommonly common sense, he was easy to work with. He also had a degree in Philosophy of all things. I quickly found that we saw things very much alike.

Gipson had a quick, inquiring mind, a strong desire to see life with clarity, and an impulse towards self-sufficiency. Over the course of the next several years, starting in September of 2019, we had endless conversations about all manner of things related to modern life, here and worldwide.

I also found that for the most part, most everyone working at the senior center or volunteering there had a heart centered approach to work and life.

We didn't always have time to converse in a no holds barred way, because there was a clientele to be served, but there was often time to discuss current events, and when the COVID 19 pandemic set in, Chase and I had the time and opportunity to discuss current events in a deep and thoughtful way.

As it turned out, these conversations inspired much of what I've written in the Introduction and Afterword to this book.

As of this writing, I'm still driving for the Fayetteville Senior Center, and it continues to be a joy for me. We have a fascinating array of workers and seniors that demand sensitivity and flexibility, and every day is different.

Losing Rick

I guess you never know when your life can change forever. January 13, 2020, brought this reality home to me. My oldest brother, Richard, had a heart attack at home. His family rushed him to the hospital, which took the better part of an hour because they lived in a fairly remote location south of Franklin, TN. A second heart attack hit him in the emergency room and this one did him in.

All this took place in just over two hours' time.

When I think of Rick his sweetness is the first thing that comes to mind. He was a gentle spirit, too, although I think our family trait of volatility lived somewhere inside him that was less apparent than it was with most of us.

Just a few days after Christmas he dropped by Diane's house in Franklin. I always stayed with sis for Christmas and the three of us had a wonderful post-holiday visit for two or three hours. I know we reminisced about Christmases from our childhood, but don't recall so much the specifics of our conversation as the quality of our fellowship.

For some reason I now forget, we didn't have a service for Rick till February in 2021. With Richard's loss, I'd gone from little brother to *Pater Familia* in a matter of minutes and I felt it was on me to speak first when we gathered to celebrate him. I wanted to set the tone at my oldest brother's memorial.

I had enough presence of mind to begin with a joke and conspired with my nephew Michael to set up the laugh.

I stood up to begin the proceedings and the first thing I said was that I'd been anxious about what to say so I consulted with Mike about how to approach it. Then I put words in my nephew's mouth when I reported that he said; *"Don't worry, Uncle Bob, just remember what Robert Downey Jr. said in* **Tropic Thunder**. I hadn't seen the movie, so I asked Michael what Downey said. Michael replied with the epic line, *"Just don't go full retard."*

The laughs I was going for broke the ice, and then I promised to remain *Compos Mentus* to the best of my ability.

I went on to say that my primary aim in speaking was to comfort Emily, Greta and Mat; Rick's wife and two children. I said that my brother was a big man, but that he had a soft-spoken presence. I spoke of his kindness, of how I'd never seen him be mean-spirited to anyone. I paid tribute to him for always looking out for me.

Somewhere in my comments, I asserted that Rick was uniquely suited to be my father's first born, and that had I been in his position I'd be dead, in jail, or on parole for manslaughter.

This got another laugh, but with the exception of the ***Tropic Thunder*** set up, everything I said was true.

If I had a magic wand, I would have granted Rick great confidence. I would have given him a sense of self-possession and identity that was solid and unassailable. Most of all, I would have granted him the liberty to become whoever he most wanted to be.

And in the moment of writing this tribute, I would thank him for enduring the challenge of having our dad for a father, because the mistakes pop made with Rick helped him become a better father to me.

I suppose in my own way I am a person of faith. Consequently, I believe I'll see my oldest brother from this life in another incarnation yet to come, and probably in a few lives after that, too.

I couldn't have had a better friend than Rick nor anyone who cared about me so consistently and so well.

Covid

Something was fishy about the way this new strain of flu was being handled. By March of 2020, a month after Rick's memorial, when everything started shutting down, the Covid Pandemic had become politicized, monetized, and polarizing.

When businesses and people could make money from conforming to the establishment's narrative, celebrities could popularize immunizations by endorsing vaccination, and big pharma was absolved from any responsibility should their vaccines prove dangerous, the quality of information we received went off the rails.

To begin with, why the hell was a government agency tasked with public health doing "gain of function" research? Why was the setting for this dubious research in China, a country whose repressive, evil régime murdered political dissidents to harvest their organs, then sold them on the black market.

If you examined the situation in terms of how it was handled in the U.S., if you did your due diligence, the playbook the American government was using to deal with Covid was pretty much a duplicate of their approach to the flu epidemic of 1919.

And please, stop with the mask bullshit. Covid 19 is an airborne virus. Wearing a mask had no chance of protecting anyone. It was like putting up a picket fence to stop an invasion of gnats. What's more, Dr. Fauci's conflicting pronouncements put him in a league with Harvey Two-Face from the Batman movie franchise. Fauci made so many contradictory statements he appeared to have more bends and twists than Gumbi.

Nevertheless, I was ready to take the Covid vaccination, which I ultimately declined to do, because I missed and wanted to visit my family in Nashville. Had it not been for Chase Gipson, who advised me to examine some anti-jab information right before I was scheduled to get the first shot, I think I would have become vulnerable to the many negative side effects of the booster that have been well documented by watchdog groups but are still denied by the powers that be.

When I flew to Nashville for Christmas 2020, I got the virus sometime while I was in transit or after I arrived and it kicked my ass, but I made the right decision to reject the so-called vaccine.

Like with any flu, even this new, seemingly turbo-charged strain, my body developed anti-bodies free of any pharmaceutical side effects from a flim-flam cure dangerously rushed to market. After spending most of January 2020 resting at home, I slowly rebuilt my stamina and strength and was back to normal in mid-February.

In retrospect, this was classic manipulation by the powers that be to create a crisis, then offer a solution that consolidated and extended their authority and dominance, by making average folks more compliant, and thereby assured those who were in power stayed in power.

At the same time, Covid and the manipulation of information about it, probably also assured one power player, Donald Trump, lost his re-election bid. Prior to the pandemic, the American economy was on an upward trend and if that upsurge hadn't been derailed by Covid, Trump would likely have won a second term in the White House.

I'm no fan of Trump, but found him preferrable to Hilary Clinton, who I trusted and respected even less than the Donald, during the presidential campaign of 2016.

As was true in many families, my kin had a variety of viewpoints about the vaccine. I decided that the best way to deal with this was simply to say that each adult in ours or any other family had to make his or her own decision about taking the vaccine.

The most compelling argument for taking the jab was that you'd be protecting others if you were immunized. By the same token, I objected to anyone telling me what to do with my own body. My response to these opposite points of view was to educate myself as fully as possible about the virus and the machinery employed to deal with it.

In my opinion, the vaccines were dangerous, despite mainstream propaganda to the contrary, and I threw my lot in with naturally developing anti-bodies to COVID, if I got it, and as much as possible, I stayed a safe distance from everyone I met.

I'm dubious about any widespread government policy, when that policy is aligned with the profit margins of the various industrial complexes that now dominate American society.

Fundamentally, I object to any industrial complex of any kind dictating what my behavior "should" be.

At the end of the day, I'm responsible for my own health, not doctors whom I may consult but will not blindly defer to. It's my life and my choice, and so long as I take precautions to protect folks I interact with, my choice of conduct trumps any other so-called authority when it comes to protecting my health and respecting yours.

Scotland 2023

Let's face it, my golf game wasn't likely to improve as I got past my mid-sixties. Especially if I didn't work on it, which now at 70 I didn't, because I wasn't going to let golf become a job. Still, I'd been playing since I was 13 and I thought it would be nice to have a swan song. Scotland was the home of the game, although it originated in Holland, so I thought one last journey to the land of the kilt would be a grand finale.

Starting in the spring of 2022, I ran my idea past my buddy Devin Sherwood. It started as a trip for just the two of us. I liked the idea of combining my sayonara with celebrating his birthday, June 11th, 2023, which would fall in the middle of our trip.

I was good at planning, so I took on investigating places to play and stay. We expected to spend around $2500 to $3000 apiece, so our original thought was to keep things on the cheap.

The first golf course/accommodation I saw that interested me was in Kinross, roughly twenty miles north of Edinburgh. The hotel and golf course complex there seemed like a nice starting off point. I checked the dates but even though I was looking more than a year in advance, the hotel, which was being renovated, was already booked up on the prime dates we wanted in 2023.

Naturally, when I talked to my buddies from time to time, I mentioned planning for Scotland and my college fraternity brother, Jimbo Hash, said he'd like to join us.

Jimbo didn't really play much, but he was coachable, and whenever we teed it up I gave him a playing lesson that got him around the course pretty well. J-bro wasn't long, but he hit it straight and often very solid. He thought I was the greatest golf teacher on the planet. We both enjoyed the fellowship of playing, which for me is the best thing about the game, and when I asked Devin if Jimbo could join us, he said sure, so long as he could invite a buddy, too.

This was the first of many, many changes that would occur before I got there at the time I originally planned but with an almost entirely different group of guys.

I knew that the trip would be a stretch for Dev because he pretty much lived hand to mouth, either working on the staff at golf courses or as a restaurant server.

Still early in planning it all, I had one concern.

As I saw it, Devin had a drinking problem. When he revealed the friend he invited to join us downed ten to twelve beers a day, I began to worry. I had no intention of setting up a trip that enabled Dev to drink excessively because I suspected he was an alcoholic.

My discomfort at this prospect got serious when I told Dev what I was thinking. I just couldn't risk doing something that would undermine his health. At first, he said he had his drinking under control. But even if that was so, having a buddy guzzle a dozen brews a day was asking for trouble. As it turned out, Dev and his friend both dropped out.

Deep down, I felt that the trip was too much for Devin. He needed to direct his funds towards more essential needs. So, all things considered, I believe he was relieved to pull out although he never said so. If I was the villain in his eyes, so be it, so long as going on the trip didn't hurt him.

By the time all this fell out, I'd been planning the trip for several months, and I had no intention of shutting it all down. My nephews played golf, although not with the skill and passion I did, or at least had done at one time, so I invited them to join me.

To a man they enthusiastically said yes.

Now I had four nephews coming, plus a buddy of theirs, Travis Deck, Andy, my nephew David's father-in-law, plus Jimbo. The first order of business was to find a place for us to stay. The accommodation would need to be no more than an hour's drive one-way to any course we played and to keep expenses down, I set up a mix of medium and high-end venues so we could keep things affordable and have a full spectrum of links and parkland golf.

My new budget goal per man was around $3500 per player.

After consulting with my nephew Michael Crabtree, my sister's oldest son, I settled on booking an Airbnb accommodation in Dunfermline around eighteen miles north of Edinburgh's airport. It was a loft space with a large kitchen, was centrally located so we could get to our early afternoon tee times in reasonable time, and it had great views of the surrounding countryside.

Coincidentally, and for the first time in my life, I started to develop some gastro-intestinal issues. I literally didn't know when I felt the urge to go, if I would be doing number one or number two, so I started wearing diapers which I continued to do in the run up to, during and after our trip. This was more than literally a pain in my ass, but sensing I needed a positive counterpoint to this physical anomaly, I resumed working on this memoir, which I'd set aside for several years, while I kept working on the Scotland trip.

Now I started booking the tee times.

Kinross was still first, followed by the legendary Gleneagles Kings course, then we'd take the weekend off to sightsee, play the New Course at St. Andrews on Monday, the superb links at North Berwick on Tuesday June 13th, our penultimate round at Pitlochry on Wednesday, and then play our final eighteen at Crieff Golf Club on Thursday, before returning home the next day.

Three weeks before the journey, I called American Airlines to book some seats over the pond and back. I'd intended to let the damn airline put me wherever they chose so I could save money but decided I should spend a little extra to be comfortable on the ocean legs of the trip.

When I called AA, I got a heart stopping shock. *"I'm sorry Mr. Moseley, but you have no reservation!"*

This was a nightmare scenario. All the group reservations, our transportation, our Airbnb loft, and all our tee times were in my name.

FUCK, NOW WHAT?

Panicking, I cancelled what I was told was a non-existent round trip ticket with AA and booked a provisional ticket with them costing $700 more than my original, non-refundable fare. I had 24 hours to cancel this new ticket and get a full refund. Then I kept looking and found a non-stop ticket from Atlanta to Edinburgh on Delta, so I booked that. When I called AA to cancel the provisional ticket, they said they'd issue me credit, but no refund, breaking their word to me after they'd fucked up my original reservation. I went off on the agent, who only then gave me the refund as promised.

The next morning, I recalled getting an email confirmation from AA on my now denied and cancelled reservation. I went back, found and retrieved this email, called AA, where upon they confirmed that my original reservation and record locator was IN FACT VALID, but that since I'd cancelled it, I was SOL.

The so-called agent who denied my original reservation had made a major mistake. So now, I went to the Better Business Bureau for help. AA's error was so egregious they wound up refunding the original ticket price and the provisional ticket fee, but those refunds didn't come through till well after the trip, thereby tying up a major bit of credit I'd planned to use during our vacation. Moreover, I was left holding the bag on the increase I had to pay Delta for booking flights so late.

All my budget would have been taken up booking all these goddamn flights, but thanks to my guardian angels, Diane and David, who gave me $2500 for the trip, I was able to tap those funds for the journey proper and wait on the refunds without more STRAIN.

The stress of all the planning, all the changes, getting everything in place, having the airline and travel service screw up, and my wonky G.I. track, left me frazzled and exhausted before we even got to Edinburgh.

Once we arrived, however, my nephew Mat took over all the driving duties, which really, REALLY helped me unwind.

The first venue we played was the Montgomery course at Kinross. It was a parkland venue and was secluded. The course was challenging but fairly straight-forward from tee to green, with generous to adequately wide fairways. The hard part was the greens. They were filled with humps and hollows that I found excessive. When we finished playing the Montgomery, I checked off the experience but decided not to return.

At Gleneagles, a truly great golf resort founded in 1919, we played the famous Kings course, designed by James Braid and it was magnificent. Unfortunately, I started badly and couldn't find my swing for the first six holes. After I foozled my drive on the 4th hole, I lost my shit and went off in a blue tirade that embarrassed me and mortified the threesome of ladies playing just behind our group.

I made a nice bunker shot on the 6th for a tap in par that got my round going and we let the ladies pass us at the mandatory stop we made at the halfway house situated just off the 11th tee.

Each hole at the King's course felt like a work of art. The routing of the holes was constantly putting the wind at different angles to our line of play and the vistas of the Scottish Highlands were unforgettably gorgeous. Unlike Kinross, I'd play this or the King's sister course, the Queens, anytime I got the opportunity.

We took the weekend off to sightsee Edinburgh. Unfortunately, we didn't get to see Edinburgh Castle, which for some reason was closed to the public at 3 pm that Saturday. The highlight of the day, if such a thing was your cup of tea, was a walking tour we did of the places where all the most notorious executions had taken place throughout the history of the city.

On Monday we went to St. Andrews to play the New Course, which I found unmemorable, although we were lucky there and throughout our trip to get very good weather.

North Berwick, (the w is silent) was a links course we played the next day at twilight, and it tied the parkland King's course as my favorite of the trip. Like the courses at Gleneagles, I would happily play it again and again.

We got our best photographs of the entire trip at North Berwick and where able to tee off at 4pm and finish well in advance of sundown that didn't happen till after 10 pm. Unfortunately, my play there was spotty, too, and the high winds there kicked my ass.

Pitlochry, our next venue, was a disappointment. Literally cut into the side of a mountain, it was impossible to cut the fairways and greens there with modern mowing machines and I found the greens there so slow they seemed like shag rugs.

I'd anticipated this and brought both heavy and light putters to allow for this possibility, but I seemed to pick the wrong putter most places we played till we got to our last round at Crieff Golf Club.

At Crieff I picked the right short stick and felt comfortable on the greens. Although my game was off there and for most of the trip, I'd found something at Pitlochry the day before that helped free up my swing. I made an adjustment, so my backswing flowed directly into my downswing with one continuous motion, and when I got this transition right, I hit the ball well.

On number 8, a short par 4 of around 330 yards, I actually drove the green with my tee shot but couldn't see my yellow ball because we were hitting directly into the sun. Luckily, my Bridgestone stopped around four feet from the hole, and I was thrilled at the prospect of scoring a 2 on a par 4. When my eagle putt dropped it was my golfing highlight of the entire trip.

Although like all golfers, I wish I'd played better than I did, the final round eagle at Crieff did much to salve my disappointment with my play. Unfortunately, when I got home, a whole new level of stress would occur in my life while my G.I. issues remained unresolved.

Marion III

When I got back from Scotland, it had been almost fourteen years since Marion and I had been in touch. I had no idea how she might respond but we'd always had a special connection and I missed that, so I called her at the number I still had for her, hoping it was the same.

As always, Marion responded to my outreach right away. Still the embodiment of Gaston Lachaise's *Standing Woman,* still prolific, still passionately political, still dedicated to her writing, and most of all still living with an intensity that burned the candle of her colossal energy at both ends, she hadn't changed a bit.

The bigger the person, the bigger their shadow.

For years I'd heard the same story from my dear, dear friend. It was a litany worthy of Rodney Dangerfield's classic complaint, *"I can't get no respect.*

"Everyone who hires me pays me nothing. I feel unseen and unappreciated. Morons criticize my poetry who have less intelligence than a slug..." On and on she went unwilling to admit that she was projecting her abusive father's condemnation of her into her working environments and/or finding editorial work settings where she felt exploited, so she could complain about and continue her lifelong battle with feeling disrespected.

Her real addiction was battling her father's criticism which she secretly feared was justified.

In all the years I knew her, I'd never heard her praise a workplace where she felt seen, properly compensated, and fully appreciated for her amazing combination of energy, passion, and skill. Ironically, her amazing ability and prolific knowledge of all manner of things, was probably compensatory. She built a formidable set of skills to counteract how deficient she felt inside.

Marion had a siege mentality that had her working non-stop just to pay her rent, which by now was upwards of $6000 per month in a doorman building that required her to tip a staff of twenty every Christmas. Time after time I suggested she relocate, but she didn't want to be away from the action and amazing energy of the upper west side of Manhattan.

Ultimately, this toxic combination of high expenses, round the clock work, precious little sleep, and debilitating worry about how to maintain it all probably killed my friend.

I began to worry when I called her in mid-August of 2023, which I now did periodically to check on her, but this time she didn't respond. This was unlike Marion, who always got back to me right away. I asked my buddy, David Turk, to check on her and he found her obituary had just posted in the New York Times.

Sometime on August 10, 2023, Marion passed away. Everyone who knew her couldn't believe it. I tried and tried to find out what happened but couldn't get the police report because I wasn't a family member, and I had no contact information for any of her Chicago based family or Manhattan friends.

Left to guess at her fate, with a woefully inadequate obituary to go by, I think she probably died of exhaustion. It seemed most likely that the morning of August 10th she simply didn't wake up.

Marion was the epitome of English reserve. She never told me, *"I love you,"* but I know she did. And I loved her, too, which once we reconnected, I told her all the time.

I only wish she could have loved herself.

Marion was a great and abundant light in my life. When she passed I felt the loss of her warmth immensely.

"Wherever you are now, dear heart, I know you're brightening your world with the force of your astounding will and passion. I miss you beyond what I can say, but sooner or later, I'll be seeing you again."

A Forced Move becomes a Blessed New Beginning

Had I a family of my own, I'm sure I would have knuckled-under, living a much more conventional life than its turned out I have. This includes owning a home because, to me, the only reason to take on the care and maintenance of an entire house is to raise a family.

For this reason, I've always been an apartment dweller.

My neighbors from hell, Brandy and Casey, who moved in sometime during the run up to my Scotland trip, were the only neighbors I've had that made me question my approach to living spaces.

Most renters, I'm told, will stay an average of three, maybe four years in an apartment before they move on. I had happily been in my place for eight plus years and had no intention of moving till the aforementioned tenants moved in right above me. These folks had two untrained dogs that trampled the floor above me, usually before I got up in the morning, driving me crazy.

I tried everything I could to get them to respect my peace of mind, but my direct appeals, always followed by a thank you gift of a pot or plant, never led to more than a few days of calm and quiet. Then, to add insult to injury, trash started raining down from their overstuffed balcony onto my patio.

The fact that the license plate on Casey's truck read; *"My other ride has TITS"* should have told me my appeals for courtesy and civility would fall on deaf ears.

I knew Lindsey Properties, my managing company, charged monthly pet fees, which obligated them to protect me. So, I appealed to them to enforce the dictates of their pet policy but all I got was a strong sense of their annoyance, and a boiler-plate response.

In essence, there message to me was *"too bad pal, you're on your own here."* Call me old fashioned but I expected much more support than the total indifference, if not hostility, I got from my rental agents.

Home didn't feel like home anymore, and free golf aside, I had a decision to make. So, after my return from Scotland, I opted to move out and move on.

The run up to Scotland had been stressful. The trip had been great, but I discovered that my endurance wasn't what it once was. Now I was back home, in need of recovery from my golfing vacation, but instead was faced with financing and handling a move on my own to a whole new domicile.

All this, combined with my continuing health issues, made this problem almost unbearable but I had to get out of where I was living. Moreover, I'd recommitted to finishing my memoir, and needed a quiet setting I'd never recover with my sexist, insensitive and indifferent neighbors perched atop my peace of mind.

Several months prior to all this, I happened to apply at Nantucket Apartments, a charming retirement community that was walking distance from work. When they called with a two-bedroom available, I leaped at the chance to lease it right away.

This would necessitate my breaking my current lease two months early but that was OK by me. The sooner I got out from under the dogs from hell, both human and canine, the better.

My friend Devin had told me a few years prior to this that when he packed up and moved my apartment in Albuquerque it was the hardest thing he ever did. Now I found out what he meant. Working almost all on my own, it seemed the process of preparing and executing my move was endless.

When I informed Lindsey of my decision to leave, they didn't thank me for my impeccable tenancy. They just said, *"your move out date is July 28, 2023, by 5 pm."*

I made the deadline in record breaking heat, and when I turned in my keys, exhausted by my efforts, I was informed I'd be charged through the end of July. I shouldn't have been surprised. Lindsey had extorted five days of rent from me by charging me from the beginning of September in 2015, even though I wasn't allowed to move in till the fifth of that month.

I declined to pay the penalty they wanted to charge me due to their extortion. "Bill me," I said as I drove off in a rage never to return to The Links at Springdale, which had once been my happy home.

The prospect of being sued by Lindsey for non-payment of the penalty they sought to impose on me, plus some additional charges they made up that were unjustified, raised my blood pressure till I realized that they wouldn't sue me after all. The $1000 at issue was apparently under whatever amount they calculated would justify legal action.

The upside of all this is that my new digs, which was a glorified one-bedroom turned into two, was perfect for continuing to write this memoir. It was blissfully peaceful, my neighbors were chill and respectful, if also a touch eccentric, and I was able to start walking to and from work which helped turn around my health issues in a very positive way.

Looking back, I'm glad I made the move, which would have been impossible without the heroic help of my boss, Chase Gipson, and his son Hollis. Although I'll forever bad mouth Lindsey Management for the corporate thieves they are, I'm grateful to have moved on.

There's nothing more important than being happy at home, and now I feel that way again.

Finding Diane

The process of conceiving and creating this memoir has taken more than twenty years to complete. Most of that time I put it on hold because my family was worried about being shamed by me for all the world to see.

This was never my desire or intent.

My own sense of its impact, and the part my family played in my story, always felt affirming. I didn't know how, but I was clear that even dad, my greatest adversary and ally, would somehow emerge with the rest of my brethren in a loving and humane light.

Although I adopted a protocol of "ruthless compassion" in my writing and I requested that kind of criticism from friends and family I trusted to read and comment on drafts of the Goose, my purpose was always to write a book that was honest and authentic, yet redemptive and healing.

This vision of my memoir would have set my family at ease, but somehow I didn't convey it. Perhaps the rawness of what I wrote terrified them, for no one read the whole book, so they were anxious about what I would reveal and how I'd reveal it. Dad knew instinctively what I was up to, yet he was more than supportive, although he probably also knew I'd be hard on him.

In ways I can't fully explain and that we never verbalized, my father and I knew somehow that I was meant to forward our evolution and growth as a family. As it turned out, writing this memoir is how I accomplished that.

At least I hope so.

Now that the six of us have come down to Diane and me, my take on our family's odyssey and what it brings up for her, has made me extraordinarily sensitive to my sister's feelings and vulnerability.

The sister I once feared would replace me is still processing, as I am, the blessings and burdens of being a Moseley. We walk that road together and she has her own story to tell. I hope she tells her story because despite her discomfort with this book, Diane been my staunchest supporter in telling mine.

No one has known me longer, been there for me as much, or loved me more than my beloved baby sister.

In dad's last letter to me, in 2003 when we first began to address how wounded I felt by him, he closed by saying this; *"I appreciate your letter more than I can tell. It was a great and courageous statement. You and I both learned that love can cause pain as well as create joy. Like Joseph and his coat of many colors, you are our "little boy." I loved you the day you were born. I love you today. I will love you the day I die."*

These comments by my father seem to suggest I was more special to him than I ever realized, and his desire to heal our rift and make his love known to me was crystal clear.

Because she was working on her own memoir and probably feared wading into the details of our often painful childhoods, Diane didn't read *Clocking the Goose* until just before it went to print. Although this hurt my feelings, I didn't take it personally. Much as I had with Nancy, I knew not to pressure her. When sis was ready to read my book, she'd do so and not before.

Once Diane got through my entire memoir, her input improved it. The editor in her took fat off my prose and set me straight on facts I got wrong or misunderstood. She also made a wonderful suggestion that helped me bring my narratives full circle.

Most of all, I finally felt her full support and blessing.

If you don't bring forth what is inside you, what you do bring forth can destroy you.

This comment of Anne Lamott, written in her memoir *Bird by Bird*, rings true with me. Her guide for writers, blends memoir, self-help, and practical advice. The book is named after a story from her childhood, where her brother was overwhelmed by a school report on birds. Their father advised him to tackle it "bird by bird," one step at a time.

Lamott shares personal anecdotes and lessons from her life as a writer, offering insights on the craft, the importance of routine, and the value of authenticity. She emphasizes mindfulness and writing as a means of self-comfort and expression.

It's a great read and if my sister is unaware of Lamott, I intend to turn her onto *Bird by Bird*.

Sis and I are Sagittarians. We are thoughtful, intentional and inquisitive. Most of all, we have a big picture orientation towards life that drives us to understand our humanity in full and to share our discoveries about how to live in ways that enhance individuality.

I don't know the form Diane's memoir will take, nor the title she'll choose. Maybe she'll call it <u>Dodging the Lawnmower</u>.

Whatever its title and form, and whatever heat she heaps upon my head, I'm especially interested in her insights into modern media culture and her feminine take on growing up Moseley. Most of all, I look forward to reading her story because it will enhance my sensitivity and awareness as a person.

As cheesy and cliché as it may sound these days, my sister makes me want to be a better man.

<u>NOW</u>

Lasting love with a life partner has always been missing for me. Maybe what I needed was to love myself, to embrace who and how I am; to let that be enough. Then again, maybe there's no reason for my solitude. Maybe I'm just making something up to explain the hermit in me.

It's not easy to live solo, but being alive isn't easy for anyone, regardless of their circumstances. Being truly alive can be and often is hard work. As of this writing, I'm 71. Well and truly into my third act, it's high time for me to thrive.

My health, such an issue in the last year, seems to be on the mend. Perhaps as <u>Clocking the Goose</u> goes to press, I'll feel a renewed desire to partner someone I love and who can love me fully in return.

Dum spiro, spero, the Latin motto at St. Andrews, means *while I breath, I hope.*

My desire to play golf is back. I just joined a club so I can play twice a week, walking each round as a way to bring up my fitness and get better at the game I've always loved.

What's great about my game is that there are many ways to enjoy it and even as a senior now, so long as I play from the proper tee and work at my game a bit, I can have as much fun playing as I ever have.

Although I feel the need to wrap things up now with a good finish, I'm going to let my stories speak for themselves.

Today, for the most part, I live in the present moment. Much of my past has been exorcized by writing this book. I like feeling free of my history; living here and now. In as much as I'm able, I strive to keep things as simple as possible, but not simpler than they should be.

This is a crucial distinction.

Real life and real relationships are messy, contradictory, and challenging, but life these days feels relaxed and rewarding, too.

If I was the goose I clocked over thirty years ago, I'd have to say I got past that misfortune. Moreover, I learned how to make breaks that didn't seem to go my way deepen and enrich me.

Most of all, I feel connected to my truest self; to who I was meant to be. It's not easy but I embrace my contradictions. Whatever good or bad is in these stories, I've stayed true to myself.

I'm proud of that.

I hope pop's proud, too.

THE END

AFTERWORD:
Getting a Good Job on Coming Full Circle

In my Introduction to this memoir, I criticized the corporatization of American culture and how the values of big business dominate our experience today. More specifically, I condemned the narrow minded, soulless, and profit at all costs mentality of modern-day corporate culture.

Likewise, in some of my chapter introductions and stories, I expressed my view that many of our universities have lost their way. Ideally, a college graduate balances the skills necessary to make a successful living with the ideals necessary to make a soulful life.

I believe our institutions of higher learning must once again become the bastions of fearless free-thinking they once were. We need conservatories where students can risk being politically incorrect, test the boundaries and possibilities of critical, radical or even revolutionary thinking and do so irrespective of how they might *look* or how they might offend *any* group of *any* kind.

At a fundamental level, higher education is about training us to make critical distinctions and to foster innovation, growth, and excellence through **trial and error**; it's about learning *how* to think, *not what* to think.

The most basic function of college is to prepare graduates for success in the world of commerce. In the arts, sciences, and humanities, however, the university experience should also be about adventure, discovery, and the disciplined yet unfettered exploration of our possibilities and ourselves.

The sensitivity and people skills of Michaelangelo, and for that matter of J.P. Morgan and John D. Rockefeller, left much to be desired but look at the enduring legacies of these titans. We can and should debate the nature of their legacies, but the hard truth is that humanity needs greatness more than it needs diversity and inclusion, or politeness, fairness, and decency.

Surely, civility **is** important, but it should never be our **primary concern**.

What then, should our priority be?

To answer this, let's first consider where we are as a society today.

As I look at my fellow Americans, I see too much success without joy, too much status without contentment, and an emptiness that seems to gnaw at people who despite their accomplishments are at odds with themselves. Clearly, this quiet desperation extends as much to our vanishing middle class as it does to folks who live hand to mouth.

Traditionally, religion addresses these very personal concerns, but religion isn't what it used to be and never was. I don't believe conventional religion's broadband approach to spirituality is geared to address the widespread, if largely unconscious melancholy we find in America today.

Whether it is, or not, the facts are these; according to a recent Pew Research Center report, the share of Americans who say they attend religious services at least once or twice a month has dropped by 7 percentage points over the last decade, while those who attend religious services less often (if at all) has risen by the same degree.

Another relevant report by The Guardian states that thousands of churches are closing each year in the US, as congregations dwindle across the country and a younger generation of Americans abandon Christianity altogether. The COVID-19 pandemic also precipitated an overall decline in religious attendance, although religious identity has remained mostly stable.

If our religions are not up to helping us, which at the very least is debatable, it's also too easy to blame corporate-think and the Woke movement for our current social *ennui*. Corporations aren't our root problem, nor are universities with social agendas that overstep their educational mission and purview.

You and I are the problem.

We, the people, have allowed these conditions to arise, dominate and overwhelm life in America today.

Why is this so? How have we lost our way?

I believe the malaise we experience now is rooted in a loss of personal integrity. As individuals, we must first be more truthful with ourselves and then share our authentic being with each other.

This is or should be the area of our primary concern and it's where my stories and yours become relevant.

When I was a boy, if I'd been honest, I would have openly declared my anger at my father. Then it could've been addressed and even if it was evaded or denied by my parents or me, it would've been out in the open.

How can we effectively encourage kids to be open and honest when they're traumatized? How old is old enough to take on the inner anger and fear that intimidates us in our youth? How do we best go about that? What kind of support does any child need to deal with their darkest impulses? How can we teach our kids to tap the colossal energy of their shadow selves without doing harm, and in ways that make them come alive yet also inspire their empathy and compassion?

If learning to work with our shadow energy and teaching our children to do the same isn't our priority, it should share that status with increased personal integrity and authentic relationships.

At nine or ten, if I'd been straight with my father when he asked me if I was afraid of him, many of the things that troubled me might've been addressed and even healed. If I'd been a smidgeon more courageous, like I became with my bicycle after I learned how to ride it *on my own*, I could've overcome my fear and come clean with dad.

Likewise, if I'd simply admitted how embarrassed I was to have blown my very first romantic relationship with Carla Davis when I was thirteen, re-upped with her or found another girlfriend, maybe I wouldn't have become a social hermit for much of my life. The choice I made here was so counter-productive and so extreme, I wish I'd reached out for guidance. I wish someone helped me see that isolating myself at the very beginning of my relationships with women would bleed into isolating myself in life.

It was the worst choice I could have made.

Yet that very choice, that exact error, and the other pains and missteps of my youth unquestionably deepened me. They forced me to look beyond conventional wisdom for solutions that allowed for my contradictions and that made sense to me. They fueled my drive to find a way of life that worked for my entire identity, warts and all. In time, through trial and error, and even when my life was not all I hoped it would be, I found my way.

I'm still finding my way and that's a never-ending process.

The key to my self-reliance is that I've learned to think for myself. I don't pass the buck of being responsible, of being RESPOND-ABLE, to whatever challenges me. We must make things as simple as possible but never simpler than they should be because real life and real success, real self-awareness and real love are filled with challenging contradictions.

Like the ripples in a millpond, when we throw the pebble of personal truthfulness into the pool of our social interactions positive effects spread in ways that can go far, far beyond our own lives.

At the beginning of this memoir, I cited two ideas that impelled me to write this book.

All of us, everywhere, are obliged to grapple with the light and darker angels of our conflicted human nature.

What have we learned from examining this idea?

Based on my life experiences I've learned that I can't get rid of any part of me. So, the only way for me to live as a civilized human being is to stay aware of my dark side and find safe, innovative ways to use its colossal energy and to coexist with it.

I think this is true for all adults, everywhere.

I've also learned the rage which afflicted my father went much deeper than his experience of the Great Depression. I see it now as a karmic inheritance, a family issue. Dad's rage lives on in me. I can't get rid of it. It's the darker angel of my own nature. It's also inextricably linked to my passion for truth.

So, of necessity, I've found liberating ways to safely express my shadow side. Partnering with my dark angel revitalizes and renews me and helps me to be wholly human, not perfect mind you, but to be in equal possession of my light and shadowy self.

Sometimes, when I get all jammed up inside, I make up Hitler speeches which I regurgitate while I'm taking a shower. My heritage is German, but I don't speak the language, so these tirades come out as guttural grunts and groans with extreme physical gestures, all of which are spontaneous and completely made up.

At other times, I let my darker angel express his moods in the form of a dance improvisation. I ask myself, *"what's the sound and movement of this darkness I'm feeling inside,"* then I give my shadow free reign to express and explore it. I do this <u>utilizing safe boundaries</u>, let go, and then work to integrate what I discover.

These are effective ways I've learned that connect to, release, and make use of toxic energy when it builds up inside me. I call these liberating techniques *structures* and they often release, relax, and renew me when I'm upset and can't sort out why.

The upshot here is that by finding ways to <u>embrace</u> my shadow and my conflicts; *by learning to <u>grapple with</u> my dark impulses*, they become my ally; they liberate me to be fully human and alive.

Now let's examine what we've learned from the second idea that drove me to write this book.

In order to fully realize our creed as Americans, we must develop a healthy relationship with our pain.

If telling my stories has touched you, it's because I shared my pain along with my joy. Clearly, as a child, I felt *other, less than,* and was in enormous turmoil. At first, I projected my upset onto others or scapegoated them so I could avoid feelings of my own that terrified me.

What's different now is that I've learned to claim and lean into my pain.

I take it on.

I strive to see what my pain is about and look for creative, safe ways to express whatever may be troubling me. Often anger comes with my pain. Anger burns but purifies; it reduces things to their essence. So long as I work with them, keeping safe boundaries as I go, leaning into my pain and anger helps me become a deeper, more tolerant, and compassionate person because I know I can do anything, good or bad, at any time.

Having this understanding tends to make me more compassionate towards folks who deny, project, or act out their pain on others.

There but for the grace of God, go I.

Although no hard evidence for it exists, no less a humanitarian than Abraham Lincoln is *reputed* to have said; *"Most people are about as happy as they make up their minds to be."* This is a valuable sentiment and a much more important attitude than whoever actually coined the phrase.

As an antidote to our existential pain, it encourages us to take command of our own happiness. It suggests our well-being is determined by our own mindset and not by external factors. It affirms that by choosing to focus on the positive aspects of our lives, we can cultivate and increase our joy.

Things are rarely as bad as they seem. By the same token, things aren't as good as they used to be, and they never were.

So, where do we go from here?

Fareed Zakaria, the political essayist who regularly appears on CNN, thinks America's current existential malaise is unfounded. According to all the standard measures, the U.S. leads the civilized world in every marker that shows a society well-fixed to deal with whatever challenges it now or in the future. He urges those who feel lost to consider that America is better off, and by a wide margin, then any other nation on earth.

If Zakaria is right, why have we lost this perspective? Why do we feel a lack of confidence in our society and ourselves?

It's as if we suffer as a populace from *"poor little rich kid syndrome,"* a very real malady privileged children experience who have everything they should want; status, wealth, power, access; who have inherited the fully realized American Dream yet are missing the two essentials we all need; love and connection.

What I make of this realization is that we all need to do a better job of loving ourselves, of cultivating the love we have in our lives, and of tending to authentic interactions with the people most important to us.

I would also have Zakaria review a movie released nearly fifty years ago called Network. Written by Paddy Chayefsky, at the 1:05 minute mark in this two-hour feature film from1976, the TV news anchor of the fictional UBS network goes on a tirade.

Howard Beale tells his broadcast audience that TV is a boredom killing instrument and a propaganda machine that will lie like hell and tell you anything you want to hear. In essence, Beale says that the TV world cares about profits and only profits. Substitute the word **corporate** for **TV** and he describes the world we suffer from today.

This is why we lack confidence in our society.

Deep down inside we know that far too much of our lives in America today is based on bullshit. The evidence of this excrement is broadcast daily on a wide variety of reality shows from all the *Survivor* spin offs to *A Current Affair* and *Court TV*.

So, despite the fact that the U.S. is still the most powerful nation on earth, if we are honest with ourselves, we know it suffers from a kind of cultural cancer. We may well be the envy of the world, as Zakaria clearly believes, but the American Dream, even for those who seem to have fulfilled it, is threadbare, if not in tatters.

We need something that will revitalize our belief in our institutions and ourselves.

Thomas Sowell, Glen Loury, John McWhorter, Denzel Washington, and other clear-thinking Black Americans are consistent in their criticisms of Woke culture and the politics of victimization.

Their message to ALL Americans is this; pick yourself up by your bootstraps; stop demanding the system give you special preferences for ANYTHING and rise by your own efforts on your own merit.

This self-reliance is consistent with our creed. It's prescient advice for people everywhere.

The answers to human problems can never be primarily institutional; they must first be internal, experiential, and then become interpersonal. Our difficulties demand we come to grips with the complexities of our lives and find ways of being and doing that work. In this, the culture of victimization has no place.

In accepting the Nobel peace prize for Literature in 1949, William Faulkner said, *"I believe man will not only endure, he will prevail."* I agree with this perspective, but in order for us to triumph we must re-engage with our lives; we must get real about where we are and deal with it.

Finally, let me share a sentiment expressed by the character of Frank Galvin, an alcoholic, ambulance chasing lawyer who has lost his way but is given one last chance at redemption in Sidney Lumet's 1982 film, <u>The Verdict</u>.

At the end of this story, Galvin begins his final argument to the jury on behalf of his comatose client whose family is suing her negligent and corrupt doctors in a wrongful death lawsuit;

Galvin: *Well...You know, so much of the time we're just lost. We say, "Please, God, tell us what is right. Tell us what is true."*

I mean there is no justice. The rich win; the poor are powerless. We become tired of hearing people lie. And after a time, we become dead, a little dead. We think of ourselves as victims-and we become victims. We become weak; we doubt ourselves; we doubt our beliefs; we doubt our institutions; and we doubt the law.

But today you are the law. <u>*You are the law*</u>*, not some book, not the lawyers, not a marble statue, or the trappings of the court. See, those are just symbols of our desire to be just. They are, in fact, a prayer. I mean, a fervent and a frightened prayer.*

In my religion, they say, "Act as if you had faith; faith will be given to you."

CLOCKING the GOOSE

If we are to have faith in justice, we need only to believe in ourselves and act with justice. See, I believe there is justice in our hearts...

APPENDIX:
Rounding out the picture of my immediate family members

Although I've given a strong analysis of my father's character and the role his anger played in our home, as well as some insight into who my grandfathers were, my perceptions of dad's character may need to be rounded out for some readers. At the same time, my descriptions of the rest of my immediate family haven't been as full as I would like. Let me address this here and now.

My Father-Raymond Herbert Moseley

After much reflection, I now feel my father was much more fragile than we ever realized. Dad had a wounded sense of self that he was too apprehensive, insecure, and proud to acknowledge, and he had no idea how to deal with his emotional frailties. Physically, this manifested as a cardiac arrythmia suggesting suppressed panic. My father's anxieties tormented but also drove him. Emily, my sister-in-law, and a pharmacist by profession, believed that pop was clinically depressed for much of his youth and adulthood. What I know for certain is that dad experienced great internal pressure and continual turmoil. He both looked for and thrived in turbulent settings. I believe this was because he needed to create an outer world that matched his inner experience. It's no accident he chose to become a fighter pilot and then a litigator, or what we called in the south, a trial lawyer.

Dad's default strategy in any situation was to work through it. The only thing missing in this approach was working out his emotional anomalies. Whatever his anxieties were, and they were often considerable, he felt *"getting a good job"* on whatever he was facing was a great palliative. Self-mastery and excellence were his core values, a legacy of his training as a naval aviator, and although his emotional traumas remained with him his entire life, his attempt to master himself in any situation through the quality of his work served him well.

A closer look at dad's personality suggests to me he fought like a tiger to gain full use of his energy, volatility, and drive. He then methodically set out to develop a cool and calculated folksiness with a down-to-earth style that became his trademark in the courtroom. Dad's command of a jury evolved due to his natural gift for putting complex ideas in simple terms, but his effectiveness was also the product of a hard-won inner battle he had with feeling awkward and shy. The challenge of mastering his perceived failings for the sake of becoming a professional's professional is what inspired my father to overcome his weaknesses in every area of his life.

Dad's personality was forged partly as compensation for his own sense of inner inadequacy and in part due to his desire to be the best at whatever he set out to master. The cosmic mix of insecurity and dogged determination that coexisted in him made him successful. Ray's force of will became overemphasized, at least for those of us who were close to him, because he couldn't accept feeling deficient internally or externally. The fact that he projected "*feeling less than others:*" that he transferred his fight with feeling deficient onto "*snobs and social butterflies,*" and then fought like hell to prove his worth, is probably what motivated him the most. The archetypal image of the savior/protector that formed my father's inner identity begs the question as to who was saving who from what.

Be this as it may, dad did the best he could with what he was given and with what he knew. He didn't know how to distinguish his deepest personal feelings from facts. His nature was black and white and personal compromise was tough for him. Papa didn't feel he had the time to be too introspective because he was so busy making himself a success according to the world's measures of success.

Moreover, there was no tradition or support structure <u>he considered valid,</u> like psychotherapy, that would help him search for or develop his self-awareness and self-acceptance. Simplistic as it may now seem, he just had to find a way to win by society's standards and that's what he set his mind and will to achieve.

<u>My Mother-Lois Virginia Hawk Moseley</u>

Just as dad had his catch phrases like *"get a good job"* or *"there's no power like willpower"* or *"you know how to play, I'm gonna teach you how to work,"* mom had a phrase we all knew was code for **"beyond this point I will not go."** When you heard her say, *"Well, I don't know,"* you knew she'd reached her limit. Her capacity for introspection was minimal. She dumped her psychological and emotional concerns into the hopper of Christianity and relied on the ten commandments to cover whatever she refused to grapple with or address inside herself.

Mom's *modus operandi* was to obey dad in all things, although when she was upset with him, she'd passively aggressively provoke his ire. I remember dad came home from work one afternoon and clearly had a rough day at the office. I could see his temperature rising and that he was primed to blow as mom needled him in ways she knew would lead him to erupt. Right before Mt. Vesuvius exploded, I inserted myself into their immanent donnybrook and said, *"Geez, dad, you must of had a really hard day at work today."* Papa just melted and all the built-up tension in him evaporated because I saw and acknowledged where he was in that moment.

Mama's dark side rarely came out but when it did it was formidable. Although I wasn't there when it happened, I had every reason to believe Rick when he told me that for some reason I've forgotten now, she whipped him with an electric cord once because she couldn't find one of dad's belts, and he that had to physically restrain her because she wouldn't stop.

At the same time, mother had a naughty, fun-loving side that also rarely came out to play. When it did, smoking and drinking were on the menu and mama could be a lot of fun.

All things considered; however, she was most comfortable playing the role of a good homemaker/obedient spouse and she loved the perks that came with dad's success.

The core conflict between her humanitarianism and her personal remoteness, however, was something she never resolved. Despite mom's remote side, she was always curious, generous, down-to-earth, and caring.

Mama wasn't easy to know or get close to, but she was always easy to love.

My Oldest Brother-Richard Paul Moseley

Just as mom's *"well, I don't know,"* expressed her self-imposed limits, Rick has a physical gesture that did the same. Keeping his elbows at his side, his forearms would extend diagonally and down, and his hands would fully extend, as his face would silently express *"well, what am I supposed to do,"* without actually saying those words.

This gesture expressed his determination not to engage with a situation beyond a certain point. Invariably, this happened when getting involved in something would take him past his comfort zone or call upon him to reveal feelings he felt he must avoid at all costs.

In my view, Rick was too devoted to maintaining a detachment that kept him a safe distance from his shadow self.

It wasn't Rick's nature to make a fuss. And the day he died, my sister Diane believes this lowkey, "no problem" attitude might've contributed to his death. The first of the two heart attacks he had on January 13, 2020, hit him at home. It took the better part of an hour to get him to a hospital in Franklin, TN, as I understand it, and when they got him to the ER, he was probably downplaying his condition. Not making a fuss may have relaxed those attending him more than it should have. After he arrived at the ER, the second cardiac arrest that killed him might've been forestalled if the doctors and nurses there had tended to him with more urgency right away.

My best and favorite memory about Richard isn't a specific event but relates to how much quiet pleasure he got from *"getting a good job"* on whatever he was working at. Dad would be proud of Rick's delight at doing whatever he did well and always to the best of his ability.

Rick was a solid, trustworthy, reliable, and caring man. I only wish he could've become the man in full I think he longed to be.

My Middle Brother-Stephen Ray Moseley

Stephen was the star of the family when we were kids, yet something about him was remote and inaccessible. In those days he gave the impression that he was totally self-sufficient and didn't want or need anything

As popular as he was among his peers, in the family he kept to himself and went his own way.

At the same time, his large appetite for everything was clear. He had an eye for the best of everything and that's what he wanted from himself and others. I had no idea how sensitive he was or how deeply his habits and patterns were rooted in his day-to-day life.

My best and favorite memories of Steve come from a specific event that was repeated year after year, as well as an experience we shared near the end of his life.

The event was every Thanksgiving celebration we shared as a family. I can see my brother going through the annual buffet as clearly as when it happened. Stephen would construct his dinner plate like an artist. Meat was placed from 5 to 7 pm, as he usually opted from a combo of prime rib or roast beef and turkey, mashed potatoes with gravy occupied 10 am, greens beans at 2 pm and stuffing at 4. 8 pm was usually reserved for broccoli casserole, then just above it, fit in between 9 and 10 am, something like cucumber salad, if it caught his fancy that day.

Once he found his seat, always at the head of the table when we gathered at his place, he would take a moment to assess his work. You could see him making this final review before he began to enjoy the victuals he'd assembled. When he was sure he'd been through and complete in his work, when he'd *"got a good job"* putting his plate together, his preparation ritual was complete.

This was the moment I loved, the transition between preparation and execution. Then and only then, when everything passed muster, would he "*go in for the kill.*" This was a beautiful moment. It was never rushed or frenetic but always deliberate, intentional and illuminated his meticulous character.

My other favorite memory of Steve was how close we got when he got cancer. From that time on, our conversations were limitless and because of that we were able to touch the fabric of our lives, individually and as brothers, in deep and meaningful ways. Our shared experience in his time of illness has been a sweet, sweet experience for me to recall every time I think of Stephen.

Steve had the biggest hands I've ever seen. When I want to talk with him in spirit, all I have to do is think of reaching out to him and putting his big right hand on my heart. Whenever I do this, I feel connected to him immediately. I also feel how much he loved me and how close we became at the end of his life.

My Sister-Diane Louise Moseley Crabtree

Sis, who is my sole surviving immediate family member, has one of the most effective defense mechanisms I've ever seen. When she meets a stranger, say a server at a restaurant or someone delivering a package to her home or perhaps a fellow traveler, she can appear to be the most cordial, engaging person and shows real interest in whoever she's interacting with. Something about this behavior gives you the impression that my sister has it all together and doesn't have a worry or concern in the world.

The truth, however, is that Diane is extremely private, has more than one personal insecurity, and has a fuse as short as anyone in my original family. What is more, she has extremely high standards and evaluates people according to how on top of things they are, and how sharply and expediently they handle their business and themselves.

My best and favorite thought about Diane is the *joie di vivre* she brings to living despite her personal struggles, and my hope for her is that when the time is right that she will share her voice fully with the world. Perhaps more than anyone in our family, Diane embodies ***all*** the abilities and frailties everyone in our family struggled to integrate and bring to bear in living a life of meaning and purpose. When the day comes that she feels safe feeling how unsafe she feels, and then shares her power, pain, and perspective with the world anyway, which I predict will be in the form of a memoir, she's gonna shake things up in ways that better all of us.

The Corporate Cosmology of Arthur Jensen from Sidney Lumet's film *NETWORK* 1976

There's no substitute for experience, of course, so I hope you'll see this film if you've never watched it or view it again if you haven't seen it for a while. The following dialogue from NETWORK is the antithesis of what I hope this memoir has convinced you is most important in our troubled age; personal integrity, individual expression, the sacredness of every single human being, and the fulfillment of people's spiritual potential. The background of Arthur Jensen's speech below is that Howard Beale has caused a public uproar so severe that it has stopped an international business deal Jenson's corporation wanted to complete...

Arthur Jensen: You have meddled with the primal forces of nature, Mr. Beale, and I won't have it! Is that clear? You think you've merely stopped a business deal. That is not the case! The Arabs have taken billions of dollars out of this country, and now they must put it back! It is ebb and flow, tidal gravity! It is ecological balance! You are an old man who thinks in terms of nations and peoples. There are no nations. There are no peoples. There are no Russians. There are no Arabs.

There are no third worlds. There is no West. There is only one holistic system of systems, one vast and immane, interwoven, interacting, multivariate, multinational dominion of dollars. Petro-dollars, electro-dollars, multi-dollars, reichsmarks, rins, rubles, pounds, and shekels. It is the international system of currency which determines the totality of life on this planet. That is the natural order of things today. That is the atomic and subatomic and galactic structure of things today! And YOU have meddled with the primal forces of nature, and YOU... WILL... ATONE! ...Am I getting through to you, Mr. Beale?... You get up on your little twenty-one-inch screen and howl about America and democracy. There is no America. There is no democracy. There is only IBM, ITT, and AT&T, and DuPont, Dow, Union Carbide, and Exxon. Those are the nations of the world today. What do you think the Russians talk about in their councils of state, Karl Marx? They get out their linear programming charts, statistical decision theories, minimax solutions, and compute the price-cost probabilities of their transactions and investments, just like we do. We no longer live in a world of nations and ideologies, Mr. Beale. The world is a college of corporations, inexorably determined by the immutable bylaws of business. The world is a business, Mr. Beale. It has been since man crawled out of the slime. And our children will live, Mr. Beale, to see that... perfect world... in which there's no war or famine, oppression, or brutality. One vast and ecumenical holding company, for whom all men will work to serve a common profit, in which all men will hold a share of stock. All necessities provided, all anxieties tranquilized, all boredom amused. And I have chosen you, Mr. Beale, to preach this evangel.

Howard Beale Why me?

Arthur Jensen: Because you're on television, dummy. Sixty million people watch you every night of the week, Monday through Friday.

Howard Beale I have seen the face of God!

Arthur Jensen: You just might be right, Mr. Beale.

The counterpoint to Jensen's philosophy is the content of this memoir as a whole. Every human being is a star-seed. If you've been moved by this book, sow your stardust in the world, wherever and in whatever ways make sense to you.

RM